Young People and Youth Justice

Young People and Youth Justice

Kevin Haines
and
Mark Drakeford

MACMILLAN

First published 1998 by
MACMILLAN PRESS LTD
Houndmills, Basingstoke, Hampshire RG21 6XS
and London
Companies and representatives throughout the world

ISBN 0–333–68760–4

KL
227
- 1
H34

A catalogue record for this book is available
from the British Library.

This book is printed on paper suitable for recycling and made from
fully managed and sustained forest sources.

10   9   8   7   6   5   4   3   2   1
07 06 05 04 03 02 01 00 99 98

Printed in Malaysia

Contents

v

List of Tables and Figures

Tables

Figures

Acknowledgements

All books are the product of far more than their authors and this is no exception. Our particular thanks are due to those who have helped us along the way by reading and commenting on earlier drafts. Brian Littlechild and Denis Jones were both especially helpful in making positive suggestions for amendments and improvements. We think the book has benefitted from their suggestions and hope they will too. Catherine Gray of Macmillan has provided a steady mixture of encouragement and guidance on the disciplines which meeting deadlines and responding to comments require.

The contents of this book and our deeply held views about the issues it addresses arise from the direct contact we both have with youth justice practitioners and the young people they work with. More than anything else their contribution should stand in these acknowledgements.

Finally to thank our families for the pressure which they absorb and the impetus they provide in bringing such a book to fruition. The long passage from proposal to final manuscript is one which has its inevitable difficulties and families bear the brunt of this – we remain very grateful for their support. The views expressed in this text, and the arguments it contains, are, of course, our own responsibility.

KEVIN HAINES
MARK DRAKEFORD

The authors and publishers are grateful to the following for permission to reproduce copyright material: Department of Health, for Tables 2.2 and 2.3; Carol Hayden for Table 5.1; Children's Legal Centre for Table 5.2; NCH Action for Children for Table 5.3; Figure 6.1 is reprinted by permission of the publisher from

Crime in the Making: Pathways and Turning Points through Life by Robert J. Sampson and H. Laub, Cambridge, Mass.: Harvard University Press, Copyright © 1993 by the President and Fellows of Harvard College. Every effort has been made to contact all the copyright-letter, but if any have been inadvertently omitted the publishers will be pleased to make the necessary arrangement at the earliest opportunity.

Introduction: Young People and Youth Justice

This is a book about working with young people and the youth justice system, but it differs in approach from more traditional treatments of this topic. It does not set out, in any systematic way, to review the literature on juvenile and youth justice; nor does it aim to provide a comprehensive synthesis of the 'what works' research. The arguments set out do not rely on detailed discussion of a limited number of projects, undertaken in the hope of discovering some generalisable ideas. This book is, however, rooted in research and what is known about children in trouble and the social systems that surround them. It is about applying accumulated knowledge to the operation of the youth justice system and to work with young people.

The central theme of the book is that there is much to be learned from the successes of recent juvenile justice practice, but that it is important for youth justice to continue developing in ways which meet the changing challenges faced by and presented by young people in our society. To meet these challenges this book proposes that youth justice workers develop practices in line with a philosophy of putting children first.

A Children-First philosophy embraces much from previous juvenile justice practice. Putting children first must still mean that youth justice workers should aim to maximise diversion from the formal criminal justice system, doing all that they can to avoid custody for young people – indeed the children-first philosophy requires re-invigorated efforts aimed at the abolition of custody for children in the light of expansionist custodial penalties for young people aged under 18 years. But such a philosophy goes much further than maximum diversion, minimum custody.

In a society with increasingly sharp social differentials of wealth and well-being, youth justice practice must adopt a much more proactive strategy towards children generally. Diversion from the criminal justice system must remain an essential systems strategy, but it is no longer justifiable to marginalise children in need, no longer justifiable simply to divert children if diversion means that their lack of access to full-time education, their lack of adequate housing and their other social needs are ignored. Youth justice practice must develop in ways which devise effective methods for supporting children in trouble and difficulty outside the criminal justice system, as well as within it.

Avoiding custody for children must remain a central goal for youth justice practice. But, increasingly, a systems management approach heightens the importance for avoiding custody of a whole series of interventions at other stages of the criminal justice process. An effective Appropriate Adult service and intervention can reduce the chance of an ultimate custodial sentence. Effective bail support programmes are essential for avoiding remands in custody or other closed institutions, and can reduce the likelihood of a custodial sentence. Well-developed community sentences are essential as alternatives to institutional and custodial sentences. The arguments set out in this text remain committed to a systems management approach animated in strategies designed to avoid custodial experiences for children in this respect.

But systems management alone is no longer sufficient. Systems management must be informed by the principles of a Children First philosophy and by knowledge of what effective intervention with children actually means in practice. Keeping children out of the criminal justice system is important, keeping children out of custody is even more important. The rationale which underpins this way of working is based not only on what is best for children themselves, but proceeds from a firm commitment to the better social health of the whole community. Keeping children out of the criminal justice system in general, and its most damaging components in particular, is the best way of ensuring that such individuals do not grow up to be more prolific and more dangerous offenders.

The approach advocated here is one which addresses issues of community safety and crime reduction with every seriousness. In the argument of this book, however, these goals are far less likely to be achieved in a climate which regards them as in competition with, rather than arising from, a determination to protect and promote the immediate and longer-term interests of each individual, and children generally. But it is not acceptable to act instrumentally to achieve these objectives if the interests of individuals and children generally are compromised. Youth justice practice must achieve its objectives in ways which are sensitive to the interests of children. This means placing children in their proper social context and distinguishing their behaviour from the responsibilities that others have towards them. Where society, its structures and institutions, fails children this must be made clear. Structured work which aims to integrate not marginalise, which aims to improve the social situation of young people and to maximise their chances both now and in the future, must be the goal.

The Children First philosophy, which is developed in this book, does not involve the mechanical application of routinised procedures to children in difficulty or danger. Effective youth justice practice can only be the product of knowledgeable, thinking and skilled practitioners who set about their work in an adventurous and innovative manner. Consequently one of the main aims of the book is to provide current and prospective youth justice practitioners with the necessary tools to carry out their work in an informed and determined manner. Putting children first does not mean rigid adherence to pre-determined procedures, ticking the boxes of anti-oppressive or anti-discriminatory practice. A Children-First philosophy means being proactive on behalf of children; it means working hard to educate others to understand more and to dispel the myths about, for example, serious or persistent offenders; it means constantly developing and redeveloping effective systems management strategies and supervision programmes, of reinvigorating appeals against harsh or inappropriate judgements. Above all it means adapting and constantly striving to put children first.

To achieve a Children First approach, youth justice practitioners must have a thorough understanding of the nature and experience of youth, and knowledge about the way society and its social structures treat children. Chapter 1 aims to provide an introduction to this topic and to outline the sorts of knowledge and information that are relevant to understanding children and their social context.

Chapter 2 comprises a more detailed analytical review of juvenile justice. If youth justice in the future is to be able to build on the effectiveness of the past then an adequate understanding of that past must be achieved. The aim of Chapter 2, therefore, is to describe that past, to give due recognition to the complex dynamics of, for example, the new orthodoxy of the 1980s, and to highlight the realities of juvenile justice practice and signal the components of a remarkable criminal justice success story. The reason for doing this, however, is not to glory in the past, but to learn from the past to make a success in the future.

People do things for reasons. These reasons may not always be totally explicit, to individuals or others, but they are always there. It is absolutely essential that youth justice practitioners not only know what they are doing but also why they are doing it. Knowledge and skills are important components in this process, but alone they are insufficient; purposeful action is meaningless unless it is given some direction. Understanding the purposes of action, the objectives which action is directed to achieve, can only be realised if we are explicit about matters of philosophy. In this context philosophy is not some abstract theory but an understanding of the principles that motivate individuals to behave in particular ways. Such is the importance that this book attaches to matters of philosophy that the whole of Chapter 3 is devoted to the development of our ideas of a philosophy for contemporary youth justice practice, including putting children first in systems management.

Chapter 4 gets down to more practical matters with an exploration of issues of managing youth justice systems. This chapter is concerned to discuss the principles and practices of criminal justice systems management updating this important topic in the light of an assessment of previous practice and the needs of the future. Seven key points within the youth justice system are identified and the development of effective practice discussed in relation to each one.

Chapter 5 is similarly rooted in systems management, but is innovative in the way it advocates the extension of these techniques to systems outside the criminal justice sphere. Young people live their lives in a range of systems, formal and informal, ranging from family and peers through schools, employment, health, housing and welfare support. Increasingly these systems are becoming hostile to an ever more marginalised youth population; a young and marginalised population whose treatment by other systems, including the criminal justice system, is often more of a negative reaction to their 'system status' rather than to them as individuals. Adopting a Children First philosophy necessitates an extension of systems management techniques to maximise the opportunities for children to benefit from all formal and informal systems of support. Chapter 5 discusses the principles and practices of managing these other significant systems.

If direct work with young people is to be effective then it must be based on the research which seeks to produce this specialist knowledge. Chapter 6 turns to the literature on the effects of various interventions on future behaviour, beginning with a brief examination of what does not work, and what does harm. Knowing what does not work, and what not to do, is as important as knowing what does work and how to do it. It is argued consistently in this book that youth justice practice must be about doing good, as well as avoiding harm, but avoiding harm remains a primary duty of any practitioner. Practitioners must develop skills in persuading others that some approaches and some treatments are negative and can do much more harm than good – being well-informed about these matters is, therefore, important. The bulk of this chapter, however, is devoted to a discussion of what is known about effective offender interventions. The research is presented in such a way as to build a model for intervention based around control theory and a normalising principle.

Finally, Chapter 7 takes the opportunity to address in more detail some issues of contemporary importance. These issues are: National Standards, risk-assessment, restorative justice and young people, and criminal responsibility. There are dangers in all these areas, but positive aspects too. This chapter attempts to map out these dangers and to suggest more proactive strategies which will assist youth justice workers to meet emerging challenges.

1
Youth and Society

Our society does not like young people. In comparison with our continental partners Britain shows little of the warmth and tolerance which extends to young people in public places or on communal occasions (AMA 1995). Politicians and commentators may offer occasional and sentimental obeisance to the notion that our future, too, lies in their hands. Yet the practical recognition of young people as an asset which requires investment and development is one which, at the level of policy or public attitudes, is strikingly absent from the dominant discourse. As Jeffs and Smith (1996) put it, 'a widespread belief is circulating in America and Britain that young people are in some way turning feral'.

This pervasive negativity forms the essential background to the treatment of the particular group of young people with whom this book is concerned. If young people generally are poorly regarded, then the small minority who end up being brought to the attention of the criminal justice system is the legitimised target for all the harshest and most destructive impulses directed against their contemporaries as a whole.

Young people are, of course, not alone in facing the difficulties which this chapter unfolds. Social and economic policies pursued over the past 15 years have produced a general reification in society, in which the fortunate have become more powerful than ever, while the excluded – older people, women, black people – are characterised by economic poverty and debilitated social rights.

In the case of 'young people', too, many of the same fault-lines are to be found. There are young people who are privileged and powerful, who by virtue of birth or parental advantage are able to

1

transcend the constraints which increasingly fall upon their peers. Equally, for many young people, additional issues of health, disability, gender, sexuality and ethnicity will act as 'intensifiers', making more acute the trends which are outlined here. Our society remains one, for example, in which definitions of 'acceptable' and 'unacceptable' behaviour for young women and young men are differentially constructed according to gender – producing real consequences in the criminal justice sphere with which this book is primarily concerned.

Moreover, as Coppock (1996: 55) has pointed out, negative stereotyping of particular groups such as black and minority ethnic children and families has 'been incorporated into the knowledge-base and practices of professionals, constructing them as "pathological" and "deviant"'. In recent years, based on such an understanding, social work practice generally has come to recognise the pivotal position it can occupy in attempting to resist or redress the ways in which discrimination is perpetuated in the lives of those with whom it is in contact. That strategy is endorsed in this book, without always reiterating the arguments which have powerfully been made elsewhere (see, for example, Ahmad 1990; Worrall 1990; Hood 1992; Browne 1993; Thompson 1994; Dalrymple and Burke 1995; Dominelli *et al.* 1996). The sort of practice which this text aims to outline begins from an axiomatically anti-discriminatory standpoint, dealing as it does with the interface between the least powerful actors – children – and those elements of the state which have the most dramatic powers to intrude upon and alter their lives. In their actions at that interface, youth justice workers should aim to redress, rather than reproduce, the inequalities and barriers to opportunity which are structured into the lives of the children and families with whom they are in contact.

This chapter sets out to explore the position of young people in general within Britain today, linking together a series of continuities and changes. Its argument will be that the objective circumstances of a large proportion of such individuals are more problematic and surrounded by greater uncertainty than at any time over the previous 50 years. At the same time, attitudes towards and opinions about young people remain at best ambivalent and, at worst, characterised by outright hostility. This combination forms part of the essential background to the radical changes currently being pursued by government policies within the criminal justice system.

Attitudes die hard

It is important to begin with attitudes since the way in which young people are regarded in our society has the most formative influence upon public policies towards them. At the risk of simplification, it will be argued here that two dominant and contradictory strands may most readily be detected in public perceptions of young people – strands, moreover, which while contradictory are nevertheless capable of being held powerfully and simultaneously.

In the first strand, young people are regarded with a set of attitudes which are most powerfully linked by envy. Here is the testimony of Charles Hendry, at that time MP for High Peak who, during the summer holidays of 1996, seized his brief moment in charge of Conservative Central Office to declare that, 'There has never been a better time to be a young person than in the Britain of 1996' (the *Guardian* 26 August 1996). Across a spectrum which unites commerce and commentators young people are regularly portrayed as having the times of their lives, untrammelled by responsibility or restraint, a group for whom life is simply an extension of a Club 18–30 holiday in which sex, stimulant and sleep are mixed in a cocktail which was never on the market when the commentators themselves were their age. These are the beautiful young people of the colour supplements and advertising hoardings, high priests of the consumer culture, wearing pairs of trainers which cost more than a family of four had to live on for a month only shortly before they were born.

In the second strand, by contrast, young people are viewed with fear. These are the youngsters who are out of control, who do not know how to behave, who have been brought up by parents who are too soft, who congregate on street corners in order to intimidate passers-by, who have no respect and show no consideration. There is a physical menace which is never far from the surface in these encounters. These young people are dangerous. They need to be avoided or, better still, kept away. Suspicion, hostility and oppression are the products of fear and, in the demonising of young people which has been the hallmark of the 1990s, full rein has been afforded to them. Geoff Pearson's book *Hooligan* (1983) is a text which is insightful, informative and a pleasure to read. It provides a key context for some of the arguments set out here – as well as a warning about claims to novelty in perceptions of young people. In a contextual sense, Pearson establishes the deep and enduring character of many of the attitudes set out above within British culture. In his words, 'A profound historical amnesia has settled around the youth question, whereby it is imagined that in the past young people were orderly, disciplined and well behaved' (in Maguire *et al.* 1994: 1163). 'Twenty years ago', as Pearson repeatedly uncovers, there existed a magical period in which young people knew their place, respected their elders, behaved with circumspection and control, devoted themselves to self-improvement and were generally a credit to their communities. 'Today', by contrast, young people are always on the brink of riot and revolt. The curbs of yesteryear have been abandoned. The traditional sources of guidance and restraint have culpably abrogated their responsibilities: school, church and parents are all to blame. But, young people themselves are most at fault. Driven by hedonism and a swaggering display of the courage afforded by their collectivity (rather than the cowardice which they would, of course, show if they were alone) they are alarmingly and overwhelmingly out of control.

Young people today

The recrudescence of these themes in our own times is easily traced. Turning briefly to that journal of record *The Times* and its sister the *Sunday Times*, the year 1995 begins with the considered views of a Scottish correspondent, apparently taken by surprise at witnessing scenes of Hogmanay. The problem lay in a familiar litany:

> It is an axiom amongst the politically correct media commentators, social workers and sopping wet churchmen that young people today are wholly admirable and the axis around which a civilisation should revolve. In reality they are a graceless, Godless, sullen, illiterate and unmannerly blight upon the landscape of a formerly civilised nation. This description applies to the more innocuous amongst them who are

not involved in drug-taking, murder or other criminal activity. (Warner, *Sunday Times* 1 January 1995).

By the middle of the year, academic commentators were being cited in order to assist readers of the newspaper make sense of this disturbing state of affairs. Dealing with a report by Rutter and Smith (1995), readers were informed that 'For most young people today, discipline is an alien concept not something against which they have rebelled, simply an experience to which they have never been exposed. The fault lies with parents who have abdicated responsibility in the increasingly rare situations where there is more than one.' In the days of Disraeli, the 'youth of our nation...were "trustees of posterity"'. Today, they had been replaced by 'a rising generation of affluent, ill-educated, spiritually dead and amoral androids' (*Sunday Times* 4 June 1995).

From amorality to criminality is but a small step, as readers of *The Times* were swift to recognise. Within three days Mrs Beryl Houghton of Leeds was sufficiently concerned to put pen to paper. Her views on youth crime were considered striking enough to warrant publication and may be repeated here in full:

> Sir, It seems to me that the increase in the incidence of crime committed by young people is due largely to the power of peer-group approval.
> Like company directors and large financial institutions, many young people today are happy to disregard public opinion and applaud and support one another in their search for self-gratification. They suffer no shame when their lack of morals is exposed. (*The Times* 7 June 1995)

And, of course, Mrs Houghton is not alone. She shares a world view with the Chief Rabbi Jonathan Sachs for whom contemporary problems began just over 20 years ago in the desperate decade of the 1960s, 'when leaders of all kinds suddenly lost the confidence in handing on moral traditions'. The predicted results were suitably apocalyptic: unless we 'recover values of integrity in business and fidelity in human sexual relations, then we shall see the collapse of 4000 years of Judaeo-Christian civilisation' (*The Financial Times* 9 March 1996).

For the purposes here these views are not just the latest in a line which stretches back to Horace and beyond. They are significant because of the extent to which they have come to dominate the ways in which young people in trouble are regarded and treated.

In the last years of the twentieth century a new hegemony has been built up, shared by both main political parties, in which the only competition appears to be in occupying the most barbarously reactionary ground. The 'yob culture' of John Major and the 'squeezie merchants' of Jack Straw are recognisably the same target. They are but amongst the latest in a long line of earlier targets, summarised by MacDonald (1995) as: 'The squatter, the Raver, the New Age traveller, the single mother, the dole fiddler, the inhabitants of the "yob culture", the "lager lout" (whatever happened to him?), the ones who want "something for nothing", the "welfare underclass", the "bail bandit" and the "persistent young offender" have all taken their places in the Tory Hall of Shame, offered up as wraiths to haunt the public imagination.'

For both parties, to be young, homeless and obliged to find an existence amongst the dangers of the street is a cause for concern only as an affront to tourism and as an inconvenience to those who have to step over sleeping bodies on their exit from the opera. Condemning more and understanding less is no departure in British social policy. It is a course of action which resonates in a set of time-honoured attitudes, never far from the surface of popular consciousness and easily available for exploitation. Youth justice practitioners ply their trade at a time when, as others have suggested, 'Britain . . . is dominated by competing claims, from left and right, to have a formula for the "re-moralising of the young"' (Stenson and Factor 1995). This all lies, of course, at very far remove from the Children-First approach which was outlined in the Introduction to this book and which is developed in subsequent chapters.

Real change: for worse, not better

Pearson's findings caution us against a reflex reaction, in which the circumstances of today are always worse than those of the recent past. Yet, it can forcefully be argued that the objective position of large numbers of young people in contemporary society has deteriorated sharply over just the 20-year period discussed above. Chapter 5, in particular, deals in some detail with the major social circumstances which shape youth justice practice today, including health, housing and education. Here the focus is upon the economic explanation which, in terms of factual data at least, is largely uncontentious. A few instances may stand for the larger picture.

Work and money

In 1976, the year before the introduction of the first Youth Opportunities Programme, 53 per cent of young people went directly into employment at the end of formal schooling. These young people stood, in many ways, near the end of a 30-year generation in which the transition from school to work was unproblematic, at least in terms of employment opportunities. The National Child Development Study, for example, in tracing the lives of all young people born in a single week in 1958, found that most managed the move to adulthood without undue difficulty or delay (Kiernan 1992). For the young person leaving school at 15, in the 1960s, a typical employment career would have seen an immediate move into full-time and regular work. Thereafter, a pattern of relatively swift job changes might follow, with little or no interval between leaving one place of work and taking up another. Jobs were plentiful and opportunities for betterment – or at least for change – were in equally regular supply. The impact of this economic status is shown in a series of sociological treatments of young people which were published during the 1970s (Brake 1980; Hebdige 1979) and which emphasised the sub-cultural vitality of particular groups such as teds, mods and rockers, punks, skinheads and so on. What linked these very diverse groups together was the capacity to exercise some control over their own lives, to make decisions about consumption and expenditure in a pattern which linked them together in important and significant ways. While, as MacDonald *et al.* (1993) and others have subsequently argued, these writers may have under-estimated the mundane realities of the lives of most young people, they nevertheless captured important aspects of contemporary reality in their portrayal of sub-cultural stylists as lively and powerful collective actors. The individualist consumer culture of the 1990s, explored more fully below, gives rise to a very different set of behaviours and ambitions.

By 1986, ten years later, the proportion of young people moving into such employment at the end of compulsory education had fallen to 15 per cent. By the middle of the 1990s the proportion is even smaller, at one in eight of 16-year-olds in ordinary full-time

employment (Courtnay and McAleese 1993). Now, too, individuals
in these circumstances emerge into the labour market from an
education system which has itself become more segmented and
driven by market considerations to identify potentially successful
and unsuccessful students from an ever-earlier age (see Chapter 5
for a fuller discussion). Average unemployment amongst 16 to
24-years-olds is almost double the national average as a whole
and proportionately they make up a declining part of the workforce (TUC 1996a). The situation for black young people is bleaker
still. One in three black school leavers faces life without a proper
job – twice the rate for their white contemporaries. The collapse of
paid work is the single greatest change to have overtaken young
people in recent history.

   If the facts are uncontentious, explaining them is far less so.
Youth unemployment is best understood by placing it in the context of wider changes in young people's participation within the
economy. The 1980s were a decade in which unemployment grew
rapidly and where the government of the day sought to explain
this rise either as an international phenomenon – about which
nothing could be done – or as voluntary. This latter explanation –
unemployment as a self-inflicted wound, in the words of Ronald
Reagan – proved particularly potent in the case of young people.
During the long and undistinguished history of government-spon-
sored schemes for mopping up youth unemployment – from the
Youth Opportunities Programme to the Youth Training Scheme,
and on to its successor of YT (Youth Training) – the official
explanation of the problem requiring attention was never an
absence of work. Young people were unemployed because they
lacked the necessary working habits, because schools were failing
to meet the needs of industry, because skill levels were not properly
developed and so on. But never because there were not enough
jobs. Instead young people were required to equip themselves with
the abilities sought after in the fast-food industry and then, in the
argot of the times, get on their bikes and to price themselves into
work. And so they did. The Labour Force Survey of autumn 1995
found that of employees aged 16–19, 37 per cent worked in whole-
sale and distribution trades – compared with 15 per cent of all
employees – with a further 16 per cent employed in the low-paying
hotels and restaurants sector. The TUC (1996b), drawing conclusions from this and other evidence, concluded that more than half

of all workers under 20 are now employed in industries 'typified by low pay, limited training opportunities, high rates of staff turnover and little union protection'.

When exhortation failed, government stepped in to take action more directly. In 1988 benefit entitlement for 16 and 17-year-olds was abolished. It was a scandal, Ministers argued, that young people should be afforded the morally sapping choice of living off the largess of the state when a place upon a youth training scheme could be guaranteed to anyone unable to find a 'real' job or continue in education. At the same time, pricing oneself into a job became easier when the abolition of Wages Councils for under 21-year-olds removed the floor from under some of the lowest paid occupations. The Low Pay Unit published an analysis of the impact of these changes in 1996. It found that nearly 55 per cent of jobs for 16-year-olds and 48 per cent for those aged 17 paid less than £58 a week, the National Insurance threshold. In 1990 the comparable figures had been 10 per cent and 7 per cent and the average hourly pay for school leavers was £1.69 an hour. This had *fallen*, in cash terms, by 1995 to £1.63 – a collapse of just under 19 per cent when taking the cost of living into account.

The changes which confront young people at the end of formal education are thus not confined simply to the availability of employment. The 1960s school-leavers encountered earlier did not only move into a world where work was plentiful and replete with choices: they also entered a world where the rates of pay and working conditions which they were afforded were recognisably linked to those enjoyed by older employees in the same occupation. Thirty years later, the argument that given time and application a young person might expect to witness an improvement in her or his own prospects has, in the eyes of such individuals themselves, become less and less credible (TUC 1996b). For most of us, ambition is shaped by attainability. We are motivated towards those prospects which have some realistic hope of being achieved and our present conduct is shaped, at least in part, by the extent to which we believe it to add to the prospect of future improvement. When the chain of attainability is broken, so the behavioural link is also shattered. Young people who come to the attention of social welfare agencies are, far too often, those for whom the chances of fulfilling even the modest ambitions of wider society – a place to live, a car, a holiday – appear remote from any legitimate route which they might travel. In these circumstances, as discussed more fully in later chapters of this book, either ambitions shrivel, or a different route is chosen. Later in this chapter the idea of *transitions* is considered, as a useful way of understanding that phase in the life course in which young people attain a level of adult independence. The information here illustrates the way in which, for most young people, this process has become elongated, delaying and deferring the achievement of goals which had previously been regarded as unproblematic (see Irwin 1996 for a more detailed development of this argument). For youth justice workers, however, it is not the elongation but the fracturing of the process which has become most significant amongst young people with whom they work.

Youth and citizenship

Even more significantly, however, in the argument of this book, is that the explicit economic agenda of the 1980s and 1990s has been matched by a wider, and more covert, set of social policies. The effect of separating young people ever further from participation in the economic mainstream has been to separate them also from the wider powers and abilities which economic independence confers. In its place has come a new and pervasive emphasis upon the subordinate position which young people occupy in all the important institutions – family, education, employment and so on – in which they operate. In social policy terms, this subordination has been codified in a series of Acts of Parliament which, over a 15-year period, have delineated a new and secondary form of citizenship for young people.

The whole notion of citizenship is one which during the 1990s has become the focus of major political and sociological interest (France 1996). The dominant Marshall (1950) paradigm, in which citizenship was essentially defined by a series of claims against the state which it had a duty to supply, has come under substantial challenge from the New Right. In this formulation, collectivity and rights have been supplanted by an understanding of citizenship constructed around notions of individualism and responsibility in which the state has only a closely qualified duty for the dispersal of benefits on the basis of citizenship. In this sense, of course, as Evans (1995) argues, citizenship is not a neutral term, but one which is shaped by political ideologies and firmly linked to ideas of social control. In the case of young people in particular, the outcome of most recent shifts in the understanding of citizenship has been 'the growth and development of new forms of social controls which limit young people's choices and restrict their opportunities to become autonomous adults' (France 1996: 40).

The dramatic departure which this represents should not be underestimated. The 1960s school leaver entered an economic world which recognisably linked her or him to older workers. Once compulsory education was at an end, the state, in so far as it sought to provide for or regulate that individual, made little or no distinction between the citizen at 18, 28 or 58. Employment laws, housing laws, social security provision and so on provided for rights and responsibilities which were largely age-neutral. By 1996 that position had been radically reversed.

Housing and citizenship

Housing may stand as an example of these wider changes. In 1985 the government changed the board and lodging regulations under which claimants were able to obtain help with certain types of rented accommodation. Ministers pointed to the disgrace, as they saw it, of the unemployed flocking to the fun palaces of seaside landladies in places like Margate and Southend, there to live a life of sybaritic hedonism at the taxpayers' expense. Only young people, however, were singled out for particular legislative attention. Time-limits were introduced which, for claimants under the age of 25, fixed the period which might be spent at any one location before entitlement to board and lodging payments would be withdrawn. An apparently random pattern was announced in which a two-week limit at one location was matched by four and eight-week limits at others. The Elizabethan Poor Law re-emerged as young people were obliged to move from parish to parish in pursuit of such basic accommodation.

Board and lodging changes proved to be only the first attempt to devise entitlements which would treat young people as a distinct and subsidiary group of citizens. The social security changes of 1988, which abolished benefit entitlement for 16 and 17-year-olds, introduced a new category of claimant, the 18–24 year old, whose needs were to be met through a lower level of benefit. In 1990 students were denied Housing Benefit. By 1994 a further re-ordering of social security policy proposed the abolition of Income Support and its replacement by the Job Seekers Allowance. Under the new arrangements claimants in the 18–24-year-old range were again singled out for particular treatment. Murray (1994) estimates that anyone in this group with savings of £8000 now faces a 60 per cent loss in weekly income, those with savings of £3000 will have a weekly benefit reduction of 30 per cent, while those with no savings at all face a loss of 20 per cent.

In 1996 these difficulties had been further exacerbated by a general move to restrict the scope of Housing Benefit entitlement which had included a series of particular reductions for those aged under 25. Under the new system the housing benefit entitlements of young people under 25 will be limited to the cost of a bed-sitting room, meaning that the cost of one-bedroom flats, studio flats, shared two-bedroomed flats and some shared houses will not be met. The most vulnerable groups will be amongst the worst affected. As other commentators have made clear, young people leaving care, for example, 'will be pushed further into the worse end of the private rented sector and if they are unable to get help with rent charges which are over and above the assessed rent will be unable to maintain the accommodation' (Social Action Today, 1996).

Citizenship, housing and crime

Pat Carlen (1996: 23) has recently explored the nexus through which the nature of youth homelessness has come to be defined by a particular version of political criminology. As she suggests, at the root of this process lies the belief that, 'people who do not own their own homes, or, worse still, are actually homeless, are not only lacking in self-reliance but their existence is a threat to British society'. A political vocabulary which equates homelessness with criminality bears particularly harshly upon young people. It pro-vides a legitimacy for what Carlen calls 'the antisocial repressions of modernist techno-bureaucracies' (1996: 121) in a general assault upon the citizen rights of a whole generation.

In the European Union, and more widely, discussion of citizenship at the end of the twentieth century has come to be centred around the concepts of inclusion and exclusion. The conceptual shift from poverty to social exclusion is one which emphasises the processes through which individuals become detached from participation in mainstream society, rather than simply the condition of marginalisation itself. In the words of Jacques Dolors (1993), 'although exclusion includes poverty, poverty does not cover exclusion'. In the social policy treatment of young people in Britain within the 1980s and 1990s these developments are vividly illustrated. To an extent unimaginable only two decades ago, harsh and enduring destitution has become a defining characteristic of whole sections of a generation brought up in poverty and inheritors of the same condition in their own lives. Many commentators have suggested that social rights, and a fully enacted citizenship, depend upon economic independence (see, for example, Lister 1991; Jones and Wallace 1992). In the case of young people, however, that relation has been carried a stage further. Around the defining core of economic relations, a set of other social relations have been accreted in which inadequate social participation, lack of power and absence of integration have been institutionalised into the experience of becoming an adult in contemporary Britain. This self-reinforcing pattern inflicts particular damage upon those young people who find themselves in trouble with the law. The process emerges powerfully in research conducted at the University of Wales, Bangor, which 'initially set out to explore the processes involved in the criminalisation of homeless youth, focusing on criminal justice and other agency responses to activities such as begging, shoplifting and prostitution' (Wardaugh 1995). The researchers quickly discovered that this narrow focus failed to reflect the broader experience which surrounded the nexus of homelessness and criminalisation with which investigations had begun. As reported by Wardaugh, 'In conversations with homeless young people it quickly became apparent that lawbreaking activities and subsequent criminalisation were processes that took place within the wider context of their exclusion from society.' The young people interviewed in Manchester, Birmingham and Stoke-on-Trent were characterised by continuous attempts, on their part, 'to negotiate some degree of inclusion within society', only to be met by systematic exclusion 'from the social, economic and political structures of our society'.

Youth transitions

The shifting boundaries of age-related entitlements alerts us to the more general difficulties which have surrounded attempts to define 'youth' by chronology. Any text which deals with the criminal justice system and the ways in which it impacts upon young people must, of necessity, be interested in age-boundaries. Yet as Springhall (1986) points out, age boundaries themselves are subject to the 'historical fluidity underpinning the definition of youth within cultural and legal meanings'. In attempting to develop an understanding of the ways in which the move from childhood to adulthood is negotiated, the notion of *transition* is preferred, as developed by Banks *et al.* (1992), Jones and Wallace (1992) and others. Following Coles (1995: 8ff) and Crane and Coles (1995), three core transitions may be identified as facing young people generally in moving from dependant to independent status and these, in turn, are mirrored by three ways in which transitions have come to be negotiated. The shifts to be accomplished are the economic transition from school to work, the personal transition from family of origin to family of destination and the spatial transition from parental home to separate accommodation. The ways in which these may be achieved can be summarised as *traditional transitions* in which young people left school and, with relative speed and ease, obtained employment, found partners and established independent households and families of their own; *extended or protracted transitions* in which the achievement of jobs, family formation and leaving home are delayed and embarked upon at a later age (see for example Banks *et al.* 1992; Jones 1993); and, finally, *fractured transitions* in which young people are faced with a protracted struggle ever to obtain reliable work in the formal labour market, or to form stable partnerships in secure and independent accommodation.

Transition and choice

In making these transitions young people face a series of choices which, according to individual circumstances, are characterised by greater or lesser constraint and opportunity. For some theorists, such as Coles (1995), the degree of choice is best reflected in the concept of *career*, in which differing paths through major transitions are understood to be the product of different decisions made by individuals. Such choices are shaped and limited by factors outside immediate individual control, most importantly including the decisions made by adults which 'help to shape and re-shape the opportunity structures with which they are faced' (Crane and Coles 1995). Nevertheless, choice remains real and available in almost all circumstances. The exercise of choice itself shapes and limits future decisions which, in turn, produce individual careers from child to adulthood. Coles is a liberal writer whose purpose is to rescue some sense of young people exercising control and influence over their own lives. An emphasis upon individualism, however, is also one of the hallmarks of the New Right and a continuing legacy of Thatcherism. Its impact is to be found in those theoretical models which, during the 1990s, have come to supplant those of the sub-cultural stylists outlined above. Here, instead of an emphasis upon collective action, attention has shifted to the individual as *consumer* (see, for example, Roberts and Parsell 1991; Ford 1992; Stewart 1992; Bocock 1993; Lee 1993). Miles (1995) suggests that 'their experience as consumers provides young people with the only meaningful role available to them' in which particular acts of consumption provide a symbolic means of asserting individuality while, at the same time, forging a link with a wider set of peer identities.

An emphasis upon choice is also a hallmark of the postmodernist sociologists who emphasise the ways in which the certainties of previous generations have given way to the risks faced by young people in a fragmented and uncertain present (Beck 1992; Giddens 1991; Lash and Urry 1987). This position is contested by writers such as Roberts (1986, 1987, 1993), for whom transitions and choices continue to be so determined by factors such as class, gender, locality and ethnicity, as to be better understood as *trajectories* rather than *careers*. Trajectories emphasise the limits of choice which face many young people. Rather than a plethora of individualised pathways from dependence to independence, transitions are better understood as clusters in which structural advantages and disadvantages propel different groups of young people towards a different series of group destinations. Escape from the powerful currents which drive such cohorts together is difficult and unusual. Even consumerism is an illusion. Young people do not make creative decisions about their own identity and their links with others. Rather they have the *illusion* of choice, constrained entirely within the very narrow range provided by consumer capitalism. Even less ideologically couched investigations, such as that of Morrow and Richards (1996) emphasise the mismatch between 'young people's expectations and ambitions and the reality of their everyday experiences, as they move into adulthood'. Choice and consumerism are more problematic in practice than the growing theoretical emphasis upon their importance in establishing identity might allow.

Amongst these competing explanations, the position adopted in this book is close to that set out by Furlong and Cartmel (1997). In their argument, young people do now face making important personal transitions at a time when 'points of reference which previously helped smooth processes of social reproduction have become obscure' (1997: 1). This obscurity, however, does not mean that the potencies of class, gender and race have not evaporated. Rather, as they argue, 'existing patterns of inequality are simply being reproduced in different ways' (p.7). Whichever explanation is adopted, for the young people with whom this book is particularly concerned, a series of common problems emerge. To pursue the consumerist perspective briefly, whether the role is better understood as embodying robust individual choice or the pre-determined parameters of more powerful external forces is of little practical consequence for the young person without the basic resources required for participation in the culture of consumption. Without such resources, as Miles (1995) suggests 'young people appear, in effect, to be disenfranchised'. The social circumstances of young people who get into trouble with the law are set out more fully in Chapter 5 of this book. The point to be emphasised here is that the withering room for manoeuvre in their circumstances and the cumulative impact of fractured opportunities, in turn, places a shrinking limit upon their capacity to make real choices which produce a real impact upon their immediate or future prospects.

Young people in trouble

The final section of this chapter concentrates more directly upon those prevailing public attitudes which shape policies towards young people in trouble. A paradox immediately presents itself.

In real life young people have fewer and fewer choices and are afforded a debilitated form of citizenship in which they are denied responsibility over a widening area of civic life. In the increasingly unreal world of criminal justice, however, the same young people will increasingly find themselves regarded as having made decisions – or choices – for which they must now be held responsible. This emphasis upon responsibility and obligation goes unmatched by any reciprocal conception of young people as possessed of rights or duties owed to them by the wider community. As 'politicians . . . vie to convince a cynical public that, if given the chance, they will impose discipline on an increasingly recalcitrant youth where others have failed' (Stenson and Factor 1995), two competing paradigms emerge which purport to make sense of those young people who find themselves in trouble with the law.

The new barbarians?

On the one hand, such individuals are presented as the 'young barbarians' of the underclass (Murray 1990, 1994), cut off from the values and behaviours of the civilised, pathologically devoted to a self-reinforcing cycle of poverty, unemployment, drug-taking and crime and held in this state of irresponsibility by the enervating largess of the welfare state. The sexual coupling of young males in these conditions, with young females determined to use motherhood as a route to their castle in a council flat, produces a progeny genetically inferior to their contemporaries in the moral majority (see Holman, 1995, for a fine refutation of these propositions). Such young people are not to be treated as capable of a mature and moral responsibility for their actions. Instead, only the stick, without the relief of carrot, can be expected to keep them in some sort of order. Lower wages, cancel benefits, remove the vote and fill the prisons is a prescription list which best holds out the hope of keeping these barbarians from the door.

Responsibility

On the other hand, young people in trouble are to be treated as though wholly and entirely responsible for their actions. The Labour Party policy document *Tackling Youth Crime: Reforming Youth Justice* is instructive here. At the age of 10, the lowest age of criminal responsibility, the document regards such a child as, 'plainly capable of differentiating between right and wrong' and in no need of protection by the niceties of *doli incapax* which the paper proposed sweeping away (see Chapter 7 for a further account of the arguments concerning *doli incapax*). Instead, such children are to be 'confronted with their behaviour' because it is '*their behaviour* which is destroying their own life chances' (emphasis added). When children are responsible for their own life chances then failure to measure up to that responsibility has to be taken seriously. Labour's policy document proposed a programme of social authoritarianism in which recalcitrant parents would be made to shape up, supervision made more rigorous, lay magistrates removed from findings of guilt or innocence and young people properly punished. During the election campaign of 1997, youth crime appeared amongst Labour's five key pledges, in a promise to curb by one half the time taken to process persistent young offenders from arrest to sentence.

The thinking which animated such proposals was perhaps best summed up in the way in which Labour leader Tony Blair and his Home Secretary-designate Jack Straw appropriated the term *zero tolerance* in their own public vocabulary during this period. Asked directly in a pre-election interview conducted by the Big Issue magazine if he agreed with zero tolerance policies in which 'every minor law break is clamped down on hard by police', Mr Blair replied simply 'Yes, I do' (Rogers 1997). In the British context, the phrase had previously been the province of municipal and feminist socialists who had succeeded, as Bea Campbell (1997) suggests, in developing a campaign against domestic violence which 'neither degraded the victim nor beastialised the culprit'. The appropriation of the term for a very different purpose was matched by a very different tone. Zero tolerance, when applied to young people in trouble, identified them as an enemy to whom the decencies of understanding, assistance or even basic tolerance need not be extended.

In government, the Labour administration moved swiftly to give effect to some of these core ideas. Its first legislative programme included a Crime and Disorder Bill which Jack Straw, making his first House of Commons statement as Home Secretary, declared would speed up juvenile justice and thus 'ensure that young offenders are made to see the clear link between crime and punishment, and to face up to the consequence of their offending for their victims and for themselves' (Hansard 1997a). The 'absurd' and 'archaic' *doli incapax* rule was to be replaced and 'from the outset it must be made clear to young people that they will not get away with offending' (Hansard 1997a). Youth justice also formed a major component in the Home Secretary's final speech to the Commons (Hansard 1997b) before the new government broke for its first summer recess. The 'statement about improving the criminal justice system' was, in effect, the government's manifesto for action and, as such, its main points are worth recording in some detail. The government's approach was rooted in a determination to 'tackle antisocial behaviour, particularly from young offenders, which makes a misery of the lives of so many law-abiding people of our country'. In order to do so, the following elements were to be part of the Home Secretary's armoury:

- 'On custodial sentences for young offenders, the courts need a more coherent and flexible set of powers to lock up that small group of persistent young offenders who wreak havoc in their communities. As I announced on 3 July, the courts will have available to them from April 1998 the secure training order. We are also proposing to give the youth court the power to order the secure remand of such offenders.'
- 'I shall also pilot tagging for those on bail as well as for fine defaulters, persistent petty offender and juveniles.'
- 'We must intervene early to change the behaviour of young offenders. We shall make it clear that the aim of the youth justice system is to protect the public and reduce reoffending. A national network of youth offender teams will implement much tougher regimes of community interventions. A new national board for youth justice will oversee change.'

Britain is a country where, in the words of one leading social commentator, the principle which seems to link social policy towards young people is one of giving 'responsibilities early and rights late' (Freedland 1997). Youth justice policy appears to be in the forefront of this development, denying young people rights which, in some cases, have been theirs for centuries, while exacting a higher idea of 'responsibility' in return. The elements in Labour's approach, outlined above, appear to carry this policy tendency forward rather than take it in any new direction. The detail of these measures receives attention in later sections of this book.

Perpetrators or victims?

This section begins with the first of a series of case studies which are used in this text to illustrate particular themes and to provide the reader with real-life material against which to test questions raised and solutions suggested. The case of Stuart, which follows, raises an issue which receives scant attention in the daily discussion of young offenders – the extent to which young people are themselves the victims of crime.

Case study: Stuart

Stuart is 13 years old and lives with his parents in a well-established, respectable inner-city area. His parents care a lot for him but are preoccupied with worry that he will become involved in the sort of trouble which is constantly being talked about on the television and highlighted in the local newspaper. Their anxiety has been increased because Stuart has been reported to the police on two previous occasions for 'being a nuisance' with groups of other young men in the locality.

Soon after the most recent reporting, Stuart is brought home in the back of a police car. The police had been called following a complaint that a group of boys had been throwing stones at a newly-erected council road sign, causing a disturbance to neighbours and passers-by. The police officer tells his parents that he is fed up with being bothered by Stuart and that he is considering charging him with an offence. Stuart must report to the local station in two weeks time.

At the local youth club, one week later, a discussion takes place with all those involved in the incident. It is generally agreed that Stuart had thrown a stone which had missed the road sign and hit the garage of a nearby house. The householder had emerged and thrown a punch at Stuart, nearly knocking him to the ground. The houseowner had then called the police.

On being taken home, Stuart says that his father had made him sit in a red hot bath, and had threatened to 'make it worse for him next time', if the police do go ahead and press charges. None of the other young people involved in the discussion seemed to find anything unusual or worth commenting on in this sequence of events. So it was that a young person involved in an accidental piece of urban play came to be at risk of formal criminal proceedings, as well as assaulted by one adult, and scalded by another, both of whom were able to regard their own actions, and have them regarded by others, as responsible and legitimate.

The view of young people as primary perpetrators of offending is so pervasive that it masks an important element in their own experience as victims of crime. Brown (1995), for example, in a study which involved 1000 young people and 500 adults in Middlesborough found that 62 per cent of responding adults thought that young people today were worse behaved than young people in the past. The research identifies the almost total way in which 'young people' and 'crime' had become synonymous in the minds of its older adult respondents, in particular: 'If one asked a respondent about their perceptions of young people, they would almost immediately start talking of increasing crime and disorder ...If one asked about crime, the account would again be very similar... Crime is seen as young people, and vice versa' (p. 32). While the same people were able to identify contributory causes which lay outside the control of young people – lack of employment, absence of leisure opportunities and so on – 'in the end [they] see young people not as victims, but as perpetrators and as both symptom and cause of the collapse of the moral universe' (p. 36). Yet, in the same study, the actual experience of victimisation was very different. Of the 11–15-year-olds who filled in a self-completion questionnaire, 59 per cent had been victimised by adults in the year preceding the study. Almost all reported being victimised by other young people. As a result, 35 per cent had been 'very' or 'quite' frightened by their last victimisation experience. In terms of action towards them by adults:

47% said they felt threatened by adults staring at them,
7% suffered physical assault,
18% had been followed in a car,
30% had been followed on foot, and
18% had adults ask them things in a threatening manner.

Adults in the same survey reported considerably lower levels of victimisation:

   10% reported suffering harassment or victimisation,
   21% said this was the result of threatening behaviour, and
   6% reported a physical assault.

While the experience of young people as victims of crime is a culpably neglected area, the findings reported by Brown are strongly corroborated in such other work as has been undertaken. Anderson *et al.* (1994) surveyed 250 11–15-year-olds in contrasting areas of Edinburgh. More than four in ten respondents reported worrying a lot about being attacked by strangers, rising to nearly six out of ten young women. Half of the young people in the Anderson study had been actual victims. Leaving aside offences committed at school or at home, 37 per cent had been assaulted during the previous nine months, 31 per cent had been threatened with violence and 17 per cent reported having had something stolen. Nor were these crimes committed by people of their own age. In less than half identifiable cases were offenders thought to be under the age of 16 while fully two-thirds of the girls reported having been harassed by adults, again involving being followed either in cars or on foot. Similar findings were further reported in an analysis of the British Crime Survey where six out of ten 12–15-year-olds reported having been victims of an incident over the previous six to eight months (Maung 1995). Even this level was surpassed in a study carried out by Hartless *et al.* (1995), who using a self-completion questionnaire with 11–15-year-olds found that 82 per cent reported being a victim of crime on at least one occasion during the previous year.

   Hartless *et al.*'s findings also emphasise an additional common thread in all the studies reported here. The young people responding to the self-completion questionnaire recorded themselves as unlikely to report that experience to anyone in authority, a finding which Brown (1995) explains as the product of young people believing that they, rather than any perpetrator, would find themselves in most trouble if a crime were to be reported. Indeed in the Middlesborough survey young people were less likely to report a crime the more serious it became, because of this belief: 'as the seriousness of the incident increased (for example, a physical assault and theft from the person compared with threats) the more likely a young person is to avoid reporting it because they fear they will not be believed or because they fear they will get into trouble from adults' (p. 38).

Failure to claim victim status by young people who are themselves identified offenders may be reinforced by additional considerations. As well as establishing the fluid and permeable nature of 'offender' and 'victim' categorisation, earlier research carried out for the Association of Chief Officers of Probation (Peelo *et al.* 1992) clearly illustrated the impact which offender status had upon anyone who subsequently became a victim of crime themselves. Once known as an offender, any subsequent victimisation becomes treated as questionable by a range of authorities and, even when established, denied any seriousness. Thus a burglary at the home of an identified burglar becomes an object of mockery when reported to the police, the loss of a giro by a known thief treated according to discriminatory procedures by the Benefit Agency and so on.

For young people with a reputation for trouble, therefore, being themselves a victim of crime – as is more than likely – brings with it the additional disadvantage of having the seriousness of that victimisation denied. Indeed, for a number of Peelo *et al.*'s (1992) respondents, the fact of not being able to rely on the sympathy and understanding which victims are able to claim was a more striking and enduring deprivation than the loss of physical goods which an offence against them might have entailed. How much more striking these feelings are likely to be in the case of those for whom denial of victim status is grafted onto a denial of their situation as young people and as such having some claim on the consideration and compassion of those more powerful than themselves.

In this account so far, consideration of victim status has essentially been confined to those cases where offences have taken place outside the domestic or personal spheres. Of course, young people are vulnerable to victimisation in these circumstances also. It is not part of the purpose of this book to provide an account of recent work in the fields of physical, emotional and sexual abuse of children. These are, of course, offences committed by adults against children. They raise a point which is of general consequence for the purposes of this book. Young people, it can be argued, commit their offences in the public arena, on the street or in other public space where they are likely to be visible and the chances of any wrong-doing more easily observed and detected. Adults, by contrast, commit their offences in the privacy of home, car and working environment, stealing from the employer and assaulting other members of their family in contexts where their behaviour is relatively invisible and unlikely to be detected (see Pearson 1994 for a more general discussion of these arguments). In the domestic setting, particularly, children are more likely to be victims of crime than its perpetrators. Davies and Bourhill (1997) very usefully explore the conundrum which such individuals pose for the media. Children as victims oblige the creation of a special counter-category of description. Young people in these circumstances have to be portrayed not as the vandals of dominant discourse, but rather the innocent victims of either adults' depravation or – more often – the culpable neglect of incompetent or ideologically-driven social workers.

In the case of young people caught up in the criminal justice system, however, this form of victimisation has additional ramifications. Just as being a known offender results in victimisation in other contexts being taken less seriously, so, too, abuse of a child who is also in trouble can be held to be less serious, or somehow justified, by that fact.

This has been a very brief consideration of a complex area in which many other issues which might be explored. The summary provided by Furlong and Cartmel (1997: 93) highlights those matters which are of most relevance to the particular concerns of this book:

> In many respects, the concentration on young people as the perpetrators of crimes has left us blind to the extent to which young people are victims; they frequently have crimes committed against them and their fears have an impact on their day-to-day behaviour. In particular, young women frequently experience harassment which they are reluctant to report and which restricts their freedom to go out alone. Moreover, while adults express concerns about 'lawless' youth, many crimes are also committed against young people by adults.

Lessons from elsewhere

The simultaneous denial of autonomy and responsibility on the one hand, coupled with the notion that young people who commit offences should be treated as though they had a mature under-standing of the nature of their actions on the other, has already taken root in the United States of America from where so many of the New Right and New Labour approaches to justice are derived. It is not the intention of this chapter to provide a comparative introduction to the way in which young people are treated in the United Kingdom and the United States. Nor are claims made that what happens in one sphere is easily or directly translated into another. There is ample evidence, however, of the ways in which North American influences impact on British social policy generally (see for example Oppenheim and Lister 1996) and in criminal justice policy in particular (Christie 1993; Smith 1996).

The future for such policies directed at young people has lately been explored by Tony Jeffs and Mark Smith (1996), who draw on recent experience of teaching and working in both Britain and America. Just as young people face the deliberate creation of subsidiary citizenship in the social and civic spheres, they point to a parallel pattern in the justice field: 'widespread concern regarding crime, and juvenile offending in particular, appears to be producing a control culture buttressed by a burgeoning array of legislation often specifically directed at young people'. The daily experience of such individuals is thus strewn with the products of policy-making which single out young people for separate and less advantageous treatment than other sections of society.

By the early 1980s, 12 American states had already imposed night-driving curfews on young people (Merry 1984). The Reagan Administration required states to raise the legal drinking age to a minimum of 21. Some states have gone further, making possession of tobacco punishable in anyone under 18 (Jeffs and Smith 1996). During the 1990s, 'curfew fever' (Blumner 1994) has swept across the United States, requiring young people – usually under the age of 17 – to be off the streets during the late evening and night time. In New Orleans, late evening begins at 8 p.m. Hawaii has a state-wide curfew. Thousands of small towns and three-quarters of the largest 77 cities in America employ such arrangements (Ruefle and Reynolds 1995). So popular have these measures proved that according to Jeffs and Smith (1996) 'a growing number are being supplemented with daytime curfews operating during school hours'!

While freedom, responsibility and autonomy are thus denied in the social and civic spheres, the fate of those young people who do come before the courts is to be treated as though they were wholly accountable for their actions. A recent and powerful account of such changes within the New York jurisdiction (Singer 1996) traces the process by which juveniles have come to be prosecuted as adults across a widening range of offences. The background to such changes rings a series of familiar bells. The context had been set by a coalition of academics and practitioners who complained of a lack of justice in juvenile courts which denied youthful offenders basic constitutional rights in pursuit of 'treatment' which was not necessarily in their best interests. It led, in the terms which Singer adopts, to *criminalisation* of process: a shift away from humanistic concerns and towards the formalities of criminal justice procedure. The immediate trigger to New York's changes then lay in a specific case of an individual young offender, Willie Bosket, who at the age of 15 shot and killed a passenger on the New York subway. The incident attracted a public outcry. The case emerged within six months of Gubernatorial elections in New York state in which the incumbent, Hugh L. Carey, was already under pressure from his opponent, 'in which he was repeatedly accused of being "soft" on crime'.

Singer (1996: 46–54) highlights a series of specific actors and arguments which then contributed to a recriminalisation of youthful offenders. These included:

- The role of the media:

  'they presented a version of reality that fit a recurring popular media theme of violent juvenile crime and juvenile justice. They stressed that a segment of delinquents was more violent and more chronic than the delinquents of earlier generations. At the same time, they argued that the juvenile justice system failed to keep up with the more violent behaviour of this new generation of violent delinquents.'

- In particular, reporters highlighted the limited powers which courts possessed for younger offenders and the impact which this was said to have on particular individuals. In the headline of one tabloid newspaper, one child was quoted as saying 'I Can Kill Because I'm Fourteen'. Police officers were readily available with corroborating material: 'The whole thing's a joke to these kids... As soon as you grab them they say, "I'm only 14" or 15 or whatever, and "there's nothing you can do to me"'.

• The response of the courts was criticised. Not only did judges fail to mete out sufficient punishment, 'the juvenile courts appeared to make things worse by doing nothing to punish and deter their repeated violent behaviour'.

• Public discourse contained a new emphasis on victims. 'Chronic violent delinquents needed to be even more harshly punished because they were now choosing more and more vulnerable victims... the image presented... was that of a legal process in which the victims were more afraid of the court than the offenders'.

• Finally, public debate developed a version of young people in trouble which divided them into 'the bad and the not-so-bad'. The really bad were made up of a small number of individuals who were responsible for a hugely disproportionate number of crimes. As ever, the police were reliable witnesses to this phenomenon:

> 'I would say that there are a small group of juveniles that are doing this... but if you get 50 or 60 kids in a borough and they are completely recycled out into the street for violent crimes like robbery or rape and murder, well, those 60 kids can put a crime pattern out there that would be 1800 to 2000 cases of robbery.'

Many of the elements which contributed to the changes traced by Singer are to be found in Britain today. To take just one example: the Northumbria police force has taken on itself, over a number of years, a campaigning role in highlighting what it claims to be the problems posed by persistent young offenders. Placing the criminal records of individual young people into the public domain produced the looked-for response in the tabloid press, with gratifying stories about 'Ratboy', 'Spiderboy' and 'one-boy crime waves'. The force were at it again late in 1996: Northumbria released details of 58 young people, claiming – on the basis of an imaginative approach to statistics – that these individuals could have been responsible for 6500 crimes over a 12-month period (the *Guardian* 12 November 1996). The response demanded by senior police officers in 1996 had shifted from that proposed in the earlier years of the decade. Then, the press campaign had largely contributed to the government's announcement of Secure Training Centres for persistent young offenders. Now the assistant chief constable of Northumbria called for special units to be used 'for juveniles *on the verge of becoming persistent offenders*' (emphasis added).

It is not part of the argument of this book that policy changes in one place or one set of circumstances will be easily or inevitably be translated into another. Yet, substitute the Jamie Bulger case for that of Bosket, Kenneth Clarke for Hugh Carey, Michael Howard for the zealots of the New York Republican Party, the *Sun* for the *New York Daily Post* and the Chief Constable of Northumbria for the officer in the Bronx and a pattern emerges which is more substantial than speculative. In the politicisation of crime two central traits appear to drive major actors: never admit to being responsible, and always aim to appear tougher-than-thou.

How much more disturbing, then, to find that the outcomes in America speak so much less convincingly. Singer (1996: 163–4) found that while the number of juveniles incarcerated in New York had tripled since the changes of the 1970s there had been 'no discernible reduction in violent juvenile crime'. On a broader front Krisberg and Austin (1993: 4), reviewing the American-wide changes in work with juvenile offenders, detected the same new emphasis on due process and commented that 'this new perspective emphasised deterrence and punishment as the major goals of the juvenile court... The most obvious impact of the conservative reform movement was a significant increase in the number of youth in juvenile correctional facilities. In addition, from 1979 to 1984 the number of juveniles sent to adult prisons rose by 48%.' The same authors concluded that, 'By 1990, nearly 60 000 juveniles were admitted to adult jails and approximately 2300 were in jail on any given day' (p. 76).

This incarceration of children is not confined to the justice system. There has been a parallel burgeoning, in the American context, of young people held within mental health facilities. Coppock (1996: 62) notes that, 'the rapid growth of for-profit child and adolescent mental health establishments has almost totally accounted for the dramatic increases in the institutionalisation of children and young people in the USA'. She further points to the inherent ethical difficulties which such private sector involvement entails: 'In some cases the staff in these establishments determine what is "medically necessary" for a child or young person, exposing an inherent conflict of interests when profits are dependent upon admissions.' These lessons are, sadly, unheeded in the British context. The private sector involvement in British prison building and management was established during the final years of the last Conservative administration. One of the early actions of the incoming Home Secretary, Jack Straw, was to confirm the private sector contract for the building of Britain's new 'child jails' for 12–14-year-olds. At the same time, he announced the active exploration of the merger of the probation and prison services into an American-style Department of Corrections (*Guardian* 17 July 1997). Vivien Stern (1997), former director of the National Association for the Care and Resettlement of Offenders, has recorded the market forces which drive the private prison industry in America, quoting the publicity brochure of a Texas conference entitled 'Privatising Correctional Facilities; Private Prisons – Maximise investment returns in this exploding industry'. Here, too, were the smoothly titled Children's Comprehensive Services and Youth Services International, both in fact organisations designed to make money from the incarceration of young people in this booming business. Similarly powerful incentives are now part of the British prison system, in which vested interests lie in securing a large and growing inmate population. As Stern's review of American publicity material suggests, 'Young criminals become older criminals. The future is bright'.

Conclusion

It has been the contention of this chapter that young people in our society face a broad-fronted assault upon their economic, social and civic positions which has led, for large numbers of such individuals, to a marginalisation of their involvement in mainstream society. The forces which create this exclusion are not accidental or the product of drift. Rather, they are deliberately aimed at a group which has become the legitimate target of any politician or populist commentator who seeks to create an easy scapegoat for the failure of their own ideas and promises. Young people in trouble are the softest of such targets and, therefore, bear a sharper burden of the attitudes and policies which are heaped upon their contemporaries. But this is also an intensifying cycle of disadvantage, because children in trouble are not drawn at random from the population of young people. A later chapter returns to evidence that the American experience of burgeoning incarceration has fallen in sharply unequal ways upon different groups of young people citing, for example, Krisberg and Austin's (1993: 50) evidence that between 1979 and 1982, when the number of incarcerated youth in American institutions grew by 6178, minority youth accounted for 93 per cent of the increase. The sharp rise in incarceration occurred even though the number of arrests of minority youth declined. In the United Kingdom also, in the argument developed here, those attitudes and policies which are most destructive to young people are most forcefully at work in drawing disproportionately into the criminal justice system those who are poor or black or otherwise outside the charmed circle of the contented majority.

This chapter has argued that, in order to develop itself most fruitfully, youth justice practice has to obtain a proper understanding of the wider social policy and political contexts which shape the experience of young people at the end of the twentieth century. The picture painted is not a happy one. It suggests that for very many young people the achievement of adult independence has become more difficult, and that for the individuals who find themselves in trouble with the law the stumbling blocks may be even harder to negotiate. In the view adopted by this book, young people develop a sense of right and wrong and patterns of behaviour which reflect this understanding, by learning from the way they are themselves treated by others. In a variety of Bourdieu's (1977, 1984) concept of 'habitus' it is suggested that individuals come to durable dispositions and particular ways of behaving through the cumulative ways in which messages are communicated about their worth and prospects. In the case of young people such messages come not only from family and friends but from encounters in the wider world of teachers, youth workers, shop assistants, police officers and bank managers (see Chapter 6 for a development of these ideas within the criminological framework of control theory). This is the background noise against which youth justice practitioners operate. It is both discordant and dissonant and places an even greater weight upon the capacity of youth justice services to counteract such messages from others and to act differently themselves. It is to the history of such attempts during the 1980s, and what might be learned from them, that the next chapter now turns.

2

Juvenile Justice: a Recent History

There can be no doubt that youth justice practice must change to adapt to the challenges that now present themselves. Crime in general, and juvenile crime in particular, is a perennial social problem. The extent of public, media and political concern expressed about juvenile offending, however, tends to go in waves. One way of looking at the juvenile justice experience of the 1980s, therefore, is to see it as a low point in cycles of concern about juvenile offending. From an alternative perspective the 1980s represents the heyday of juvenile justice; a remarkable criminal justice success story in an area of social policy where we are far more accustomed to talk of failure.

Setting the scene

In the 1980s there was a quiet consensus about juvenile crime and how to deal with it. This consensus, however, was not the product of some grand government plan or policy; rather it emerged from a number of sources and grew in strength throughout the decade. A Conservative government was elected in 1979, in part, on a tough law and order stance. In juvenile justice terms this led to the introduction of tougher regimes in detention centres and a government policy towards juvenile offenders based on the 'short, sharp, shock' (that is, to give young offenders a nasty custodial experience which they will not want to re-experience and which will, therefore, lead to a cessation of offending). The deterrence-based philosophical underpinning of the 'short, sharp, shock' was fairly quickly discredited by official research (Thornton et al. 1984), but it was not the findings of research which led to a change ι. government policy and the end of detention centres.

In parallel with the government's official policy towards juvenile offenders, a disparate group of academics, senior civil servants in government departments and practitioners were developing an alternative. This alternative was based, essentially, on the belief that formal state intervention into the lives of young people often did more harm than good, and that more intrusive or excessive intervention (that is, removing young people from their home and placing them in custodial or care institutions) was generally more harmful. It would be quite wrong to overstate the degree of coalescence of views between academics, government departments and practitioners at this time. There were indeed very lively debates taking place in the early 1980s, between and within these groups, about the nature of juvenile crime and the best way to deal with it. Nevertheless, by the early to mid-1980s, two distinctive sets of practices emerged and rapidly came to dominate juvenile justice practice.

It is most appropriate to see the events of the 1980s, not as a distinct chronology of causal events, but as a dynamic and fluctuating set of coincidences and developments. There was certainly an extremely active and influential practitioner-based movement which developed at this time and which took an important lead in practice-based projects. But so too did the Department of Health and Social Security (as it was then known), led mainly by officials rather than Ministers, instigate some significant policy changes and practice initiatives. A more detailed discussion of the dynamics of the 1980s is reserved for later in this chapter; for the moment it is important to note that during the early to mid-1980s an increasingly robust consensus formed between government departments and juvenile justice practitioners, underpinned by the belief in the harmful effects of intervention and based on two distinctive practices: (i) diversion from the formal criminal justice system through the development of cautioning, and (ii) the targeted provision of community-based treatment programmes operating largely with an alternative-to-custody aim and developed through the use of supervision orders.

In public the government and its Ministers continued to talk the rhetoric of tough punishment; in official policy terms, however, the government joined the quiet consensus. The development and provision of alternatives to custody received support at the highest

$\frac{\text{c}}{\text{c}}$ .o the DHSS Intermediate Treatment Initiative[1]
:h involved the provision of seed-corn monies to
;ed projects and which aimed essentially at re-
.ermediate treatment as an alternative to custody).
.oo, received official government support in the form
)ffice Circular Instructions which advocated increased
use   :asures which fall short of formal prosecution. In the
1980s this consensus was sustained by considerable policy success
– that is the use of cautioning expanded greatly and by the mid-
1980s the provision of alternatives to custody was near universal
(Bottoms *et al.* 1990) – and by considerable success in practice as
the use of custodial sentences for juveniles declined from around
8000 per year at the beginning of the decade to under 2000 by the
end, and the prevalence of juvenile crime over this period was
declining (a decline that was not linked to population changes).
Such was the extent of these changes and their widely perceived
value that Jones wrote of these events in terms of 'the successful
revolution' (Jones 1989, 1993).

Making youth justice policy today

In the 1990s, however, this consensus has evaporated. The relationship between academic research, government policy and front-
line practice is always an uneasy one and there is rarely, if ever, a
symbiosis of all three (hence talk of a quiet consensus in 1980s
juvenile justice rather than a grand plan). Historically, however,
in this country there has traditionally been some kind of relationship which has sustained a sense of criminal justice policy as social
policy. Academics, practitioners and policy-makers, while not
always agreeing, have traditionally formed a nexus through
which official policy and practice has emerged (see Rutherford
1996). In the 1990s this relationship has been stretched to breaking
point such that criminal justice policy is now much more closely
affiliated with political policy. Academics, government officials and
practitioners[2] have been replaced in political policy-making by the
media, and more typically by the 'popular press' which engages
with politicians in a race to both shape and satisfy 'public opinion'
(in the main by habitually demonising young offenders and baying
for ever more excessive punishment).

This is the context in which youth justice policy is now made and which makes change a necessity, and it is in this context that youth justice practice must develop. The overall purpose of this book is to set out a positive agenda for change, based on the principle that children who offend should be seen and treated as children first. But in setting out an agenda for change there is no suggestion that youth justice should entrench itself as a community corrections agency, or that a major change in philosophy or direction is required. Our approach is no less radical, but it is incremental. Future success requires change, but this change needs to build upon existing knowledge and build upon what is already known to be effective. There is a great deal about the 1980s which was positive and even exceptional, and it is essential to learn from that experience in building the future. There are also aspects of 1980s juvenile justice practice which are more problematic, and learning must draw on these also.

Chapter 1 located young people within their social context, tracing the development of the context of childhood and examining how society and the political establishment has shaped the context in which young people live out their lives. This second building block chapter, therefore, reviews the 1980s[3] juvenile justice experience in some detail to develop a clear understanding of what made this period such a remarkable success story.

The welfare of the child

To understand why juvenile justice became 'juvenile justice' it is necessary to know something about the treatment of young people in trouble with the law in the period that preceded the 1980s. For present purposes this period need not be discussed in too much detail (for a more detailed historical account see, Bottoms, Haines and O'Mahony forthcoming; Gelsthorpe and Morris 1994) and a brief overview will suffice.

Since its establishment in 1908, the juvenile court held both criminal and civil jurisdiction over children. The differentiation between criminal and welfare matters within the juvenile court (and the state systems which supported this court and provided services to children and their families) has varied over time; sometimes being more distinct, at other times being quite blurred. The juvenile offender and the juvenile in need have not always been treated as separate entities, and there has not necessarily always been a sharp distinction between the disposals available for those who have offended and for those who need help.

In practice, however, throughout most of its history (that is between 1908 and the end of the 1960s) the juvenile court dealt mostly with young people who had offended, and the number of civil cases brought remained relatively small. Nevertheless, it was always the intention that the juvenile court should have regard to the special needs of young people when passing sentence; an intention which led to the later enactment of a statutory principle, still in force today, that:

> Every court in dealing with a child or young person who is brought before it, either as an offender or otherwise, shall have regard to the welfare of the child or young person and shall in a proper case take steps... for securing that proper provision is made for his education and training. (Children and Young Persons Act 1933 s.44(1) as amended by the Children and Young Persons Act 1969)

The 1960s was a fairly turbulent decade for juvenile justice policy. Towards the end of the decade, however, based on the belief that there were considerable similarities between children who offend and children in need, the then Labour government formulated a policy towards the juvenile court underpinned by a single and thoroughgoing welfare-oriented philosophy. This policy was encompassed within the Children and Young Persons Act 1969 (CYPA) and would have resulted in a sentencing approach towards juvenile offenders which had more in common with traditional welfare-based systems.

In practice the CYPA 1969 was only partially implemented (due largely to a change of government in 1970). The new Conservative government rather than phasing out prison department custodial sentences for juvenile offenders, as the Act had intended, retained both Detention Centres and Borstal Training as custodial sentences for juveniles.[4] The government did, however, enact significant sections of the CYPA 1969 most notably in the establishment of a range of new welfare-based sentences (Care Orders and Supervision Orders available for both offenders and young people in need) and in doing so, in respect of these orders, shifted the locus of decision-making power away from the juvenile court to the newly created Social Services Departments (who had a great deal of say in recommending such orders to the court and full discretion in how these orders were later implemented).

The welfare philosophy tended to 'thin the mesh' of the boundaries around the juvenile court, as responding to the offence became less significant than responding to the needs of children. This change in philosophy is reflected in changed sentencing practices (selected sentencing trends for the 1970s are provided in Figure 2.1 below), but an official record of criminal sentences masks one of the most important developments of the decade – the creation and expansion of Intermediate Treatment.

Intermediate treatment

Although the term Intermediate Treatment (IT) did not appear in the CYPA 1969, and it has never been a sentence in its own right, the Act included sections from the White Paper *Children in Trouble* (Home Office 1968: para 25) where the term was first used. None of these sections, however, provide a clear definition of IT, and in fact it is quite difficult to find a precise official designation of what IT was supposed to be. A helpful definition appears in an article by the then Chief Inspector of the Home Office Children's Department:

> The proposal for Intermediate Treatment is another example of the constructive use of group situations. The purpose would be defeated if intermediate treatment were to be restricted to those labelled delinquent: rather, the facilities are to be available for adolescents who, while living at home and continuing to attend school or work, need, either by their own volition or by direction, new experiences in human relationships and in interesting activities...(Intermediate Treatment) will only be creative if it embraces a variety of young people who have the same needs but too few ways of expressing them without too much discomfort for the rest of us. (Cooper 1970 quoted in Bottoms *et al.* 1990)

In legal terms an IT requirement was an attachment that courts could make to a Supervision Order, but it was always the intention, as the above statement makes clear, that IT was to be a needs-based service available to a wide range of young people who were not necessarily subject to formal court orders. In practice the formal legal order did not comprise the central qualities of IT in the 1970s. In reality it was the activities that actually comprised IT that came to be its defining characteristics. This requires a little explanation.

The concept of intermediate treatment was introduced in the Children and Young Persons Act 1969 to mean work with children 'at risk' that was 'intermediate' between family work (working with the young person in the context of their family, and focusing on the family as the unit of intervention) and working with children in a way which entailed removal from home and placement in child-care institutions. Intermediate Treatment essentially meant direct, face-to-face work with young people in their own right, but the nature of this work was never very clearly defined or understood; it simply meant working directly with children, and the work done under the banner of IT was very diverse. In the early 1970s, Social Services Departments were allocated funds to pay for the local development of IT, but almost anything that social workers or probation officers (and youth workers or others employed by local authority education departments) did, directly with young people, could be, and was, called IT.

Not only was the nature of the activity of IT blurred and diverse, but the client group was equally poorly defined and consequently variable. To a large extent a pragmatic approach seemed to prevail in the early development of IT. As custody had not been abolished in the early 1970s (as the 1969 CYPA had foreshadowed) the intended client group for IT projects was largely still being incarcerated, thus restricting the available population to a younger age group and those not typically given custodial sentences. In reality, however, the distinctions between types of treatment (custody or community) and the range of 'clients' seemed less clear.

In the form in which it was implemented, the CYPA 1969 at the same time created a separate welfare-based system within which there was a greatly blurred distinction between the delinquent and the child in need, whilst retaining a separate punishment-based custodial system for offenders (Thorpe *et al.* 1980). In practice, in a somewhat chaotic and confused manner, the 1970s witnessed both bifurcation in sentencing (a state of affairs where the treatment offenders receive is divided around some arbitrary point and where some receive harsh treatment in the form of punishment while others receive help) and blurred sentencing practices where offenders and those in need received the same type of sentence.

As noted above, the CYPA 1969 was underpinned by a welfare-based philosophy supported by the developing power and influence of the social sciences; a discipline which held that the causes of delinquency or social distress could be discovered and determined in individual cases, and that appropriate treatment methods or programmes could be devised to cure these problems. It is sometimes difficult today to imagine the strength of this philosophy, but such was its influence at the time that the growing numbers of social workers employed in the burgeoning post-Seebohm Social Services Departments actively set out to work with more and more children.[5]

Social workers believed that formal intervention was a good thing, and commonly recommended what would be regarded today as highly interventionist sentences (in the form of Care Orders and Supervision Orders) on children with either relatively minor criminal offences or experiencing relatively minor family, developmental or adolescent difficulties. Where formal IT Orders were made, these were just one mechanism for 'getting kids into IT groups'. Even though IT in its origins had a natural place in the juvenile court, as a requirement attached to a Supervision Order, access to IT was rarely, if ever, restricted to young people on court orders but commonly open to a wide range of young people. Young people on straight Supervision Orders (with no additional requirements) were frequently involved in IT groups, and other young people were commonly involved in IT on a 'voluntary' basis without being subject to any formal court orders (Haines 1996).

Intermediate treatment in practice was inextricably linked to the philosophy of the social sciences and the welfare-based modality of treatment. If treatment was a good thing, and social workers (and others) in the 1970s generally believed that it was, then it should be available to any young person in some kind of need (however defined). The zealous pursuit of treatment and of young people to fill treatment programmes was a major defining characteristic of this period. But it was not uncommon for social workers to recommend custodial sentences for juveniles appearing before the courts; sometimes because they felt that early treatment had failed, sometimes because they experienced difficulty integrating difficult young people into treatment groups, and sometimes because they believed it was in the young person's best interests to receive a short, sharp dose of discipline.

Intended and unintended consequences

The 1970s was a period of great optimism and enthusiasm, but also one in which a wide variety of practices emerged. Whilst much of the varied development of IT can be attributed to the diverse activities of local authority social workers, it would be inappropriate to think of this decade and of these developments as a wholly planned strategy. Much of the development of IT was dependent on the interests, skills and activities of individual social workers working in separate Social Services Departments (SSDs) in a fairly independent manner (Haines 1996). But the outcomes of the activities of these social workers were not necessarily in line with their intentions; there were many unintended consequences (see Kerslake 1987) of social work interventions, and there were other agents within the system whose actions were also important.

One important and powerful group within the juvenile justice system were magistrates. Increasingly during the 1970s, Magistrates grew dissatisfied with Care Orders (primarily because of the discretion such orders gave to SSDs to decide how such orders were carried out), and over the decade magistrates made fewer and fewer Care Orders on 14–17-year-olds in criminal cases (Jones 1990). Correspondingly, the 1970s saw an increase in custodial sentences for this age group (Morris and Giller 1987).

Figure 2.1 shows selected sentencing trends for males aged 14–16 years from 1970–80. These trends clearly indicate the decline in the use of the Care Order in criminal cases and the corresponding increase in the use of custody over the same period. When interpreting the decline in the percentage use of Supervision/Probation Orders, however, it is important to remember that the 1970s juvenile court effectively became two parallel systems (one custodial, one welfare-based) such that the range of potential sentences expanded. Thus whilst there was a percentage decline in the use of such orders, overall there were larger actual numbers of children being drawn into the system and many of these were made subject to supervisory orders for relatively minor offences.

Given this overall expansion in the numbers of young people being drawn into the formal criminal justice system, and that many of these young people were receiving increasingly interventionist and often custodial sentences (often for very minor, first offences), it is perhaps not surprising that towards the end of the 1970s a

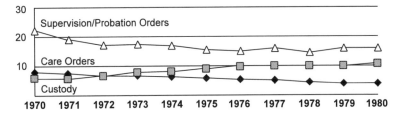

Figure 2.1 Selected sentencing trends: percentage of males aged 14–16 found guilty of indictable offences 1970–80

number of strident critiques were beginning to appear. Prominent amongst these was the work of David Thorpe *et al.* (1980) who conducted detailed research following the partial implementation of the CYPA 1969:

> If one compares the sections of the Act that were implemented and those that were not, the answer is obvious: a new system came in but the old one did not go out. Intermediate treatment arrived, but detention centres and attendance centres remained; the community homes system was created, but the approved schools retained their character and borstals were still available for 15–year-olds...What happens when a system that is intended as a replacement is simply grafted onto its predecessor and run in parallel with it?...Considered abstractly there are two possibilities, of which the first is intense conflict and abrasion. While there has indeed been a great deal of conflict at the ideological level...this simply has not happened in practice. The other possibility is that the two systems come to some form of accommodation, an implicit set of demarcation agreements and neutral zones, and that the sector served by the old system simply expands in order to make room for the newcomer. It is in this direction that all the available evidence points in the case of the 1969 CYPA. The two systems have, in effect, become vertically integrated, and an additional population of customer-clients has been identified in order to ensure that they both have plenty of work to do. (Thorpe *et al.* 1980: 22–3)

Thorpe *et al.* were clearly identifying the workers in local agencies as those responsible for ensuring that they had plenty of work to do, and that in respect of policemen, social workers, probation officers, magistrates and social service administrators:

> Quite simply, cumulatively, these disparate bodies of professionals made the wrong decisions about the wrong children at the wrong time. (Thorpe *et al.* 1980: 3)

In essence the arguments put forward by Thorpe *et al.* were critiques of system behaviour – they argued that the system, and the individual workers within it, made the wrong decisions about individual children. At the same time, however, other academic commentators were mounting an attack on the philosophy of social work in the 1980s, and there were a number of distinct strands to these critiques:

1. that the social sciences were not actually very good at identifying the causes of delinquency or social distress;
2. that the social sciences were not at all good at developing and providing effective programmes of treatment;
3. that social workers were using the social sciences to justify intensive programmes of treatment which were not only unlikely to work, but which were actually extremely interventionist and could not be justified by the levels of delinquency or seriousness of social problems;
4. that highly interventionist programmes of treatment sometimes did more harm than good in individual terms (because of the poor understanding of causality and consequent inherent weaknesses in treatment); and
5. highly interventionist programmes of treatment often did more harm than good in systems terms (because once a young person had tried and failed at treatment then punishment was the inevitable outcome of further criminal justice involvement – otherwise known as 'up-tariffing') (Kerslake 1987; Morris and Giller 1981; Morris *et al.* 1980).

It would be quite wrong to think that the debates and arguments that were conducted at the end of the 1970s were carried out in a dispassionate and clinical manner. These were fervent times and some of the criticisms of social work practice verged on outright attack:

> Because we do not understand the significance of much juvenile 'misconduct', the various reports presented to decision-makers contain valuejudgements and unfounded assumptions. As a general rule, we do not know with certainty which factors refer to, or which situations indicate which form of treatment...As such, these reports are useless guides to choosing dispositions, but these 'facts' then justify the form and content of intervention. These reports recast or reconstitute the child's

identity as a 'delinquent', 'truant' or 'troublesome'. They are in essence what one American writer calls 'character assassinations'. (Morris *et al.* 1980)

Nevertheless, these criticisms were extremely powerful and influential, even amongst those social workers who were the targets of the attack, and they were instrumental in bringing about an end to interventionist welfare-based treatment of delinquent youth as well as paving the way for the juvenile justice movement of the 1980s.

The origins of juvenile justice in the 1980s

The growth of custody and the development and expansion of intermediate treatment came to be the defining characteristics of the 1970s. It was only in the 1980s that the term 'juvenile justice' came into being. Crucial for this development was the fact that the academics who were critical of high rates of custody and the welfare-based approach did not stop at providing criticism; they also proffered a way forward. In fact there were two distinct movements amongst the academic community, each of which was influential in different ways. On the one hand there were those who were critical of what they saw as inherent injustices of 1970s sentencing and social work practice, and on the other there were those who were more concerned with a range of more practical matters. In reality there was some blurring between the activities and messages of these two groups (some even had a foot in both camps, see for example Tutt and Giller 1987; Tutt 1982), and blurring in the ways in which these ideas were ultimately used in practice.

The group who were mostly concerned with the injustices of 1970s practice, perhaps not surprisingly, argued for a more *just* (and justice-based) system of dealing with juvenile offenders (Morris *et al.* 1980). While the arguments of the other group (who were based mostly at Lancaster University) had two distinct strands: (i) by way of refuting the social–scientific explanations of delinquency they put forward a set of their own ideas about young people and offending – coupled with a research-based understanding of what actually happens to young people who become involved with the criminal justice system, and (ii) they articulated a view of the criminal justice system as a series of decision-making points and argued that, with proper intervention, the actual decisions that are made can be changed (Thorpe *et al.* 1980; Tutt 1982; Tutt and Giller 1987). It is worthwhile examining the arguments of these two groups in a little more detail.

The back-to-justice movement

The normative argument for a justice-based approach to the processing and sentencing of offenders is predicated on the belief that justice is inherently a good thing in its own right. To argue against justice is to argue for injustice – which is clearly undesirable: it is not possible to have too much justice. There is a great deal of power in the logic of this argument and it was certainly influential in the politics and practice of the early 1980s. But the back-to-justice movement did not develop in a vacuum, rather it grew out of the welfarist practices of the 1970s and a significant part of the argument for *justice* was a reactionary stance towards welfare. There was, therefore, an important consequentialist argument for a justice-based approach predicated on a faith in the ability of such an approach to iron out the perceived weaknesses of a welfare-based approach. Table 2.1 summarises in ideal–typical terms the characteristics of welfare-based and justice-based approaches. The perceived weaknesses of a welfare approach and the ways in which *justice* promised to limit or eradicate these problems is indicated.

The normative argument that justice is inherently a good thing was important at the ideological level in garnering general support at political, policy and practice levels for a justice- based approach to the treatment of offenders. In its most tangible form the back-to-justice movement was successful to the extent that justice-based legal principles were increasingly incorporated into criminal justice legislation in the 1980s.[6]

The earliest and most direct legislative examples of justice-based thinking are to be found in the Criminal Justice Act (CJA) 1982. This Act was a complex piece of legislation to the extent that it did not have an identifiable central philosophy, but brought together a number of disparate strands (some pre-existing, some new). The most obvious 'policy' clash in the Act was the way in which it consolidated custody at the centre of the juvenile criminal justice system while retaining a requirement for the juvenile court to have

Table 2.1 Justice vs welfare

	Welfare – ideal type	Problems of welfare	Justice – ideal type	Justice-based solutions
Overall aims	To serve the interests of society and children	It doesn't, but mainly serves the interests of self appointed 'experts'	To serve the interests of justice	Justice-based procedural control limits discretionary professional power
Process	The needs of children and the causes of their behaviour are investigated	The social sciences do not provide a solid basis on which these investigations can be conducted	The legal rights of children are safeguarded by legal representation and the application of the 'due process' of the law	Justice-based procedures limit the scope of factors which may be taken into account in criminal justice processing
Main concerns	The discovery of needs	These are potentially endless and open the way for excessive intervention	The determination of guilt	Direct culpability for individual acts is the only justifiable basis for intervention
Basis of sentencing	1. The needs of the young person & society 2. Treatment	1. These are socially constructed, have dubious validity and are not open to outside scrutiny 2. The effectiveness of treatment is questionable	1. The severity of the offence 2. An appropriate restriction of liberty	This establishes firm, clear and 'public' criteria on which sentencing decisions are made
Type of sentence	Indeterminate	This creates uncertainty for children	Determinate	This establishes a certainty of punishment for harm done

regard to the welfare of young people brought before it, also strengthening provisions for the supervision of young people in the community. The Act also incorporated a number of distinctive justice-based sections, for example:

- All young people appearing before the juvenile court were henceforth entitled to legal representation.
- Courts were required to give reasons, in open court, for particular sentences and to ensure that the young person understood why a particular sentence was being passed.

Perhaps most significantly, however, the Act introduced three criteria at least one of which had to be satisfied before a custodial sentence could be passed:

- that the offender is unable or unwilling to respond to non-custodial penalties, or
- that a custodial sentence is necessary for the protection of the public, or
- that the offence is so serious that a non-custodial sentence cannot be justified (s.1(4) CJA 1982, subsequently strengthened by s.123(3) CJA 1988).

Furthermore, before a custodial sentence could be passed a Social Enquiry Report had to be prepared which examined, *inter alia*, whether a community-based sentence was appropriate. It was these three criteria coupled with the central role that the Act gave to social workers in the juvenile court which were to prove central to the practitioner-led 'new orthodoxy' movement of the 1980s. In essence these three criteria gave the emerging juvenile justice specialists both the opportunity and the grounds for challenging custodial sentencing, and this they did with considerable success (Dodds 1986; Rutherford 1983; Stanley 1988).

It is important to recognise, however, that social workers were slow to realise this potential, and that early research on the impact of s.1(4) CJA 1982 showed only a very limited effect (Burney 1985). Much of the ultimate success which juvenile justice officers achieved in respect of s.1(4) is attributable to the work of NACRO's Juvenile Offenders Team (Pitts 1990) which set about a programme of work in local Juvenile Justice Teams actually demonstrating how these criteria could be used to challenge magistrates' sentencing practices. It is further important to realise that the juvenile offenders team was funded directly by the Department of Health and Social Services.

It was noted earlier in this chapter how the, then, DHSS (and in particular senior civil servants in this government department) were instrumental in juvenile justice developments in the 1980s – particularly in the sentencing arena. While the Home Office during the 1980s, perhaps more traditionally, tended to place the greater emphasis on custody, the DHSS simultaneously put a significant effort into the development of alternatives to custody. Most notable amongst these efforts was the DHSS Intermediate Treatment (IT) Initiative: a programme of providing seed-corn monies to re-articulate IT away from a more welfare-oriented youth service provision into an alternative to custody.[7] The DHSS also funded NACRO's juvenile offenders team to monitor the impact of LAC 83(3), the government circular which promulgated the DHSS IT initiative, and to support the development of these alternative to custody projects at a local level (NACRO 1987, 1991).

This official sanctioning of alternatives to custody, therefore, did much to encourage and consolidate the juvenile justice practitioner movement of the 1980s. But we are getting slightly ahead of ourselves here and need to backtrack a little to examine the other strand in the development of 1980s juvenile justice.

Systems management and the anti-custody orthodoxy

As significant as the back-to-justice movement proved to be in creating a climate for the CJA 1982, it was neither this movement, nor the Act itself, which was instrumental in bringing about much of the positive reforms in 1980s juvenile justice. Notwithstanding the role of the DHSS and NACRO (noted above), much of the credit for developments in the 1980s must go to those individuals working in the emerging juvenile justice teams in local areas. And to a very large extent these individuals, and the practices they gave life to, were heavily influenced by the academics from Lancaster University. This group, it will be remembered, put forward an argument with two distinct strands: (i) a largely research-based understanding of juvenile crime and of what actually happens to young people who become involved with the criminal justice system, and (ii) systems management. In terms of the former, the argument consisted of a mixture of research findings and beliefs (see generally, Kerslake 1987; Pitts 1988; Rutherford 1985, 1992; Thorpe *et al.* 1980):

- The *'triviality' reality*, that most juvenile crime is not of a serious nature and much of it is, in fact, more trivial and of more nuisance value than a serious threat – the so-called 'triviality' reality.
- The *'growing-out-of-crime' rationale* that most young people commit offences at some time during adolescence, and by far the majority of these will stop offending quite naturally as part of the maturation process if left to their own devices (that is, juvenile offending is not the product of social or personal pathology and, therefore, not suitable for 'treatment') – the so-called 'growing out of crime' rationale.
- The *'labelling' theory* that formal involvement with the criminal justice system can have negative consequences for young people to the extent that they are labelled delinquent and then go on to act out this label – the so-called 'labelling' theory.
- The *'up-tariffing' effect* that formal involvement with the criminal justice system can have negative consequences for young people to the extent that once they are brought into the system for minor offences they can be accelerated through and up the tariff of sanctions for future (often quite minor) offences – the so-called 'up-tariffing' effect.
- The *'schools-of-crime' argument* that custody is of itself a brutalising and harmful experience that exposes young people to older and more sophisticated offenders and thus tends to have a negative effect on future behaviour – the so-called 'schools of crime' argument.
- The *'net-widening' principle* that welfare-based approaches tend to bring more and more young people into the criminal justice system with all the negative connotations this implies – the so-called 'net-widening' principle.
- The *'radical non-intervention' thesis* that the best juvenile justice workers can do is to avoid the harm done by the criminal justice system, and its system of sanctions, by leaving young people alone – the so-called 'radical non-intervention' thesis.

These ideas were extremely influential amongst practitioners, and they underpinned and provided the driving force for the practices which were to come to define the 1980s juvenile justice experience: a strong anti-custody ethos and the provision of alternative to custody sentences, and an equally strong pro-diversionary ethos and the development of cautioning. It is doubtful, however, that the alternative to custody and pro-cautioning movement would have been so successful were it not for the second element of Lancaster-style thinking, that is systems management.

A particularly frustrating aspect of social work practice is the seeming inability of individuals to take action which changes the overall behaviour of institutional systems; as Thorpe *et al.* (1980: 135) state:

> One of the major contradictions lying at the core of social work theory and practice is the seeming inadequacy of micro-intervention (at the level of individuals and families) in situations where material stress and status-frustration appear to make a major contribution to social dysfunction... Decisions about changes in social and economic structure can only be made, by and large, at the highest political levels.

The approach advocated by Thorpe *et al.* broke this impasse through two distinctive innovations. Firstly, they recognised that changes in sentencing trends are the cumulative product, over time, of many small changes in individual cases, as Bell and Haines (1991) explained thus:

> Changes to sentencing patterns, at both national and local levels, have been progressive. Intervention in the criminal justice system is made on an individual basis and the courts take time to change their decisions... But it is the aggregated or cumulative effect of individual decision-making over time that produces overall change in sentencing patterns. (Bell and Haines 1991: 122)

And secondly, they recognised that the operation of the criminal justice system actually comprises a whole series of decisions, and that as individuals pass through the system each decision has implications for future courses of action and future decisions, for example a remand in custody is more likely to result in a custodial sentence, whereas a remand with bail support is more likely to lead to a community sentence. By changing these individual decisions, Thorpe *et al.* (1980) argued, you could change the way that the system deals with individual offenders.

In other words, arresting, processing and sentencing an offender is a process that may be influenced by targeting specific decision-making points in the process whereby the outcome for particular individuals may be changed. (Bell and Haines 1991: 121)

This process came to be known as 'systems management' (Tutt and Giller 1987) and it proved to be an extremely powerful tool in the hands of committed juvenile justice workers.

It is important to recognise, however, that systems management techniques can be utilised to change decisions in any direction – there is no automatic link between systems management and the provision of alternatives to custody.

Systems management of itself is a value free management tool that says nothing about the aims of intervention. But it is the linking of systems management with the critique of welfarism and the over-use of custody which creates such a powerful mixture. (Bell and Haines 1991: 121)

What made the 1980s juvenile justice experience such a success was the animation of systems management strategies at the local level in the service of anti-custody and pro-diversion beliefs and practices. In other words, juvenile justice workers throughout the 1980s increasingly used aggressive systems management techniques to increase the number of decisions made to divert young people from the criminal justice system, and to decrease the number of custodial sentences that were passed by the courts. Chapter 4 will go on to examine how this was actually achieved in practice: for the moment a more detailed look is required at the actual outcome of these changes.

The juvenile justice 'new orthodoxy'

It would be quite incorrect to think that all IT workers suddenly abandoned their welfarist principles and readily embraced justice and systems management approaches. Research results from a national survey (Bottoms *et al.* 1990) shed a considerable amount of light on the nature and aims of juvenile justice practice (as they stood in 1984/5 at the time of the research, for social services departments only). The following Tables 2.2 and 2.3 set out some of these results.

Table 2.2 Aims of IT identified in interviews with social services
departments

Aims	No. of SSDs endorsing aim	%
(a) Target group aims		
1. To offer alternatives to custody and/or residential care orders	87	92.5
2. To offer a credible programme to the courts, *wider than* the provision of alternatives to care and custody	16	17
3. To offer a range of services for juveniles at different points in the spectrum of tariff or need (including an emphasis on the 'middle range')	32	34
4. To provide worthwhile preventative activities for youngsters 'at risk', i.e. pre-delinquents, non-delinquents, minor delinquents, truants etc., including those at risk of voluntary reception into care	45	47.9
5. To divert children and young persons from court appearances	24	25.5
(b) Other stated aims		
6. To reduce re-offending or reduce crime	15	16
7. To focus on offending behaviour or focus especially on offenders (reduction of criminality not specifically mentioned)	29	30.9
8. To contribute to an integrated child care service within the department	10	10.6
9. To provide positive new experiences for clients and/or promote the well-being of clients, improve relationships with them etc.	14	14.9
10. To promote general community development	1	1.1
11. To intervene in and contribute to the management of the local juvenile justice system(s)	7	7.4
12. Other aims	5	5.3
	$N = 94$	(100)

Source: Based on Bottoms *et al.* 1990: 102.

Bottoms *et al.* (1990) went on to develop a typology of social services departments' IT polices which indicates the breadth of local policy aims and objectives:

1. *Prevention Pure.* Predominantly needs-based, with a welfare-treatment ethos. Little interest in clients' status *vis-à-vis* the criminal justice system. No emphasis on systems intervention or awareness of possible undesirable outcomes from welfare-based intervention. No serious attempt to compete with custody/residential care.

2. *Prevention Plus.* Still needs-based and with a welfare-treatment ethos. Significantly more interest than 'prevention pure' in juvenile justice system links and/or in a certain view of alternatives to custody and care; but such developments are nevertheless perceived within a predominantly welfarist ethos.

3. *Alternative to Custody and Care Pure* (AtCC Pure). Intermediate Treatment (IT) seen as exclusively for those at serious risk of custody/residential care. In most areas IT perceived as for offenders only, but in a few also for non-offenders at serious risk of s.1(2) care orders.[8] Programmes tend to be offence-focused, not needs-focused. To prevent stigmatisation and punitive disposals, the notion of the 'least restrictive alternative' is often advocated and this leads to the use of systems approaches, the development of diversion from court, etc. Preventive work with non-offenders may be undertaken by such authorities, but if so will *never* be called intermediate treatment, and may not be called prevention.

4. *Alternative to Custody and Care Plus* (AtCC Plus). Has many similarities with category 3 above, especially in the primary emphasis on IT as an alternative to custody or care. But IT is also seen as appropriate for a 'medium-range' of offenders appearing before the juvenile court (and, occasionally, also for non-offenders appearing before the juvenile court in care proceedings). 'Preventive' work, again, is not allowed as part of the IT programme.

5. *Broad-based.* This category comprises at least the following two key elements: (i) a recognition of the importance of targeted IT provision aimed at being an alternative to custody or care; but such provision is seen as independently important, and not simply subsumed within a preventive philosophy as in the

Table 2.3   Typology of IT policy in social services departments

	No of SSDs	*%*
1. Prevention Pure	1	1.1
2. Prevention Plus	12	12.8
3. AtCC Pure	22	23.4
4. AtCC Plus	27	28.7
5. Broad-based	32	34
	N = 94	(100)

Source: From Bottoms *et al.* 1990: 103.

'prevention plus' category; and (ii) a retention also of preventive work with non-offenders, the 'at risk', etc., as a part of the intermediate treatment remit. The combination of these two elements makes the broad-based category distinctly different from both preventive and AtCC policies.

Table 2.3 sets out the numbers and percentages of social services departments falling into each category of the above typology.

It can be seen from this research that Social Services Departments' policies for working with juvenile offenders strongly reflected anti-custody thinking – 86.1 per cent of SSDs which responded (that is, summing 3, 4 and 5 above) – although this did not entirely mean that other forms of social work intervention with offenders not in any immediate danger of reception into care or a custodial sentence was seen as being unimportant. Increasingly, however, as the decade passed the national trend was towards the establishment of specialist Juvenile Justice Teams operating almost exclusively an anti-custody and pro-diversionary strategy. Such was the extent to which this philosophy and set of practices came to dominate juvenile justice that one commentator called it the 'new orthodoxy'[9] (Jones 1984).

Corporatism?

The ascendancy of new orthodoxy thinking in the 1980s led many to believe that it represented the triumph of *justice* over *welfare*. John Pratt has argued, however, that to locate the debate about the nature of juvenile justice in terms of the parameters of the welfare vs justice debate is to fail to recognise the complexities of practice:

> We know that from the mid-1970s the march of history ceased to be on the side of welfare. The 'new orthodoxy' (Jones 1984) of the emergent 'justice model' took policy off at a different tangent and reversed many of the previous taken-for-granted assumptions about 'the way forward'. I will argue, though, that the welfare–justice dichotomy should not be seen as forming the analytical parameters of juvenile justice debate. Instead, this simply laid the foundation stones on which a third model – that of *corporatism* – has been built. (Pratt 1989: 237–8 *original emphasis*)

For Pratt, therefore, corporatism[10] not justice formed the dominant mode of practice in 1980s juvenile justice. Thus, while he concedes 'justice-model talk' assumed an ideological dominance over that of welfare:

> There has been no corresponding shift towards a fully blown justice-model legal form which puts into operation all this talk and these ideas. Against some of the prerequisites of this model, such as certainty, due process, visibility, accountability, least restrictive intervention, we see instead an increase in administrative decision-making, greater sentencing diversity, centralisation of authority and co-ordination of policy, growing involvement of non-juridical agencies, and high levels of containment and control in some sentencing programmes. (Pratt 1989: 245)

There is an element of truth to Pratt's argument to the extent that the 1980s did not witness the operationalisation of a full-blown justice-based approach and new orthodoxy adherents did make use of administrative interagency strategies. But it is difficult to sustain the argument that new orthodoxy-style practice was wholly characterised by the term 'corporatism'. As the 1980s progressed, and particularly in the early 1990s, corporatism has come to dominate the broader organisational contexts of criminal justice service delivery, but it is only in more recent times that the managerial corporatism of central government has been brought to bear on the operation of juvenile justice teams.[11]

Juvenile justice practice in the 1980s was characterised by far more conflict and abrasion than corporatism allows for. As new orthodoxy adherents set about their aggressive pro-diversion and anti-custody strategies many battles were fought between juvenile justice teams on the one hand, and the courts, the police and even with other parts of the Social Services Departments themselves on the other. We need to probe a little more deeply, therefore, to understand the nature of new orthodoxy practice.

Practitioner-led change

Although in this chapter considerable attention has been given to the diverse origins and development of juvenile justice in the 1980s, and as important as these national debates and activities were, it would be an overly simplistic interpretation of events to conclude that there was a simple relationship between the back to justice movement, the Lancaster group and juvenile justice practice. Changes at the level of practice are only ever loosely linked with national movements, policy developments and legislative change. Thus it is the differences in local Social Services Departments' policies and the aims of IT in the mid-1980s, as reported by Bottoms *et al.* (1990) above, that provide a clue to the nature of new orthodoxy practice.

The success of the juvenile justice new orthodoxy movement owes a debt to policy-makers and academics whose work is described above, but much of the credit for this success must be located in the changes brought about by those working in local juvenile justice teams. New thinking about the nature of juvenile crime and its treatment and the techniques of systems management heavily influenced juvenile justice practitioners, but it was they who transformed this thinking and techniques into practice. There was no simple relationship between the national level and the local level, and those at the local level very much made the new orthodoxy their own such that the developments in 1980s juvenile justice are commonly talked of as a 'practitioner' movement. As our account of the development of new orthodoxy thinking shows, to talk about a practitioner movement as if that was all that happened in the 1980s is misconceived, but it is equally incorrect to see the new orthodoxy as the result of national developments or 'top-down' policy change (at a national level or within SSD management). The energy and animation of juvenile justice management strategies was very much located in the vision and ability of the individuals working in local juvenile justice teams.

The way in which juvenile justice practitioners carved out their local strategies was quite distinctive. Firstly, it is important to realise that although there was diversity in the precise details and nature of local projects and practices, by and large juvenile justice workers were driven by a mission to reduce custody and increase diversion. They believed that the criminal justice system was doing mainly harm to young people, and they felt that they knew best what should be happening and that they were the ones to bring change about; as a prominent member of the juvenile justice practitioner movement said when asked about the philosophy he brings to his work:

> Abolish it and enjoy it. Abolish the work, abolish custody, do your best for the kids... that's about maximising the opportunities for their mis-demeanours to be placed in the context of them being children fre-quently coming from shitty families being caught up in a system some parts of which have very little sympathy or tolerance towards youth. (quoted in Haines 1996)

In practice 'doing the best for the kids' came to mean essentially two basic things: (i) increasing diversion, and (ii) reducing custody. To achieve these two things, however, most juvenile justice teams adopted a firm stance of being specialists who worked only with juvenile offenders and aggressively set about achieving their objec-tives.

Working with conflict

In terms of diversion, this did mean working with the police (and other agencies) in interagency juvenile liaison bureau (Bowden and Stevens 1986; Evans and Wilkinson 1990; Wilkinson and Evans 1990), but interagency working does not necessarily imply that all partners are working towards the same objectives (Blagg *et al.* 1988). The frequent interagency conflict and abrasion over indivi-dual decisions, as juvenile justice workers sought to divert as many young people as possible from prosecution, should not be masked by the rhetoric of interagency 'cooperation'.

There was conflict, too, within Social Services Departments as juvenile justice teams increasingly carved out their specialist iden-tity and role. In the change from IT to juvenile justice, the aca-demic critique of the implications of taking welfare issues into account in criminal justice processing tended to be interpreted in two particular ways: (i) an injunction that welfare issues had no place in the juvenile court and sentencing, and (ii) that juvenile justice teams do not deal with welfare issues but only deal directly with individuals' offending behaviour.

In terms of juvenile justice teams being part of larger SSDs, this represented quite a big change in philosophy and practice. Increasingly the teams focused their work on offending behaviour in quite a narrow manner, often only engaging young people in face-to-face work as it directly related to offending. Where so-called welfare issues (that is anything other than offending behaviour) arose in respect of young people on criminal court orders, many juvenile justice teams eschewed direct involvement electing to refer such cases to social worker colleagues in other parts of the SSD.[12] This, perhaps not surprisingly, often resulted in conflict with SSD colleagues as members of specialist teams sought to create and defend boundaries around their work roles (Haines 1996).

Juvenile justice workers did not demur from conflict with magistrates in the juvenile court. Although juvenile justice practitioners have always sought to play an active professional role in the juvenile court, and accept that this professionalism involved the competent provision of court services, this did not generally mean that juvenile justice workers saw themselves as servants of the court or that they played a subservient role. Aggressive custody-reducing strategies necessitated an element of challenge to existing court practices, and while this did sometimes result in abrasion or conflict, in the main these conflicts were of a professional nature.

An anti-custody orthodoxy

A very large part of new orthodoxy practices were targeted on decision-making points in the criminal justice system, and this naturally led juvenile justice workers into a degree of conflict as previous practices were challenged. This institutional or organisation dimension of new orthodoxy thinking and practice was one of the defining characteristics of 1980s juvenile justice, and one which can hardly be encompassed by the label 'corporatism'.

In professional terms the fact that the court strategies of juvenile justice teams centred on reducing the extent of custodial sentencing did not imply that attempts to avoid custody were based on any explicit justice-based philosophy. The aim was simply to avoid custody and anything that advanced this aim was justifiable at all points of individual and systems intervention throughout the criminal justice process. The following quotation from a juvenile justice officer encapsulates this philosophy:

> We are not focusing in on what is the most appropriate justice response, what we are focusing in on is the fact that we want to avoid custody. And that goes all the way down the line... The justice model is not about what's *just*, its about what's the furthest from custody, not what's just or what's right... We are not arguing for justice. We are taking avoidance of custody as the focal point of our work. That affects every bit of work we do all the way down the line. (unpublished research notes)

Thus while it remains very true that juvenile justice practitioners made every possible use of justice-based legal requirements (such as those enacted in the CJA 1982), there is very little sense in which new orthodoxy thinking incorporated a justice-based philosophy. The philosophical basis of juvenile justice in the 1980s drew on the beliefs etc about the nature of juvenile crime and its treatment outlined previously, but juvenile justice practice was far more characterised by systems manipulation with the ultimate aim of avoiding custody. When it is understood in this manner the juvenile justice experience of the 1980s was a remarkable success, as the sentencing trends shown in Figure 2.2 demonstrate.

These sentencing trends (see also Allen 1991) clearly demonstrate a proportionate decline in the use of custody over the decade of the 1980s to around 8 per cent (a figure which in absolute numbers is roughly equivalent to a decline from around 8000 custodial sentences in 1980 to under 2000 in 1990). Two further factors put this decline in an even sharper focus. Firstly, research

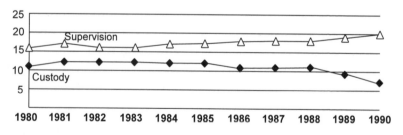

Figure 2.2   Selected sentencing trends: percentage of males aged 14–16 found guilty of indictable offences 1980–90

showed that the growth in community-based supervision was at the expense of custody, and that alternative-to-custody programmes were effectively targeted on young people who would otherwise have received a custodial sentence (Bottoms 1995). This is particularly notable because the general experience of so-called alternative-to-custody provision is that such programmes are only, at best, partially successful in reaching the target group; tending also to embrace offenders who would have received other pre-existing community sentences (McMahon 1992). Secondly, and perhaps even more importantly, account has to be taken of the impact of trends in cautioning over this same period (see Figure 2.3).

The evident growth in the proportionate use of cautioning is particularly notable as increasing the diversion rate was an explicit new orthodoxy objective in its own right. But, increased diversion also has implications for the formal criminal justice system. Put simply, if more and more minor and younger offenders are being diverted from formal prosecution then it is increasingly the older and more serious offenders who appear in court (Bottoms *et al.* 1996). If there were no changes to courts' sentencing behaviour, then an increase in diversion would be likely to lead to a proportionate increase in more severe sentences. But this did not happen in the 1980s as shown in Figure 2.2. The growth in cautioning, therefore, actually means that the decline in custody over the 1980s is far more significant than straightforward sentencing trends tend to suggest. Juvenile justice practitioners were not just successful in reducing the custody rate, they were even more successful in

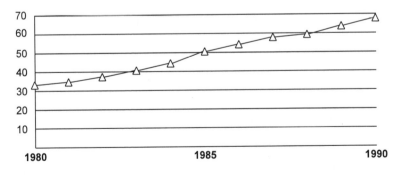

Figure 2.3   Males cautioned as a percentage of those found guilty for indictable offences 1980–90

reducing this rate for a relatively older and more serious cohort of offenders.

Committed to systems management

The achievements of juvenile justice practitioners in the 1980s are remarkable. The growth in diversion and decline in custodial sentencing represents an unprecedented criminal justice success. At the nub of this success was not any abstract philosophy or implementation of justice principles in practice, nor any particular view about the nature of juvenile crime (although the notion, *inter alia*, that young people 'grow out of crime' (Rutherford 1985, 1992) was influential). The new orthodoxy movement was so successful because of the extent to which practitioners at the local level were able to make effective use of systems management techniques to change the decisions that were made in respect of individual young people and thus to manipulate the overall operation of the juvenile justice system.

It would be clearly inappropriate to diminish the significance of a range of factors (such as those discussed in this chapter) for the success of juvenile justice in the 1980s. In particular, it is especially important to recognise that systems management techniques can be used to change decision-making in any direction; there is no explicit ethical or moral aspect to systems thinking, thus it was extremely significant that systems management techniques were combined with a strong pro-diversionary and anti-custody orthodoxy in 1980s juvenile justice.

Politicians from the left and the right, of whatever political party, like to believe that they exercise a great deal of control over the country and the institutions of the state. While it is true that legislation has an important impact, for the most part this impact is limited to setting the context in which others act; legislation is, in fact, a fairly blunt instrument. The Law may be that which is contained in Statute, but the law only becomes real when it is implemented in practice which involves decision-making by people other than politicians, and there are always many, many decisions to be made in its implementation. One of the most important lessons, therefore, to be learned from the experience of juvenile justice practice in the 1980s is that individuals at the local level have a great deal of scope and ability to shape the way in which the institutions of the state actually operate. Any local action must be tied to an explicit philosophy and this philosophy must inform the actions and decisions that are taken, but systems management techniques are the mechanism which brings these abstract philosophies into the realities of practice.

Subsequent chapters set out important principles for the way in which young people should be treated in this country; indeed the next chapter is devoted to developing a youth justice philosophy. The argument of this book remains rooted in a commitment to systems management as a way of bringing this change about.

Problems and pitfalls of juvenile justice in the 1980s

As positive as this account has been about the juvenile justice experience of the 1980s its shortfalls need also to be recognised. In practice two major problems may be identified, one concerning changes in the nature of social work with children generally and the implications of the highly specialist stance adopted by juvenile justice workers in the context of broader changes in Social Services Departments, and the other concerning the direct work with young people on Supervision Orders.

Changes in the nature of social work with children

In the 1970s social workers dealt with relatively high numbers of children. It will be remembered from what has been said above that the prevailing philosophy of this time was interventionist; welfare and treatment-based. It was a positive thing, therefore, to be involved with children, and social workers (some of whom were designated Intermediate Treatment Officers) actively sought to engage young people in treatment programmes (see Haines 1996). Much of this work was done under the general heading of Intermediate Treatment. This was partly because Social Services Departments had been provided with funds (by the DHSS) to develop such work, and partly because IT was fairly loosely defined as (almost any kind of direct) face-to-face work with children in their own right and this became a somewhat fashionable tool of social work intervention.

The children who were involved in 1970s-style IT represented quite a wide spectrum. Because IT Orders could be attached to criminal Supervision Orders there was an in-built propensity for IT to have a role in the court system and for it to involve work with offenders, but such work was far from an identifying characteristic of 1970s IT. Table 2.4 presents a schematic of the typical range of IT programmes that existed during the 1970s and the types of children commonly found in these programmes. 1970s-style IT was, therefore, extremely broadly based. Some of the activity that comprised it was fairly focused – including, for example, the heavy-end IT – but much of it was less directed and had a general preventive ethos. As noted above, almost anything that was done with children (where the child was the focus of the activity rather than, for example, work with the family as a whole) could be, and was, called IT. And in practice this amounted to an enormous amount of work of tremendous variety carried out with large numbers of very different children (for example, in some areas 'IT projects' ran education programmes for school-excluded children). In reality, 1970s IT was very much more characterised by programmes that fell into categories 3–5 in Table 2.4 than those which fell into categories 1 and 2.

In the 1980s, however, with the development and growth of juvenile justice, much of this changed. In contrast to the 1970s, 1980s juvenile justice increasingly came to be characterised by programmes that fell into categories 1 and 2 in Table 2.4. Intermediate treatment workers, who by now were calling themselves juvenile justice officers, were mainly working with identified offenders at a fairly high point on the criminal tariff.

It is important to realise that as the change from IT to juvenile justice took place, there were other broader changes taking place also. One significant change concerned the actual social work staff who were conducting most of the IT programmes. Intermediate treatment was a new concept in the 1970s, and initially there were few specialist staff who were called designated IT officers. Intermediate treatment was more of a social work method than a specialism, and as such it was a method utilised by a wide range of social workers. It was only later that IT developed as a specialism (in large part because it mainly comprised groupwork, and organising such groups was a task better performed by an individual who specialised in such work – it proved quite difficult for busy social workers with

Table 2.4 Schema of IT programmes

Type of Programme	Court order	Description	Profile of children
1. Heavy-end IT	Supervision Order plus specified activities or IT requirement	A group focusing on offending behaviour, probably with some activities mixed in	Mainly older children (14–16 years) who have committed relatively serious offences
2. Offenders group	Supervision Order plus IT or Criminal Care Order	A group mixing activities with some work on offending	Middle age-range children (13–15) who have committed less serious offences
3. Activity group	Supervision Order or Care Order or voluntary attendance	A group focusing on constructive use of leisure time	A wider age-range of children (possibly split into more age-specific groups) some of whom have committed offences but others with a wider range of social or family problems of a middle–serious nature
4. Social skills group	Supervision Order or Care Order or voluntary attendance	A group based on developing relationships and improving social skills	A wider age-range of children (possibly split into age-specific groups) some of whom have committed offences but others with a wider range of social or family problems of a less serious nature than above
5. Befriending group	Voluntary attendance	A group comprising general activities designed to provide a focus for children	A wide age-range of children (possibly split into age-specific groups) from deprived social or family circumstances

heavy caseloads to devote the time necessary to groupwork organisation). As IT took on a specialist identity, in practice, the work tended to be divided up. Increasingly, during the 1970s, newly appointed specialist IT officers took on the court-oriented, middle to heavy-end range of IT work, but many generic social workers continued to run a diverse range of IT groups with a much broader range of children – often alongside the IT specialists (see Paley and Thorpe 1974 and their notion of the 'continuum of services').

In the early 1980s, as IT began to transform itself into juvenile justice, it was mainly those IT specialists who engineered the transition, and in practice those social workers who had been conducting IT groups tended to drop IT as a method of working with children; in part because, as happens in social work, it was superseded as a method by other new developments (mainly a more family-oriented approach). To a large extent, therefore, that activity that had mainly characterised IT in the 1970s (programmes 3–5 in Table 2.4) simply waned as alternative methods of working with children and families emerged.

Coincident with this change were broader developments within SSDs themselves. Notable amongst these were radical shifts in the workload of Children and Families Social Work Teams. The early 1980s witnessed the explosion of child abuse onto the national agenda, with considerable ramifications for SSDs. The national pattern is mixed, but it is no exaggeration to say that SSDs were overwhelmed by child abuse and child protection from the early to mid-1980s such that this type of work came to dominate the delivery of social work to children and families almost to the complete exclusion of other services. To a very large degree, therefore, work in a Children and Families Team came to mean child protection work, and what was lost in this shift was the wide range of work that was being done with children from deprived social or family circumstances.

In the 1980s, therefore, as juvenile justice increasingly developed its specialist role, so too Children and Families Teams were taking on a new specialist role and much of the work that had been done with a wide range of deprived children was no longer being undertaken. Large numbers of children who had been receiving a service in the 1970s were no longer receiving services in the 1980s (Haines 1997). The failure to establish an entitlement to welfare-oriented services independent of the criminal justice interventions has, in practice, further marginalised an already disadvantaged group within the population.

Direct work with young people on Supervision Orders

It has already been noted how, within the new orthodoxy, juvenile justice workers tended to adopt a firm stance of working only with offenders and that, in practice, this tended to be interpreted to mean that juvenile justice workers did not get involved with the 'welfare' problems experienced by many young people. The justification for this stance was rooted in the juvenile court experience of the 1970s, and the fact that many young people were being made subject to long-term, intrusive court orders on the basis of social or family problems. This practice of sentencing by need rather than by the severity of the wrong done by the young person was seen as inherently unjust (because, for the most part, these needs were not matters the young people had any control over), and it was also believed to lead to young people being accelerated up the criminal tariff ultimately resulting in punitive custodial sentences for relatively minor offences or, once again, because of their social or family needs.

Taking a firm stance on excluding welfare matters from the juvenile court, therefore, was seen as a very necessary action central to the achievement of systems management objectives (that is, excluding welfare matters from decisions about sentencing, and focusing on the severity of the offence, was integral to changing these decisions). The principle of excluding welfare matters from the juvenile court, however, tended to be carried over into direct work with young people. Thus a principle that was central to systems management strategies for the processing of juvenile offenders became part of the orthodoxy for direct work with offenders post-sentence. Juvenile justice officers, therefore, found themselves working with young offenders made subject to Supervision Orders bound by the injunctions of juvenile justice managers not to engage with welfare problems.

In practice it would be naive not to recognise, firstly, that many of the young people on criminal Supervision Orders were experiencing considerable social and family problems (see Bottoms 1995), and, secondly, that many juvenile justice officers did carry out direct work to ameliorate these problems. But technically speaking such work was proscribed by new orthodoxy thinking and it remained a covert and underdeveloped activity. Many young offenders are not only troublesome but troubled, thus juvenile justice officers found themselves confronted by young people experiencing high levels of deprivation and unable to ignore such problems, and having to make some kind of response; but the professional development of appropriate responses had not formed a significant part of 1980s juvenile justice. Juvenile justice officers, on the whole, were not equipped with the skills or techniques to work effectively with difficult young people.

Moreover, the nature of direct work with young people on Supervision Orders has tended to be limited to work that dealt directly with the offending behaviour; and this has primarily been interpreted very narrowly. There has been little explicit recognition that offending behaviour can be related to social, family or material circumstances (as these have a link into the welfare continuum). The kind of direct work with young people sanctioned by new orthodoxy thinking has largely been limited to offence-focused work. In practice this has meant a number of very limited things:

- Offence confrontation work – reinforcing the unacceptability of offending;
- Developing a victim perspective – educating young people into the impact of their offending on victims;
- The offending curriculum – teaching young people how to avoid situations where offending can occur.

Anyone experienced in working with young people will be familiar with the sterility of these limited methods. Integral to any type of long-term human interaction is the development of a relationship which forms the basis of continued contact. Establishing a relationship with a young person who has offended simply in terms of their offence, to the derogation of any other aspect of their lives, is inhibiting for the worker and insulting to the young person. Research has shown that young people value, and get the most out of, supervision that is engaging and where work is done to tackle the problems they face in their day-to-day lives (Bottoms 1995 and Chapter 6). New orthodoxy thinking is an extremely powerful professional tool for systems intervention, but it was professionally sterile for face-to-face practice with young people.

The key to future success lies in retaining an effective systems strategy while building in effective methods of intervention in the lives of young people in trouble.

3

Developing a Youth Justice Philosophy

The importance of philosophy cannot be overstated. Such is the significance attached to this topic that it is placed immediately after the two review chapters and first among those chapters which aim to set out strategies for the future of youth justice. It may seem strange, however, for a book about youth justice policy and practice to contain a chapter on philosophy at all. Indeed, one rarely finds significant attention paid to such issues in criminal justice and criminology texts, or in texts about child care. This book aims to remedy this failure in the field of criminal justice. Although the book is about young offenders and the youth justice system, and the various chapters directly address this topic, it is also therefore about the philosophy of youth justice, and such issues are implicit in all the chapters in this book. It is crucial that professionals within the youth justice system understand the aims of their work, and in order to do so it is essential to be explicit about this philosophy and its importance.

What do we mean by philosophy?

The academic discipline of philosophy may seem esoteric and remote from aspects of daily life, both personal and professional. But a notion of philosophy, in a general sense, informs all that we do. When we act in a purposeful manner, this action is shaped by particular ways of thinking which can be conceived in terms of a philosophy. It is helpful in this sense to think about action in terms of three components: (i) knowledge, (ii) skills, and (iii) philosophy. Each component may be defined in the following terms:

- *Knowledge*. The range of information, and nature and level of understanding gained from experience or study.
- *Skills*. The degree of expertise demonstrated in undertaking tasks.
- *Philosophy*. The system of thought that motivates and directs action in the service of particular objectives or principles.

In professional terms, for youth justice workers, knowledge in this context means understanding young people and their behaviour; its causes and how it can be changed. It means understanding criminal justice legislation and the system and how it works. It means understanding the role of youth justice workers in the courts, with young people and as employees of large organisations.

Skills, in this context, are the abilities professional workers possess and use in the discharge of their duties. They are typically presented as a discrete list, for example obtaining information, report-writing, verbal presentation, problem-solving, objective-setting, use of technology (telephones, faxes and computers) and so forth.

Knowledge and skills are intimately linked, to the extent that one may possess knowledge but without skills be unable to apply this knowledge to concrete situations. But whenever knowledge and skills are combined in some form of action, this action is always (although often implicitly) informed by a particular philosophy. A philosophy, therefore, gives purpose to action: philosophy shapes the way in which we use knowledge and skills to achieve certain outcomes.

Philosophy, then should not be taken to mean some abstract system of thought, or some high-brow idea of how society should operate or could operate in an ideal world. In the sense used here it is about a more down-to-earth normative concept that allows meaning to be given to actions. It is a way of making sense of what we do.

Before concentrating upon the philosophy which is important for the future of youth justice, something needs to be said about the importance of such matters generally and about how this sort of thinking informs or shapes our actions. Once this has been completed, some recent practical examples of different criminal justice philosophies – that is juvenile justice in the 1980s, government, the CJA 1991 and the youth court, and of managerialism – will be examined. Finally, the motivating ideas of an overarching philosophy for youth justice practice will be set out.

Why is philosophy important?

The previous section separated out knowledge, skills and philosophy as the three components of action. In practice, in our daily personal and professional lives, these three components are highly interrelated. They do not occur in any order of priority, they do not form a linear chain of thought,[1] and they do not have meaning independent of one another. Knowledge, skills and philosophy are inextricably intertwined in action to the extent that action is dependent upon the way in which we make sense of these three components in particular situations. This process is not always wholly reflexive: in other words we do not always make explicit in our own minds or to others the reasons why we act in particular ways. A certain action sometimes feels right in a given situation, but this feeling of the appropriateness of a particular course of action is based upon a coincidence between our knowledge, skills and philosophy (however imperfect this process sometimes is!). It may be helpful, at this stage, if some examples are given of the importance of philosophy for everyday action to show how it shapes these actions.

Actuarial practices

In the modern world, whenever we apply to insure ourselves against some future risk we are subjected to what Simon (1988) calls *actuarial practices*. In other words, when we seek to insure our cars against theft or damage or our houses against loss or damage, when we apply for life insurance and when we apply for credit, insurance companies base their decisions on whether to grant credit or on how much we should pay to receive loss or damage insurance on our position within a variety of categories. These categories include: where we live (postcode), whether we smoke, our age and sex, employment status and salary, and so on.

Insurance companies use an actuarial approach because they cannot know in advance precisely what risk we as individuals present. Actual decisions about, for example, how much we should pay in premiums to insure our lives are based, therefore, on statistical aggregates of how long *people like us* have lived in the past. The extent to which we fit into a variety of categories (smoker/non-smoker, male/female and so on) will determine our risk status, and insurance companies' assessment of our risk status will determine how they treat us. These decision-making processes, therefore, have little to do with us as individuals, but recast us as points in actuarial risk tables: risk tables which have been calculated on the basis of what is known about the previous behaviour of large numbers of people. At face value one may see nothing wrong in this process – it may appear to be 'value free' – but is this the case?

In the late 1980s in the United States a woman challenged her employer's decision to charge her a higher pension premium because, according to actuarial data, as a woman she would live longer than a man and, therefore, present a greater insurance risk. The courts ruled that the company had acted illegally, and that it had discriminated against this woman on the grounds of gender. The insurance industry responded with indignation:

> They expressed a kind of shock that what appeared in their paradigm as a value-free technical decision (to use gender in setting benefit premiums) had been adjudged as discrimination. (Simon 1988: 779)

This example is particularly useful because it highlights the relationship between knowledge, skills and philosophy; it shows how philosophy is often hidden or implicit in human action, and it shows the importance of philosophy in power relationships and in shaping institutional order.

The *knowledge*-base of actuarial practices is to be found in the vast database of previous human experience: information about life expectancy, victimisation rates of particular neighbourhoods and so on. This knowledge-base is accumulated and used through *skills* in statistical data-collection and analysis, and could not be accumulated without these skills. The skills are only relevant by virtue of being applied to a particular population, and this knowledge is only given value because there are skills to manipulate basic raw data. This knowledge and these skills alone, however, are not sufficient;

one must also know what to do with the knowledge and skills to give them meaning, and it is at this point that philosophy becomes crucial.

In actuarial practices there is a coalescence of two primary philosophical positions: (i) that knowledge derived scientifically is value-free in the same way that the scientific method of collecting that knowledge is value-free, and (ii) a market philosophy that if you receive certain goods to a particular value, then you should pay the 'proper' price. It is this philosophical component that allowed the insurance company to believe it was right to charge a woman higher premiums because women live longer.

Hidden philosophy

It is interesting to note how this philosophy was implicit or hidden within these actuarial practices: the decision to charge women more was presented as a decision based purely on the information (knowledge + skills) held by the company. It is further interesting to note how the insurance industry acted with indignation at the decision of the courts; they could not believe that they had acted in a discriminatory manner. There is nothing in the information held by the company that could justify such an indignant response; it is only because this information was given meaning or value by a particular philosophical position which the industry believed implicitly to be right that they were bemused by alternative interpretations of their behaviour.

The fact that philosophy is often implicit within human (and organisational) behaviour, and yet so crucial in shaping that behaviour, is an important point to grasp. As Simon said of the actuarial practices he studied:

> Insurance classifications differentiate people in ways that would normally be considered offensive. The ideological power of actuarial practices is their ability to neutralize the moral charge carried by these forms of difference. As a consequence, the political power of these forms of difference to generate identity and thus mobilize constituencies for change is diminished while patterns of domination remain. (Simon 1988: 794)

The often hidden, yet pivotal role of philosophy (in the knowledge, skills and philosophy complex) can, therefore, lead to and

justify practices which may be judged alternatively as discriminatory. This is a property not restricted to the insurance industry and
the particular knowledge, skills and philosophy interaction that is
characteristic of it. In the criminal justice system, for example, the
Home Office is showing increased interest in the use of risk predictors in sentencing. Similarly in this context, some of these risk
predictors are actuarially-based and could be used to justify, 'in a
value free manner' for example, extremely harsh and punitive
sentences for black people or young people – if it can be shown
that being black or being young is generally associated with offending (issues of risk assessment and youth justice are addressed in
more detail in Chapter 7).

It is not necessarily the case that the knowledge, skills and philosophy complex is discriminatory or results in practices which are
harmful to groups within the population. The determining factor
in this relationship is the operational philosophy of the decision-
maker. Knowledge and skills are only given meaning by a philosophy which directs that knowledge and those skills in the service of a
particular objective. It is not only important, therefore, to be aware
that knowledge, skills and philosophy are inextricably intertwined
in action; it is also important to be aware of the contribution each
makes to the complex of behaviour. As shown above, it is frequently
the case that the philosophical component of action is implicit or
hidden behind knowledge and skills which are presented as logical
or value-free. It is absolutely essential that we make the implicit as
explicit as we can, both in our understanding of the behaviour of
others and in understanding why we act in the ways that we do. To
act purposefully depends upon a clear articulation of philosophy.

The philosophy of juvenile justice in the 1980s

It is popularly believed, particularly by some politicians and some
groups within the criminal justice system, that the philosophy of
juvenile justice in the 1980s was minimal intervention – this was not
the case. It is true that minimal criminal justice intervention was a
strategic target for many juvenile justice workers who believed that
the excessive involvement of young people in the criminal justice
system could have more negative than positive consequences. But
minimum intervention was a tactic, not a philosophy. Strategic

minimum intervention was only relevant to certain specific criminal justice decision-making points: there were, in fact, a number of typical juvenile justice practices in the 1980s that were extremely interventionist, running completely counter to and remaining inexplicable in terms of a minimal interventionist philosophy.

It has also been argued by some that the philosophy of juvenile justice in the 1980s was essentially justice-based (Morris and Giller 1987) or corporatist (Pratt 1989). In fact it was neither of these, as the practices one would expect to follow from either a justice-based or corporatist philosophy were, as shown in Chapter 2, not the defining characteristics of the period. To expose the philosophy of juvenile justice in the 1980s it is necessary to probe beneath a simple examination of particular practices or strategies, and to uncover the reasons *why* juvenile justice workers acted in the way that they did.

Chapter 2 argued that the 1980s juvenile justice new orthodoxy was essentially based on an anti-custody philosophy (see also Bottoms *et al.* 1990). In other words, it was the avoidance of custody for young people that justified and gave meaning to the actions of juvenile justice workers. These workers used their knowledge and their skills to manipulate, through systems management, the way in which the criminal justice system made decisions about the processing of juveniles to maximise the chances of avoiding a custodial sentence. Table 3.1 looks at the range of key decision-making points in the juvenile justice system and highlights how the anti-custody philosophy shaped the actions of juvenile justice workers.

In practice the sophistication of anti-custody systems management techniques has increased markedly over the years. In the early 1980s when the new orthodoxy was forming, the strategy was limited to offering the courts a community-based supervision as an alternative to custody – which magistrates accepted or not, largely according to their preferences. By the end of the 1980s, as Table 3.1 indicates, systems management techniques were being utilised in the service of the anti-custody philosophy at every possible opportunity within the juvenile justice system. At all times, however, the driving force to develop ever more sophisticated strategies has been the continuing goal of reducing custody for young people.

The juvenile court was superseded by the youth court in the early 1990s. The Conservative government intended that this new

Table 3.1 The influence of the anti-custody philosophy on the actions of juvenile justice workers at key decision-making points in the juvenile justice system

Decision-making point	Juvenile justice actions/aims	Influence of anti-custody philosophy
Charge or process	To divert young people from the juvenile justice system through cautioning or other non-process options	Keeping young people out of the juvenile justice system altogether is the most effective way of avoiding custodial sentences. Delaying entry of young people into the juvenile justice system reduces their chances of ultimately receiving custodial sentence because greater opportunity is afforded to use non-custodial sentencing options
Bail/remand decision at police station	Efforts are made to achieve the least restrictive bail conditions and to avoid, wherever possible, institutional or custodial remands. If young person is a danger to self or others, or if a 'grave crime' has been committed, then the preference is for remand to local authority secure accommodation	If a young person is made subject to strict bail/remand conditions or is remanded in custody this sends a message to magistrates which may result in the young person penetrating juvenile justice system sanctions further than necessary following first, and subsequent, court appearances
Bail/remand decision in court	Efforts are made to achieve the least restrictive bail conditions and to avoid, wherever possible,	If a young person is made subject to strict bail/remand conditions or is remanded in custody this sends a message to magistrates at subsequent court appearance which may

Table 3.1 *continued*

Decision-making point	Juvenile justice actions/aims	Influence of anti-custody philosophy
	institutional or custodial remands. If young person is at risk of remand into custody, or is a danger to self or others, or if 'grave crime' committed, then preference is for bail support programme or remand to local authority secure accommodation	result in a higher tariff or custodial sentence. Intensive bail support is only justified in: (i) keeping the young person in the community until sentence, and (ii) demonstrating to magistrates the viability of a community sentence thereby reducing the risk of an ultimate custodial sentence
Sentencing	Efforts are made to achieve the lowest possible tariff sentence. Targeted provision of intensive community supervision options to avoid custodial sentences	Sentencing tends to reflect: (i) the seriousness of the offence, and (ii) progression up the tariff. Keeping sentences at lowest possible point on tariff maximises opportunities to avoid custody. Intensive community sentences are justified only where these are targeted on individuals who would otherwise receive a custodial sentence. The most intensive community sentences are used as a last resort to avoid custody
Appeals	Efforts are made to encourage and facilitate appeals against custodial sentences	Appeals are promoted in individual cases to remove a young person from custody, but also strategically to raise the position of intensive community sentences on the tariff

youth court (and the CJA 1991 which introduced it) should embody a new sentencing philosophy – that of 'just deserts'. In practice the 1990s has seen little change in the philosophy of juvenile (now youth) justice workers. Youth justice workers have remained as committed to an anti-custody philosophy in the 1990s as much as they were in the 1980s, but this philosophy is no longer sufficient to match the challenges of the youth justice system and the challenges presented in working with young people. This is not because young people have changed, or that custody has become acceptable, it is because the context in which youth justice workers work is changing. A viable new philosophy for youth justice must be placed within an explicit understanding of: (i) the philosophy of the CJA 1991, (ii) the philosophy which underpinned the implementation of the youth court, (iii) the philosophy of social services departments' and probation services' managers in implementing the youth court, and (iv) more recent philosophical changes shaping the Labour administration of criminal justice policy generally. These alternative philosophies, which as we shall see are sometimes competing with the philosophy of youth justice workers, shape the context within which the challenges of the future must be met.

The philosophy of the CJA 1991

Arguably the CJA 1991 represented the first time that a British government clearly enshrined in a comprehensive piece of criminal justice legislation a single coherent sentencing philosophy and policy. That the Conservatives certainly saw sentencing philosophy and policy as a matter for government was clearly demonstrated in the White Paper *Crime, Justice and Protecting the Public* (Home Office 1990):

> No Government should try to influence the decisions of the courts in individual cases. The independence of the judiciary is rightly regarded as a cornerstone of our liberties. *But sentencing principles and sentencing practice are matters of legitimate concern to Government*, and Parliament provides the funds necessary to give effect to the courts' decisions. (para. 2.1, *added emphasis*)

The government's sentencing policy had at its core the achievement of *justice* through a more consistent[2] approach to sentencing:

To achieve a more coherent and comprehensive consistency of approach in sentencing, a new framework is needed for the use of custodial, community and financial penalties. (para. 2.3)

Just deserts

This new sentencing framework was based on 'just deserts'.[3] At the core of a desert-based sentencing framework is a more structured approach to sentencing. Courts are required to make an assessment of the severity of the offence, or offences committed in combination, and balance this with information about the individual offender (culpability, age, attitude, level of maturity, nature and reasons for the offences and so on), and then select the most appropriate sentence from an *à la carte* menu of sentencing options. In a desert-based approach, this sentencing principle is often combined with restrictions on the ability of courts to choose particular options. In particular, there is usually an injunction which requires courts to limit the severity of the sanction to assessments about the seriousness of the offence. As it was put in the White Paper, courts:

> have to be satisfied that the seriousness of the offence justified the severity of the restrictions on liberty which would be imposed by the order. (para. 4.6)

The desert element in sentencing, therefore, is linked to various amounts of restrictions on the offenders' liberty; restrictions which can be applied either through community sentences or through a custodial sentence. It was clearly the intention of government, therefore, to do away with notions of alternatives to custody and to enshrine a ladder of sentencing options with escalating levels of control/restriction. Offenders found guilty of the most serious offences would receive custodial sentences. Those found guilty of minor offences would receive discharges or fines. And those found guilty of offences of intermediate seriousness would receive a 'community sentence'. These community sentences should still represent an appropriate level of restriction of liberty for the severity of the offence committed, but the precise nature of the community sentence was to be decided according to the individual characteristics of the offender. As the White Paper said:

In using community sentences, the courts will need to consider the seriousness of the offence, the totality of the punishment and the *characteristics of the offender*. If an offender needs advice and training to tackle problems which are at the root of his offending, then the court is likely to opt for a probation order. If, on the other hand, the aim is to deprive him of leisure as a punishment and to make some reparation to the community, then community service would be preferable. The order of severity is not fixed; a short community service order of less than 60 hours would be less severe than a probation order with 60 days specified activities; and both might be less severe than a probation order without requirements combined with a heavy compensation order. The courts will have to look at the overall effect of the sentence on the offender. (para. 4.8, *added emphasis*)

On the basis of this individualised desert-based approach to sentencing, the CJA 1991 included various re-formulated and new sentencing options for 16 and 17-year-old offenders in the newly created youth court. This individualism in sentencing firmly established a need for individualised assessments about individual offenders. It was expected that courts themselves should make certain individualised assessments (for example concerning the severity of the offence), but the adumbration of a fully individualised desert-based sentencing framework consolidated the role of community-based agencies in providing certain information about individual offenders, and in the provision of a range of community-based sentencing options.

The philosophy of the CJA 1991, therefore, was clearly desert-based, that is it was intended that sentencing should reflect assessments about the seriousness of the offence balanced with relevant information about the individual offender. Such was the importance of the role of community-based agencies in making a success of this new philosophy that the Conservative government was concerned to ensure that local agencies acted appropriately in implementing the provisions of the Act. This concern was manifested in a strategy for the local implementation of the CJA 1991, and this strategy, too, had a philosophy of its own.

The philosophy of government–local implementation

It is a public sector truism that government has little control over the local implementation of legislation once it has been enacted.

Government creates legislation, but it is implemented through the decisions and actions of many individuals working in a wide range of local organisations and agencies; and these individuals have traditionally enjoyed a degree of discretion in their decision-making. From a government perspective, therefore, it can appear that the intent or purpose behind a particular piece of legislation is subverted in implementation by local organisations.

This apparent subversion of legislative intent became a particular target for the Conservative government, and increasingly over the 1980s and early 1990s it mobilised a variety of strategies to ensure local compliance with its policy objectives. At the root of these strategies was financial control, as embodied in the Financial Management Initiative (an initiative which had its origins in the office of Prime Minister Thatcher and which borrowed heavily from the business sector, see, HCC 588, Gray and Jenkins 1986, Humphrey 1993, Jackson 1985). The process of financial control within business has a number of key features. Firstly, a central core of strategic decision-makers is established to determine the size and purpose of financial budgets. Secondly, devolved units of management responsibility are created. And lastly, key performance criteria are determined by the strategic core to be implemented by unit managers and according to which unit managers may be financially audited. While financial control has been an extremely significant, and often locally quite negative, feature of modern government strategies, also of great importance has been the general development of *managerialism*, based partly on the FMI experience.

Managerialism

Managerialism represents an extension of financial management to the extent that it borrows certain of its key mechanisms. In the context of centre–local relations, firstly, government establishes its key policy objectives; secondly, it requires certain specific actions of managers in local agencies which are intended to bring this policy into implementation; and lastly, it monitors local managers' actions to ensure that they have acted in accordance with government intentions (see, generally, Pollitt 1993).

The CJA 1991 was the first time that a piece of criminal justice legislation was implemented locally under the managerialist strategy of the Home Office. This strategy was contained essentially in

Home Office Circular 30/1992 *Young People and the Youth Court.*[4]
This circular reiterated the government's individualised desert-
based sentencing philosophy and set out clearly what it expected
local agencies to do in implementing this philosophy:

> The new provisions for dealing with 16 and 17-year-old offenders bring
> together elements of both the juvenile and adult court systems, for which
> there are separate practices and procedures. Their implementation will
> need to be carefully planned locally, in order to make the best use of the
> opportunities and resources for constructive work with offenders in this
> age group and to avoid conflicts in objectives and working methods,
> duplication of effort, or failure to provide necessary support...
> A crucial part of the planning process will be to decide the local
> arrangements for the management of the community sentences for
> which the probation service and social services have formal responsibil-
> ity. Formal responsibility for the supervision of offenders made subject to
> probation orders, community service orders and combination orders will
> lie with the probation service. Formal responsibility for supervision
> orders will lie with either the probation service or social services. How-
> ever, subject to that, day to day responsibility for managing these orders
> and working with the offenders may best be carried out by or shared
> with one or more other agency or organisation. The actual arrange-
> ments will need to be decided locally. It will be necessary to identify
> the resources available locally to support young people under statutory
> supervision, and to plan the distribution of work in such a way as to
> ensure that they are used most effectively...
> Whichever statutory service has formal responsibility for supervising
> the young person, there should be as much flexibility as possible in the
> use of facilities that other local services and organisations are able to
> offer. For example, where a probation order has been made and it is felt
> that the offender would benefit from part or all of the local authority's
> specified activity programme, arrangements should be such as to allow
> this to take place. (HOC 30/1992, paras 11, 18, 19)

In its concern to ensure that senior managers in local agencies
acted effectively to implement government policy objectives the
Home Office went on to provide a checklist of action points in
the circular, under the general heading '*Making it work locally*',
'which need to be covered in making local arrangements for dealing
with 16 and 17-year-olds in the community under the 1991 Act.'
(HOC 30/1992, para. 28). Thus the circular encouraged local
agency managers, acting together in interagency groups, to produce a series of policy and implementation documents detailing the
precise arrangements for delivering services to the youth court,

including local action plans which were envisaged as important documents in the planning and implementation processes of providing services to the youth court (see, HOC 30/1992 Annex D).

It is this specification of managerial/organisational action points which is quintessentially managerialist (see Haines, Bottoms and O'Mahony 1996), and although this strategy was intended to bring about the implementation of the government's criminal justice philosophy, the managerialist strategy itself was based on a control philosophy (see generally, McWilliams 1992, Vanstone 1995). In other words, the purpose of the managerialism was to achieve greater control over local agencies and their practices. The philosophy of government in the implementation of the CJA 1991, therefore, was one of *control*.

The philosophy of local agency managers

There is an important, and crucial, difference between financial management control and managerialism. While both are based on a control philosophy, in financial management this control is largely achievable because outputs are specified and measurable: a given budget is set for a particular purpose, and the way in which the money is spent is directly recorded and subject to audit. In managerialism, as it is applied to the policy context of centre–local relations, outputs are much more difficult to specify and not always directly measurable. The managerialist approach, therefore, tends not to get embroiled with setting outputs but focuses instead on specifying procedures. Compliance with the specified procedure is intended, in a managerialist model, to achieve the desired output.

In HOC 30/1992 the procedure which senior managers in local agencies were expected to follow was quite clear: establish senior management interagency groups, agree a local policy for the implementation of service provision in the youth court, and manage this policy into practice. The Home Office vested considerable importance in local compliance with HOC 30/1992, and this sort of managerialist approach also tends to carry with it an implicit threat; because non-compliance with the stated procedure would be clear to the Home Office on subsequent inspection, and those agencies or managers who did not fully comply with the circular would be judged negatively. It is perhaps not surprising, therefore, that research demonstrated a very high level of local agency compliance with the procedural requirements of HOC 30/1992 (Haines and O'Mahony 1995a).

The nature of this compliance and the type of outcomes it tended to produce are worthy of further examination. As noted above, senior managers in local agencies tended to comply with the procedural requirements of HOC 30/1992 in the production of inter-agency youth justice policy documents. In doing so, however, they tended not to focus on the government's philosophy, as contained in the provisions of the CJA 1991, of achieving individualism in sentencing; rather, they tended to focus on the much more obvious requirements of HOC 30/1992 to specify the organisational arrangements for the provision of youth court services (that is to specify which agency would provide what services to which age-groups of young people). Thus, for example, it was quite common for local agency managers to agree that probation services would not routinely prepare pre-sentence reports or offer probation-based disposals for young people aged 16 or below. While courts retain the power to make such sentences despite these agreements, this potential is effectively greatly diminished by these interagency arrangements.

In their concern to comply with the procedural requirements of HOC 30/1992, therefore, senior managers tended to establish local arrangements which operated contra to the philosophy of the CJA 1991. This is significant not only because it shows how the procedural control mechanisms inherent within a managerialist approach are not necessarily guarantees of achieving the desired objectives, but it also shows how these procedural requirements can come to dominate the thinking and actions of those they are targeted at such that compliance with the procedures becomes the goal and not the achievement of the original objective (Haines *et al.* 1996). For many local managers, therefore, their philosophy in implementing arrangements for service delivery in the youth court was one of instrumental compliance or fear of failure.

More recent philosophical changes shaping government criminal justice policy

Chapter 2 discussed the changed criminal justice and political context of youth justice in the 1990s. There had traditionally been a nexus between academics, practitioners and policy-makers (government), however imperfect, through which criminal justice policy emerged. Arguably there is no greater demonstration of this nexus than the CJA 1991 and, in particular, the emergence and consolidation of a consensus around the desert-based approach to sentencing. More recently, however, this consensus has been stretched and possibly even broken. These developments are perhaps best captured, in ideological essence, by John Major's (1993) statement that as far as offenders are concerned 'we should understand less and condemn more', and by Michael Howard's 'prison works' statement. But similar sentiments have been expressed by the Labour Party with Tony Blair and Jack Straw's official support of 'zero tolerance' street policing. The increasingly unpopular and desperate Conservative government promoted a Home Secretary who, with little apparent regard for the voice of reason, set about a programme of increasingly retributive and anti-liberal reforms. In 1997 a Labour government was elected and contrary to the hope that the voice of reason would be restored to the Home Office, the new Home Secretary produced plans (Labour Party 1996) to build on the work of Michael Howard.

The logical and reasoned approach to criminal justice policy formation which might be claimed for the 1991 Act was thus followed by a period of less subtlety. To a large extent the Conservative administration of the 1980s and 1990s had won the ideological battle to sever the link between individual action and its social context (Gelsthorpe and Morris 1994). More particularly this government was successful in severing, in the minds of the public, the link between 'problem' behaviour (like crime) and social problems (like unemployment, inadequate housing, social distress and so on). This paved the way for a doctrine of individual responsibility and an increasingly punitive approach towards those who 'fail to discharge this responsibility appropriately'.

This manner of thinking was not limited to adults, but generally extended to include young people who were the targets of much damaging criminal justice policy.[5] Subsequent legislation, supported by both Conservative and Labour administrations, has seen the introduction of new prisons for children aged 12 to 14 years (and increased secure accommodation provision), powers to allow courts to take previous convictions into account when sentencing, the abolition of the unit fines system, the attachment of 'aggravated' to car theft as a mechanism for imposing stiffer sentences, the introduction of previously 'adult-only'-type sentences into the youth court, and the lengthening and toughening-up of community sentences.

Guidelines issued by successive governments has reflected this recent trend. There has been a tightening of control and restrictions (on both criminal justice workers and offenders) through revised National Standards, and a significant toughening in the policy towards cautioning.

More generally, however, major political parties in England and Wales have made increasingly draconian statements about their proposals for dealing with young offenders. Recent proposals have included abolishing the principle of *doli incapax*, removing the right to free legal advice and representation, diminishing/removing the right to have an appropriate adult present during questioning, introducing curfews for all young people, and a generally negative and punitive approach to all young people who have committed even minor offences based on confrontation and offence-focused intervention (to the neglect of welfare issues or needs).

Politics, philosophy and policy

How, then, in terms of a general philosophy, can recent developments be explained and understood? It is not sufficient simply to state that criminal justice policy is now more closely affiliated with political policy. Something of the relationship between them and of the nature of political policy itself must also be understood.

From the late 1970s, and throughout the 1980s and early 1990s, the Conservative government saw themselves (and perhaps were judged by the majority) as the party of law and order. Rhetorically, the interpretation of being the party of law and order has meant being tough on crime and criminals. For much of the 1980s, however, get tough law and order political rhetoric was balanced by criminal justice policies which did not wholly reflect the rhetoric (certain 'get tough' practices were introduced, but community sentences and diversion were also emphasised). It is only more recently that there has been a greater degree of congruence between the rhetoric and reality of criminal justice policy.

The political significance, however, of winning the ideological battle of law and order has been immense. At the time of the 1979 general election a MORI poll placed the Conservatives 30 points ahead of Labour – the biggest cross-party difference on all policy issues tested (see Downes and Morgan 1994). Being the party of law and order came to mean the difference between being in government or opposition, and the political battleground of law and order has become an increasingly important one. To try to close the gap between the parties Labour has consistently moved towards a much more punitive set of policies; in response the Conservatives reinvigorated their punitive rhetoric and backed this up with increasingly punitive policies and practices in an effort to deliver on their promises. The outcome has been a spiralling competitive punitiveness as each party/government seeks to satisfy the lust for punishment it nurtured.

It is tempting to conclude that the spiralling punitiveness that has arisen from these developments is linked in some simple or straightforward way to public opinion. But as Bottoms argues, the concept of public opinion, especially when related to criminal justice issues, is a very complex one:

> While considerable popular support can be produced for punitive policies when rather general and abstract survey questions are asked, that is much less likely to be the case when questions are asked about specific situations concerning which survey respondents have detailed knowledge (including crimes of which they are themselves the victims). In these latter cases suggested penalties are likely to be much closer to those actually imposed in the courts. (Bottoms 1995a)

There is no simple relationship, therefore, that links public opinion with an overtly punitive criminal justice approach. Rather, Bottoms suggests that a punitive approach has been adopted, *inter alia*, because politicians believe that such a stance 'will satisfy a particular electoral constituency'. It is not so much that public opinion leads political policy, therefore, but because the evidence in general and abstract opinion polls suggest that there is popular support for punitive policies, politicians believe that there is political advantage to be gained from a punitive approach. Bottoms calls this approach 'populist punitiveness' and he sees it as an overtly political philosophy:

Hence, the term 'populist punitiveness' is intended to convey the notion of politicians tapping into, and using for their own purposes, what they believe to be the public's generally punitive stance. (Bottoms 1995)

The contemporary political populist punitive philosophy, therefore, is a motivating factor which animates much current criminal justice policy.

A philosophy of youth crime

The intensity of the political significance of law and order has been noted above. Since the 1980s this has tended to result in a political discourse overly preoccupied with crime and criminals. The mechanisms at play during this period are complex but extremely significant. Despite a material worsening in the social conditions of larger numbers within the population (Hutton 1995), and the increasing marginalisation of youth (see Chapter 1), the connections between multiple deprivation and crime are seldom established. Arguably, one of the most significant ideological successes of the recent Conservative era is the disconnection between 'social ills' and offending. The negation of the notion of 'society' and the doctrine of individual responsibility have combined to justify a diminution in general welfare provision and a harsher response to personal failure – including a failure to be law abiding.

Crime prevention fits neatly into this dynamic. It allows government to make (legitimate and popular) claims that it is doing something positive about crime, while at the same time responding more harshly to those who offend because they have failed to take advantage of the opportunities offered. The type of thinking behind this approach has tended to skew political, media, academic, professional and public thinking such that, for example, we no longer see young people who offend as children in need or distress, rather we tend to see children in need or distress as potential criminals. This potential to become a criminal is in all children (but particularly those who live in deprived or depraved circumstances), thus a significant aspect of social policy towards young people is sold under the banner of crime prevention (rather than the prevention of social distress). And following this line of thinking, children in extremes of social deprivation or danger who commit the most minor of offences are rearticulated away from being the most deserving cases for protection or assistance into potentially serious criminals who require harsh punishment to deter them from future offending.[6]

The rearticulation of 'in need' groups within the population as potential problem groups is fairly widespread in modern political discourse. Thus we talk about the unemployed, the homeless, offenders, the sick and so on in such as way as to make them distinct from ourselves. The separation between 'us' and 'them' that this type of thinking creates establishes a distancing which allows *us* to tolerate quite harsh and unsympathetic treatment of *them*, that is groups to which we do not belong.

Young offenders and the welfare state

It is important to locate this type of thinking in the context of the modern state. In short, the ideal of a comprehensive welfare state with equality of provision for all according to need is no longer a shared objective. Modern states compartmentalise problem groups, the homeless, unemployed, offenders and so on and target policies on these populations. But this componentiality allows for the development of distinctively different policies for each of the identified groups – even where this may mean no provision at all, or a punitive approach, for the less or undeserving. This approach tends also to result in policies and practices predicated on the worst possible case but generalised to the wider population.[7] Thus the administration of benefits is built around the 'need' to prevent benefit fraud; and criminal justice policies are developed with the most serious offenders in mind.

This book argues that this general approach is fundamentally flawed and morally unacceptable. While large-scale positive social change is unlikely in this respect, youth justice workers need to develop strategies that take full account of the realities of social policy and the reality of young peoples' lives – rather than some wished-for ideal. As shown above, and in the first two chapters, the political context and world of young people has changed. Youth justice practice needs to take account of these changes while building on the strengths of the past. An alternative-to-custody philosophy alone is no longer a sufficient and justifiable animator of youth justice strategies.

If anything may be learned from the juvenile justice experiences of the 1980s, however, it is that bottom-up change is possible. To be sure, in a managerial culture it is much more difficult for front-line service providers to exercise the levels of discretion previously enjoyed to re-animate government policy and legislation in more humane directions. It is also the case that both front-line workers and those people who receive services are generally in a much worse and more hostile social position than previously. But bottom-up change is still possible. The challenge for youth justice is to articulate a philosophy which is capable of shaping the nature of these bottom-up strategies.

A children-first philosophy

The overarching objective of youth justice practice must be to see all young people under the age of 18 years treated as children. The philosophy for youth justice must be to treat all young offenders as children first. This children-first philosophy should inform, guide and shape all that youth justice workers do in and for children in the criminal justice system.

A basic principle of this children-first philosophy is that children should be treated differently from adults and in a separate manner which recognises the special status accorded to them because of their youth. Children do not have the ability or maturity of adults to influence their social situation and make choices within it; children act within the social situations established by adults. The limitation upon such choices has to be recognised and the need to protect and invest in children for the future. Treating children differently and in a manner which minimises harm and maximises their potential for the future is a central feature of the children-first philosophy.

Where young people have committed offences, therefore, our first objective must be, wherever possible, to treat them as children first and only secondly to treat them as children who have offended. When one investigates the social circumstances of young people charged with a criminal offence it is quite typical to uncover significant amounts of unmet need: inadequate housing (or homelessness), no income and living with families who exist below the poverty line, unchecked violence or abuse,

unemployment and no realistic prospects of work, grossly inadequate leisure provision and no ability to buy access to commercial
leisure-time opportunities, school exclusion or marginalisation
within the education system, poor health and inadequately tailored
health education/provision, and exposure to drink and drugs, and
so on. Frequently, however, the only reason these unmet needs
have come to notice is because the young person has been charged
with a criminal offence; the needs were there before, and they are
present not just in those who are identified as offenders but much
more widely in the youth population; and these needs are generally unmet within this population. These needs should be met
through mainstream social welfare provision and, crucially, not
through the criminal justice system, what is not an appropriate
mechanism for distributing social welfare.

Putting children first in the youth justice system

How then does the children-first philosophy translate into the
operation of the youth justice system? It is helpful in this respect
to examine some key decision-making points and actions within the
youth justice system, and to give examples, as shown in Table 3.2.

The conundrum for youth justice and for society's general
response to young offenders is the need to do something about
juvenile crime and young offenders, while not:

1. inadvertently over-reacting to minor delinquency,
2. doing harm or worsening a young person's prospects, and
3. inappropriately using criminal justice interventions where welfare needs are present.

Current political solutions to this problem tend to emphasise either
a harsh punitive response to confront the young person's behaviour and deter them from future criminal activity, or advocate
intrusive interventions into a morass of welfare issues that is not
justified by the seriousness of the offence. Both of these approaches
are highly problematic.
  Chapter 6 reviews the literature on the effectiveness of interventions in reducing offending. The research conclusively demon-

Table 3.2 Principles of a children-first youth justice philosophy

Decision-making point	Youth justice actions	Children-first principles
Arrest/charge	To act as an 'appropriate adult' and safeguard the interests of the child	SSDs have a duty to protect, and act in the best interests of, children; this applies with equal force to children in the CJS, whose rights and interests must be protected. This includes not only protection from harm but positively securing access to services etc. that promote the health, well-being and future prospects of children
Bail/remand	To maintain children, wherever possible, with their family or community. To provide services as necessary to achieve this objective	It is the right of all children to live with their family or in the community; action which promotes this is in line with a children-first philosophy
Divert/prosecute	The promotion of diversion and the provision of services which supports this aim	Children should never be prosecuted because of welfare needs. If welfare needs come to notice at this stage, excessive criminal justice intervention is not justified. Referral to other support systems which ensure services are provided for children and families is appropriate
Sentencing	To maintain a focus within sentencing on the seriousness of the offence. To place the offending within its social and individual context. To avoid custodial sentences	Welfare needs have no place in justifying excessive criminal justice intervention, but can helpfully be used to contextualise an individual's behaviour and aid constructive sentencing. Referral to other support systems which ensure services are provided for children and families is appropriate
Supervision	Forms of supervision, or community sentences, should be made available to ensure children are maintained within the community. Content of supervision packages should reflect the seriousness of the offence and the social circumstances of the young person	Supervision should not be punitive, but should reflect the relative immaturity of the young person and invest in them for the future. Intervention should be based on knowledge about 'what works' and take account of the reality of children's (often deprived) lives

strates the futility of punitive approaches which at best have no discernible impact on offending (although they may cause harm of various sorts), and which at worst amplify delinquent behaviour. Excessive intervention predicated on welfare need is inappropriate because it tends to punish those living in deprived circumstances when these children have no control over and are not responsible for their social circumstances, but it also has a number of additional problems:

1. Those with high levels of welfare need but low levels of offence-seriousness tend to be treated more harshly than those with low levels of welfare need and higher levels of offence-seriousness.
2. Early intervention based on welfare needs tends to lead to a rapid escalation of sentences and, ultimately, higher levels of custodial sentencing.
3. High levels of perceived injustices in the operation of the criminal justice system.

Neither of the contemporary 'solutions', therefore, are adequate to the challenge.

The children-first philosophy is a more adequate solution to juvenile offending as it avoids the traps other approaches fall into in the following manner:

1. By retaining an emphasis within the criminal justice system on responses to delinquency based on the seriousness of the offence.
2. By limiting these responses with the injunction that young offenders should be treated as children first.
3. By responding to the social problems of minor delinquents through appropriate referrals to other community-based agencies (a normalising principle).
4. By responding to the social problems of more serious offenders on community sentences through the inclusion of appropriate elements in supervision packages (see Chapter 6 for more details).

The achievement of an operational children-first philosophy will require an active professional response from youth justice workers.

The articulation of such a strategy needs to be supported by professional knowledge about children, their behaviour and the various systems that exist to provide children's services; and mobilised with a variety of skills in assessment, working with children and their families and systems management. Effective use must be made of, for example, international conventions relating to the rights and welfare of all children, including the 'Beijing Rules' (1995) on the administration of juvenile justice, the Directing Principles for the Prevention of Juvenile Delinquency 'the Riyadh Guidelines' (1990), the Minimum Rules for the Protection of Minors Deprived of Liberty 'the Havana Rules' (1990), and the United Nations Convention on the Rights of the Child (1989). These international conventions set out the rights of children regarding, *inter alia*, access to proper education and welfare services, and our domestic practices must be made to reflect them. There are many practical steps that can be taken in this respect. For example, avoidance of the term 'offender' in favour of young person or child, use of interagency relationships to ensure all children have proper access to education, and use of domestic legislation to protect children in trouble or danger (that is using the Children Act 1989 to protect children in prisons from abuse).

Putting children first in systems management

Continued emphasis must be placed in a children-first approach on the management of the youth justice system. Much of the success of youth justice strategies during the 1980s was based upon a firm and thoroughgoing commitment to the principles of systems management. Put simply, the approach suggested that even in complex and contentious circumstances, changing systems rather than individuals is likely to be more successful in leading to changed outcomes. The idea that social work practice should operate across this broader canvas, and in a thoroughgoing and theoretically informed fashion, was not new. The 'unitary methods' of Pincus and Minahan (1973), for example, were particularly influential and the subject of much dispute between those who saw systems intervention as preoccupied with maintaining the status quo (Leonard 1975), and those who believed it to involve an active assertion of clients' needs, against those of inert or hostile systems.

There is a phenomenon in the fields of social welfare thinking and practice which produces the risk that success in any endeavour gives rise to exaggerated claims for the efficacy of particular models of understanding and acting, and calls for their more generalised application. In the hands of its more fervent supporters (see, for example, Ross and Bilson 1989) systems intervention became a fashionable dogma rather than a useful and relatively modest tool in pursuit of particular objectives. Following the work of Raynor (1991, 1995) those elements of a systems approach within the field of criminal justice which, in the colder climate of the late 1990s, seem to have stood the test of empirical investigation and sustained practical application are now set out. Some claims for systems management are identified which now seem less robust and which require modification or abandonment if the considerable strengths of the approach are to be harnessed to the needs of contemporary policy and practice.

It is important to be clear that the arguments of this book retain a firm commitment to the basic principles of systems management, confident that a focus upon what is done to young people, as well as what they do themselves, continues to be a cornerstone of effective youth justice action. In rapidly changing times, however, even the most central tenets have to be re-examined and recreated in order to meet new circumstances and challenges.

The claims for a systems approach which continue to make it a central part of any ongoing strategy for youth justice may be summarised as follows:

- Systems are best understood as a series of components which are interdependent and which influence one another.
- These interdependencies emerge most significantly at critical decision-making points which form part of a process. Here different trails of influence come together, are shaped by one another, and particular outcomes made more or less likely.
- That criminal justice and other social systems are, nevertheless, more characterised by loosely rather than closely integrated elements in which the pathways of cause and effect are understood only with difficulty.
- That *actual* rather than *intended* inputs and outcomes have to be the focus of such an understanding.

- That unintended consequences are the likely product of complex interactions, rather than simply occasional or aberrant outcomes, and therefore need to be kept under constant consideration.
- That monitoring forms an essential component of a systems approach. Systems cannot be influenced if the consequences of intervention within them are unknown.
- That systems management strategies instigated by youth justice services have to rely on influence and persuasiveness, rather than on authority, to decide outcomes. Youth justice workers can help to shape systems behaviour; it cannot be determined by them.
- That influence is most likely to be exercised effectively when proposed changes are discussed and debated openly with others, and based upon a confident and distinctive vision of criminal justice rooted in such social work values as inclusion and reconciliation, rather than exclusion and revenge.
- That efforts to influence criminal justice processes are a basic and fruitful investment in influencing the future behaviour of individuals who get caught up in them. Systems approaches of this sort have a direct benefit for youth justice strategies which aim to influence the offending of their clients.
- That, in the field of criminal justice in particular, there is empirically-informed evidence that more intervention often produces more harm than good, both for specific individuals and in terms of more general net-widening.

Some of the difficulties with systems management are the result of over-ambitious claims for the strengths suggested above. As Raynor (1991) suggests, the process is one of an 'over-extension of a good idea until it becomes, at least in some of its applications, a rather bad idea'. Three particular extensions which have become entrenched in some parts of youth justice practice, and which seem to be particularly unhelpful, may be summarised as follows:

- Social welfare intervention can only lead to harm and must always be avoided.
- Social systems are capable of being thoroughly understood and intervention within them precisely targeted and routinely applied with predictable and reliable results.

- Power differentials between different players and interest groups within such systems are relatively unimportant. Interdependence means that outcomes can be affected by any determined group.

A systems management approach has to avoid the difficulties which these more florid formulations contain. Each of the three assertions set out above needs modification for contemporary practice and our reformulations of them now follow. When these changes are added to the enduring strengths of the method noted earlier, systems management still provides a necessary and capable foundation for successful practice. A modified model could be characterised in the following way:

- Systems intervention is capable of being delivered in a way which preserves the possibility of doing good, as well as avoiding harm. Not all the things which social welfare services have to offer intrinsically or inevitably rebound to the detriment of young people. Indeed there are social rights which such individuals are often denied in other systems and which, if criminal justice outcomes are to be affected, need to be pursued with them and on their behalf. The application of systems management principles to the housing, employment and medical rights of young people is explored more fully in Chapter 5. In the meantime, it is our firm contention that positive intervention by youth justice workers is possible within a systems management approach which still remains consistent with the enduring strengths outlined earlier. Indeed such positive action is not simply capable of being encompassed within the systems approach, it is a necessary component of it if the prospect of worthwhile outcomes is to be enhanced.
- Systems management remains a more provisional, imprecise and unpredictable enterprise than purists imply. While the broad outlines of systemic patterns remain clear – least intrusive interventions lead to least problematic futures, for example – the individual careers of young people who become caught up in the criminal justice processes remain just that: *individual* progressions in which particular combinations of systems components and decisions are worked out in different ways. For practitioners this means that an uncritical or mechanical applica-

tion of systems management will always be deficient. The essential challenge of social work lies in the refusal of social circumstances ever to replicate themselves in a neat or exact fashion. In the hands of over-ambitious systems theorists, youth justice workers seem sometimes to have been thought of as dangerous individuals who must not only be kept from doing harm to individual young people, but whose general practice would be much improved by reducing it to a series of formulaic rules, the rigid application of which would best be ensured through a rigorous process of non-negotiable gate-keeping. This is a view which this book rejects. It is the practical implementation of policy by individual workers which has the greatest impact and that implementation is most frequently in the hands of workers at team and local level. Systems management works best when carried out by informed and critical practitioners, capable of exercising judgement in order to apply its principles effectively in the unique circumstances which characterise even the apparently simplest or most routine of criminal justice encounters.

- Systems management approaches underestimate the issue of power differentials within the criminal justice system in a way which is likely to lead to unhelpful distortions in the understanding of the impact which youth justice social work services can hope to produce. Such difficulties are two-fold. On the one hand systems theory can appear to underestimate the very real power which lies in the hands of particular actors at different points within the criminal justice process, and the discriminatory ways in which these powers can be applied. A sturdy application of systems principles will be incomplete if it does not include a positive determination to advocate and advance the best interests of particular individuals against whom that system may move especially sharply. At the same time, such an approach has to avoid a naive confusion of influence with power. Raynor (1995) has pointed out that the rhetoric of Probation Service influence upon the criminal justice process has not been matched by its performance – or, indeed, by a necessary willingness to act in a way which promotes influence. Rather, it has been over-preoccupied with the development of its own programmes and procedures to the neglect of understanding the ways in which these activities might influence other parts of the criminal justice system. Part of the reason for this preoccupation has been an inflated sense of its own importance. Indeed Raynor lays particular emphasis upon the importance of attitude change, independent of legislative or organisational amendments, in altering outcomes.

Youth justice workers need a dual strategy which, in many ways, is a mirror image of the least successful systems strategies. In poor practice, services have developed fierce-sounding policies matched by a timidity at the point of application. Workers are unlikely to stand out for unpopular policies in court if they fear that such actions will put them not just on the line, but out on a limb. The prescription set out here would turn such a pattern on its head. Achievable policies matched by determined application in individual cases is a combination which needs to command a greater degree of support from managers and a more challenging approach from workers. The next two chapters set out the basics of this challenging approach, firstly in Chapter 4 for the criminal justice system, and secondly in Chapter 5 for other significant systems.

4

Managing Youth Justice Systems

Chapter 3 summarised an understanding of systems management in the youth justice field, and suggested some important modifications to that approach. This chapter now moves on to consider the contemporary application of such techniques in practice, providing a detailed discussion of the implementation of effective systems management strategies at the different points at which significant decisions come to be made about young people in their contact with the criminal justice agencies. These are the points at which the different interest and power groups within the system combine in different formations and where the opportunity to shape the behaviour of systems rises most accessibly to the surface. The discussion here is set out around the following key decision points within the youth justice system:

- At the police station
- Pre-court diversion\
- Bail
- Remand
- Preparing pre sentence reports
- Supervision and breach
- Custody and post-custodial work

At the police station

It is a central lesson of a systems management approach that decisions taken early in complex and interrelated processes can have a significant impact upon later outcomes. The initial arrest and detention of a young person by the police therefore represents a critical point of entry into the criminal justice system and, where that entry involves the presence of a social welfare worker, it needs to be managed in a way which is consistent with the principles outlined earlier in the previous chapter. Changes in the right to silence introduced in the 1994 Criminal Justice and Public Order Act have placed additional significance upon these initial encounters and upon the actions needed to protect and preserve the rights of vulnerable young people.

Appropriate adults

The role of the appropriate adult demands both a thorough knowledge of systems and the ways in which they can be operated to the benefit of young people together with a capacity to apply this knowledge critically and assertively in the particular circumstances of individual cases. Sadly, however, the most recent evidence of social work practice in this area is not encouraging (see Evans 1993). For this reason and when it is done properly, the work undertaken at the appropriate adult stage can form the foundation for effective work at a systems and individual level. The discussion which follows does not aim to provide a detailed guide to appropriate adult practice. Information of that sort is well set out in other texts (see, for example, Littlechild 1996). The emphasis here is upon those points within the process where systematic actions should be triggered, rather than upon responses to the particular dilemmas posed by different individuals.

The role of the appropriate adult is set out in the Codes of Practice of the Police and Criminal Evidence Act 1984. The Codes were revised in 1991 and again in April 1995 – the current version – and they set out to provide additional protection for vulnerable people during detention and questioning by the police, helping to maintain the 'fundamental balance' between the parties involved. Young persons under 17 are deemed to be vulnerable on the grounds of their age and understanding. Interviews at police stations with such individuals must include the presence of an 'appropriate adult', defined as a parent/guardian or a social worker or, in the absence of either, another responsible adult who is not a police officer or employee. A solicitor attending to offer legal advice may not act in this capacity.

The best evidence for contemporary practice in this area comes from a specific study undertaken for the 1993 Royal Commission on Criminal Justice. Professor Roger Evans investigated the techniques used by the police in interviewing juveniles, including the impact of appropriate adult presence on these interactions. It is important to emphasise the general finding that the presence of an extra adult within the process by itself alters interaction and provides, even in a simple social sense, a support system for the detainee. Against that general background, however, the evidence concerning specific performance of the appropriate adult role was not encouraging.

Evans and his team analysed 167 taped police interviews with juveniles. They found that 'When solicitors are present in interviews they rarely contribute to the proceedings. Neither do social workers. It appears that appropriate adults, including parents, do not normally offer advice to juveniles during questioning or take any steps to ensure that interviews are conducted fairly.' This inaction was characteristic, despite the researchers finding that persuasive or oppressive techniques had been used in about a quarter of the sample: 'By any standards there are examples of oppressive questioning in the sample of cases discussed here. On occasion juveniles are for example harangued, belittled or directly and indirectly threatened.' Social workers were present as appropriate adults during 29 of the 167 taped interviews. Persuasive tactics were used on 18 of these occasions. A challenge was mounted by the appropriate adult only once.

Improved practice has to be rooted in proper training. It demands a combination of improved knowledge of the law and relevant procedures and a greater willingness to act assertively on the basis of that knowledge in the difficult conditions of a police interview. Knowledge begins with a recognition that anyone undertaking appropriate adult work is not involved simply to assist the business of 'processing' a detained young person. There should be no question of simply *observing* what goes on in order to lend the process some spurious legitimacy. Rather, the job is an active one with a duty to intervene within the process in order to defend certain basic principles. These include:

- having regard for the individual's physical and emotional welfare;

- safeguarding their rights and civil liberties;
- checking their understanding of process, and supervising interviews to make sure they are properly and fairly conducted and free of oppressive behaviour or harassment; and
- making communication with the young person easier.

In the case of young people known to youth court workers these principles take on a fresh importance. The Evans study found that police officers interviewing juveniles took a different attitude and approach to those whom they believed (because of previous contact, background or address) to be 'criminals' and those who were not so identified. Individual suspects falling into the first category were significantly more likely to be subjected to unfair questioning or pressure. Such attitudes have, of course, been widely legitimised by senior officers and politicians intent on demonising young people generally and that sinister 'small group' responsible for a disproportionately vast proportion of offences in particular. These are, also, of course just the individuals who are likely to be known to youth justice workers and to require their services at police stations.

Against that background four main stages in the process can be identified where systemic points of intervention arise: initial request, on arrival at the police station, during the interview, and after the interview has been concluded. At each stage a series of key questions can be identified for practitioners.

Initial request

The first question for anyone asked to attend at a police station as an appropriate adult should be 'Am I the best person for this job?' Are there family members or friends who may, because of their familiarity to the young person, be better placed to provide the sense of solidarity, commitment to that individual's best interests and determined advocacy of those interests which the role requires? Have factors such as race, gender and the possible need for a translator also been properly considered at this initial request stage?

On arrival at the police station

Police stations are intimidating places, even for those whose jobs bring them into regular contact with police officers and those parts of the station which lie behind the front desk. It is thus important for appropriate adults to act with the confidence which will establish their independence in the action which is to follow. The following questions can help to ensure that the basis for that confidence is located within the role itself, rather than in the characteristics of any individual worker:

- Has a check been made of the custody record, in order to be satisfied that the Codes of Practice have been followed and to obtain preliminary details of arrest and length of detention?
- Has an interview between the appropriate adult and the young person alone been considered in order to allow for an assessment of the cause and extent of that individual's 'vulnerability' and a preliminary response to any particular needs?
- Before any police interview begins, has the formal caution been administered and the rights of the young person explained to them by the investigating police officer in the presence of the appropriate adult?

During the interview

At the start of the interview the physical arrangement, as well as the tone in which proceedings are conducted, should be tested to ensure that they provide an aid rather than a hindrance to communication. Seating arrangements in the interview room should be checked, for example, in order to ensure that they allow for proper eye contact between the young person and the appropriate adult. Thereafter an active part in the process must be maintained. Are unfair interviewing techniques, such as statement-questions ('You hit him, didn't you?') or persuasive tactics being employed? If so, are they being challenged and recorded? Has the reserve power to leave the interview thus ensuring that it comes to an immediate end been considered where unfair practice continues?

After the interview

If the young person is being charged with an offence, the appropriate adult should accompany her or him through the photo and finger-printing process. Key questions to consider before leaving the station include: has the custody record been examined again?

Have any issues of concern been noted in it and has the record been signed? Has the copy of the record to which they are entitled been obtained for both suspect and worker? The responsibilities of the appropriate adult end when s/he leaves the station. Other aspects of a youth justice worker's role, of course, may only just have begun and bail, to which this chapter now turns, will be amongst the earliest and most crucial.

Police bail

One of the most important decisions to be made at the police station will be taken in relation to bail. Section 27 of the 1994 Criminal Justice and Public Order Act introduced new powers which have allowed the police to grant conditional as well as unconditional bail. In general the police now have the same powers as courts in this regard, except that they may not require an individual to live in a bail hostel, Social Services accommodation or to make her or himself available for inquiries or reports or to undergo medical tests. In a systems management context this means that local authorities need to ensure that arrangements are made to liaise with the police in order to discuss, and if possible agree, the types of condition which would be appropriate in a range of different situations. It will also mean making full use of the procedures – through police internal review and by court application – for variation or lifting of the conditions where these are unreasonable or oppressive. This in turn requires a notification system for those instances where youth justice services do not provide appropriate adults at interview, in order that police bail decisions can be reviewed in all cases prior to court hearings.

At the time of writing, the effects of these new police powers are largely unreported. Preliminary evidence does suggest, however, that one effect has been to sharpen the categorisation by the police of those for whom bail is likely to be opposed. The capacity to attach conditions to bail means that only those who in the estimation of the police cannot be bailed under any conditions are brought before the court for determination. The onus upon youth justice services to intervene at this point is thus all the more acute.

Two other changes brought about by the 1994 Act need to be noted here. The automatic refusal of bail in serious cases is unlikely

to impinge upon day-to-day youth justice practic
as part of the general encroachment upon cou
which is characteristic of contemporary crimin
making. The removal of the presumption of bail \
of the Act introduces when a defendant is chargea
able or either-way offence which was allegedly comi
bail is considerably more serious. As Paul Cavadino (1   , suggests:

> The removal of the presumption in favour of bail in these cases means in
> effect that the burden of proving why bail should be granted is on the
> defendant. Yet at this stage the defendant is still presumed in law to be
> innocent of the charges. The presumption in favour of bail is linked with
> the presumption of innocence.

From a systems management perspective decisions made in relation to bail at the police station will be of crucial importance. Bad
decisions made at this early part in the process will have an enduring impact far beyond their immediate significance. Neglect of
essential systems outside the narrow criminal justice sphere may
create equal difficulty. Short-term targeted intervention within
family systems, for example, may prevent breakdown or improve
the chances of reconciliation just at the point where the availability
of such support is likely to influence future decision-making. This
chapter now turns to these issues.

Pre-court diversion

More perhaps than any of the other initiatives of the systems
management approach, diversion came, by the end of the 1980s
and early 1990s, to be widely accepted as a hugely successful and
beneficial way of dealing with the mass of young people who
become peripherally involved in crime. In retrospect, its very
achievements have clearly contributed to the astonishing turn
around and assault upon one of the very few success stories of
British criminal justice policy which has subsequently characterised
the policies of both major political parties. In its hey-day, two main
arguments underpinned the diversion approach: firstly, the notion
that crime is an ordinary and normal part of growing up which for
most young people goes unnoticed and which readily extinguishes
itself as individuals mature; and, secondly, the notion that greater

volvement with the criminal justice system acts to delay and disrupt such maturation, thus increasing rather than lowering the risk of further offending (see, for example, Sampson and Laub 1993). The more young people could be prevented from entering the formal system, therefore, the better their individual chances of being untarnished by crime and the better the chances for the community generally of avoiding the consequences of their increased criminality in the future.

In a systems management approach, the practical method of pursuing diversion is to focus upon the point at which decisions about formal prosecution are most often taken. As John Pitts (1995) has suggested, organisational changes which embodied this approach were rapidly and widely achieved:

> By the late 1980s, a nation-wide structure of multi-agency juvenile justice panels had been established in England and Wales. The panels, composed of representatives from welfare agencies, the youth service, the police and education departments, reviewed apprehended children and young people entering the system and, wherever possible attempted to divert them away from court.

The police and panels have at their disposal a range of possible actions which do not involve further intervention of any kind including decisions to take No Further Action or to issue an informal warning. At a more formal level, a remarkable rise occurred in the use of police cautions as a way of dealing with young people.

Diversion policy and practice

The climate for diversion was clearly established by a series of circulars issued during the 1980s by the Home Office, in which local authorities and police areas were urged to extend the cautioning of young people as a demonstrated method of keeping such individuals from becoming further enmeshed in the formal criminal justice process and developing into more sophisticated criminals, and avoiding the stigma of conviction which as the Crown Prosecution Service points out 'can cause very serious harm to the prospects of a young offender or young adult'. Indeed, the extension of the cautioning approach to the 17–20 age range was firmly endorsed in Home Office Circular 59/90 which asserted that 'The courts should be used as a last resort, particularly for juveniles and young adults' (Home Office 1990). Systems management received a powerful endorsement in the same document:

> Participation by other agencies in the decision-making process can do much to improve the quality and consistency of cautioning decisions...Chief Officers should consider inviting juvenile liaison panels ...to review any case where the police are in doubt whether or not to caution a juvenile, for instance, where he has been previously cautioned or convicted.

In 1992 a group of respected commentators could still declare that, 'The 1980s was a remarkable decade for juvenile justice practice in England and Wales' (Ashworth *et al.* 1992: 20). Figure 2.3 earlier illustrated just how far that progress had rested upon the increasing use of cautions as a means of dealing with young people in trouble. The proportion of cautions applied to known indictable offenders aged 10 to 16 rose from 50 per cent in 1979 to 81.6 per cent in 1992 (source: abstracted from *Criminal Statistics, England and Wales* 1989, Cm 1322, London HMSO, 1990: 120 and *Criminal Statistics, England and Wales* 1992, Cm 2410, London HMSO, 1993: 110).

Just as the proportion of young people dealt with by means of cautioning increased, so too the hard evidence for the success of cautioning was substantially strengthened by a national survey of juveniles cautioned during a week in November 1991 and subsequently widely reported (see, for example, Spencer 1994). Of 1244 juveniles cautioned, 73 per cent had no previous cautions and a further 16 per cent had one previous caution. Of the remaining 11 per cent only three in a hundred had been dealt with by cautions on more than two previous occasions. As a report of the study in the *Justice of the Peace* concluded, the figures 'illustrate that multiple cautioning is largely myth' (Spencer 1994).

The early patterns of service delivery which followed the 1991 Act were reported upon by both Social Services and Probation Inspectorates (Department of Health 1994; Home Office 1994). Although the focus of both reports is upon matters specific to that Act, both also comment upon the continuing achievements of pre-court diversion and cautioning schemes in keeping non-serious young offenders from the formal system. Success was the product of considerable investment in this area of work, most often by social services departments. Yet, just as the evidence for these reports was being gathered, and less than a year after its October 1992 implementation, the 1991 Act had come under severe attack and had been, in significant measure, amended (Home Office 1993a).

Diversion in retreat

In all of this the whole business of young people and the courts was thrust to the front of the public agenda. The months covered by this study witnessed a remarkable repudiation by government of an approach to young people in trouble which had been painstakingly assembled and happily endorsed by that same government for more than a decade. The latest Home Secretary, Michael Howard, decried the actions of those following the advice his own department had provided about cautioning. A draft circular of November 1993 now accused authorities of 'bringing cautioning into disrepute' (Home Office 1993b, para 7) and, amongst other changes, laid it down that 'It is only in exceptional circumstances that more than one caution should be considered' (Home Office 1993b, para 7).

In contrast to the 1990 circular which had drawn on research evidence commissioned from the University of Birmingham, circular 18/1994 made no claim to empiricism. It contented itself with a display of synthetic indignation that a minority of children received more than one caution,[1] and on that basis proceeded to three distinct discouragements to previous policy. The prohibition of repeated cautioning – other than in exceptional circumstances – was confirmed. The development of cautioning-plus schemes was consigned to that limbo reserved by the Home Office for imaginative and worthwhile initiatives.

The general approach adopted in this book suggests that caution-plus schemes should be organised within a particularly careful framework. At their most questionable such schemes descend into the unscrutinisable waters of administrative justice, bringing young people further into the system on a random basis. At best, such schemes are capable of nudging the system towards developing extra ways of providing help for those young people who need it, with the minimum formal obligation or connection. The triumph of the Home Office was to throw out good and bad schemes without discrimination. Finally, in the same circular, the carefully constructed pattern of interagency systems management was undermined. Ample evidence is available of the practical difficulties which inter-agency diversion schemes have to negotiate in reaching real levels of cooperation (see, for example, Karabinas *et al*.'s 1996 evaluation of the Craigmillar Youth Challenge project in Edinburgh). The encouragement of panel and cooperative arrangements of 1990 was replaced by advice of a very different character: 'The decision to caution is in *all* cases one for the police, and although it is open to them to seek the advice of multi-agency panels, this should not be done as a matter of course' (Home Office 1994, para 3. emphasis original).

As Spencer (1994) in the *Justice of the Peace* concluded, 'If the letter of HOC 18/1994 is followed...then the era of concern to avoid labelling, stigmatization and the accelerated development of youthful criminal careers out of frequently very transient phases of delinquency is over'. Such concerns have, if anything, been increased by the plans of the 1997 Labour administration. Setting out his curriculum for youth justice the new Home Secretary told the House of Commons that, 'We will end the practice of repeat cautions. There will be a single final warning, which will usually trigger effective intervention by youth offender teams' (Hansard 1997).

Reinvigorating diversion

It was argued at the start of this chapter that systems management approaches have to be kept under regular review if they are to remain relevant in changing circumstances. This is particularly true of pre-court diversion arrangements where so much productive work has been achieved in the last 15 years. It will not do to think of diversion in the past tense, as something which belongs to a former era as for example it sometimes appears in the statement of Directors of Social Services and others (1995) – 'throughout the 1980s, and into the next decade, considerable emphasis *was* placed on the desirability of diverting young offenders out of the youth justice system...Community based interventions *were* encouraged' and so on (emphasis added). Rather, diversion has to be re-shaped to meet the new and more hostile circumstances. One such example is to be found in Northamptonshire. An early and outstanding leader in 1980s diversion, Northampton was clearly in the firing line when the tide appeared to turn so rapidly against its central tenets. Yet, as Adrian Bell (1996) Director of the Northamptonshire Diversion Unit has suggested, new strategies can be developed to meet the changing times building on former practices to meet the prevailing 'culture of severity'. Two examples are worth noting here: changing use of cautioning, and work with victims.

In response to changing attitudes towards cautioning, Northampton now deal with the majority of first-time offenders by way of informal action (warning) at source by police officers and custody sergeants and without the involvement of the diversion unit. During 1994/5 the proportion of informal actions for young people was 55.5 per cent and continues to rise. The diversion unit itself has a narrower remit, coming into action as Bell explains:

> when people come back to notice at least once or when they commit offences for which we have a special service. These include all sexual offences; whenever offenders are perceived to have special mental health needs; or where officers have a specific concern related to the offence or the offender (such as the offence being committed in order to 'survive' by way of food or shelter, and when unless a critical change occurred further similar offences would be likely).

From these sources the diversion unit accepts referral of between 15 per cent and 20 per cent of all those coming to notice. The large majority of these receive cautions, while those referred because of special concern are most often resolved by informal warning once intervention has taken place. During the current year the proportion of young people dealt with by cautions in Northamptonshire is 14 per cent. When the figures for informal action and cautioning are combined, the county's experience provides an overall diversion rate of 76 per cent for 1995/6. As Adrian Bell concludes, whatever changes have to be made to adapt a diversion system to meet new demands, 'ensuring that only those who need to be in court go there must be a basic tenet of any Youth Justice strategy.'

Tactical and pragmatic approaches such as those developed in Northamptonshire, are an inevitable component of practice within the tainted waters of the criminal justice system. Some principles have to be applied, however, in order to negotiate the border-zone between the dilemmas and dangers of instrumentality (a sort of anything-goes-so-long-as-it-works approach) and the possibility of still making practice gains. The principles of Children First provide a way of addressing these difficult areas, placing a boundary around what youth justice services ought to be prepared to do on the basis of treating young people in trouble as children first and offenders second, and placing the best interests of such children at the centre of practice approaches. Northamptonshire, for example, rely heavily on working with victims of offences as a way of making their overall strategy marketable in current circumstances. Considerable reservations exist about such work, as the discussion of restorative justice in Chapter 7 indicates. While diversion remains a keystone to any successful systems management approach, the problems and costs of operating such a policy in a hostile climate cannot be heaped upon young people themselves.

Bail decisions

This section is concerned with allied attempts to influence decisions made at pre-trial points within the process. It is worth noting of course that decision-points exist within the court system which allow proceedings to be discontinued in a diversionary fashion. The Islington Mentally Disordered Offenders Project, although aimed primarily at adult offenders, provides a useful example of a court-based diversion scheme. In their evaluation of the project's work Burney and Pearson (1995: 308) point to systemic issues which arise in its operation, emphasising that 'A relatively tiny number of people passing through a myriad of decision-making points in the criminal justice system cannot be dealt with by posting a gatekeeper, like a cat at a mousehole, at every opening'. The need for youth justice workers to be properly informed and skilled to act across a range of court-based circumstances is a central message.

Bail information and bail support services aim to influence decisions which courts might make, either by providing information which allows the Crown Prosecution Service not to oppose bail or to allow the courts to avoid a remand into custody. These decisions are of great importance in at least three different ways.

- *The immediate impact upon the individual and her or his ability to maintain vital aspects of their lives during the pre-trial period.* Successful maintenance of accommodation or education, for example, will have a continuing impact upon the quality of life which a young person is able to experience and may be influential in final determination of court outcomes. Equally, family, domestic or general living conditions which break down at this stage can have dire consequences within the criminal justice system, as well as being calamities in themselves. For young people whose circumstances are difficult or volatile, youth justice workers have a systemic interest in remaining actively involved in order to remain influential at later points within the criminal justice process.

- *The decision as to bail has an immediate impact upon the number of young people held in custody.* The Howard League *Troubleshooter* project (discussed in more detail below) found that 42 per cent of the young men with whom it was in contact received a sentence of imprisonment at the conclusion of their court proceedings, while the remaining 156 young people (58 per cent) were either acquitted, discharged or were given a community sentence (Howard League 1997: 36). It is plausibly argued within the justice field that the fact of remand will have contributed to a less serious final sentence in a considerable number of these cases. It is nevertheless difficult to see how individuals who are suitable for community sentences following remand have had that suitability brought about by the brutalising experience of imprisonment. In the case of young people, particularly, these arguments have additional force. Unambiguous scope exists for reducing the number of those on remand whom the Courts have not seen fit to detain after sentence.

- *The availability of bail produces a series of significant impacts upon the final sentencing decision.* Youth justice research has shown (Haines 1996) just how significant the very earliest decisions within the arrest, charge and bail process are in shaping final sentences. Decisions which mark out young people as too difficult or dangerous to be allowed home or transferred to local authority accommodation live with them throughout the process, casting views of them into a particular mould which persists beyond the seriousness of any offences they may have committed or changed information about their circumstances which may subsequently have come to light. Not only are defendants remanded in custody faced with additional and significant difficulties in mobilising their defence cases and at high risk of losing those social props – accommodation, education, work, family contacts, – which influence court decisions, they are also identified as 'serious' by the very fact of appearing from custody.

In a systematic way, therefore, influencing bail decisions has an impact well beyond the immediate court hearing.

Nevertheless, a series of important safeguards are required if bail support or supervision schemes are not to have the unintended and unhelpful consequences which remain a risk of all social welfare initiatives. A recent study of conditional bail in the adult courts (Hucklesby 1994) has highlighted a series of relevant reservations. The proportion of bailees subject to conditional bail has increased steadily since its introduction in 1967, and a very large number of restrictive conditions are routinely applied – 33 per cent of conditional bailees in the Hucklesby study were subject to four or more conditions. These conditions are often difficult to reconcile with the personal circumstances of individual bailees or with the grounds of objection to unconditional bail but seem, rather, to be used in a routine or undifferentiated manner.

Finally, and most importantly, the view is widely held amongst those most closely connected with the process that rather than replacing custody, conditional bail is too often a substitute for unconditional arrangements. Provision of services in relation to bail more generally must therefore be grounded in the central systems management principle of providing only the level of intervention necessary to change decisions. The practices which are described below should be rigorously judged against a test of their non-net-widening operation. Additional services which are provided at the bail stage can only be justified, in a systems-management sense, if they lead ultimately to less rather than more intrusion into the lives of young people.

Bail information

Two forms of intervention at the bail stage are most widely to be found in youth justice practice, of which bail information usually occurs first within the court process. It involves the provision of any information which a youth justice service might be able to place before the Crown Prosecution Service, or the court itself, and which could contribute to a bail decision. In best practice such services should be available to all young people when the possibility of not granting bail is under consideration. Youth justice workers are well-placed to seek and provide relevant information concerning:

- the status of any address offered by the young person, including any support which might be available there;
- the availability of alternative addresses within the locality, such as with the extended family;
- the effect of denial of bail upon education or employment;
- any previous periods of bail without breach; and
- any current or previous involvement with the Social Services Department and the effect of denial of bail upon any ongoing work being carried out with the young person.

The essential point which needs to be made about bail information concerns the ethos in which it needs to be conducted. To begin with, bail information work needs to be given full value within the range of duties undertaken by services. It cannot be adequately tackled as an add-on extra, to be passed from worker to worker or squeezed in around other urgent tasks. Thereafter, bail information has to be an *active* duty. It is not simply a matter of gathering routine information and passing this on to others. Bail information work needs to take a far more dynamic stance, exploring possibilities, pursuing different avenues, checking information and challenging assumptions. In a systemic sense this means that as well as having a thorough knowledge of the way in which chains of decisions are made, and how the outcome of that chain might be influenced at different points in its progress, bail information workers need to maintain a considerable degree of *independence* from other players in the system and be prepared to push for unfashionable or uncomfortable outcomes, rather than becoming trapped into the collusive world of insiders which is otherwise so characteristic of criminal justice arenas.

In more general terms, as the National Association for Youth Justice (1993) amongst others has pointed out, bail information services have to be embedded within a wider courtroom strategy which has within it 'a range of strategies and techniques which can influence what decisions are made by the courts and how they make them'. In rural areas, where specialist posts for bail work are unlikely, these links to wider principles stand out all the more clearly. Here bail information and support work is likely to relatively *ad hoc*, undertaken by Court Duty Officers. It is all the more important, therefore, that representation of the youth justice service by 'confident and competent advocates', properly trained and supported by accessible advice and guidance from colleagues and line managers, is a fundamental building-block in such a strategic approach and runs through all the different elements of the process with which this chapter is concerned.

Bail support

Bail support initiatives move beyond the provision of information to the direct supply of services designed to offer the court an acceptable alternative to a remand to local authority accommodation or custody where bail or conditional bail appears inadequate. Such intervention has to be subject to stringent gatekeeping. When unconditional bail is not acceptable to the court, for example, the first consideration should always be to maximise the use of conditions which do not involve additional supervision of the young person. If supervision of any sort is required, then the formal requirements of such intervention must be tested directly against their relevance to the reasons for refusal of unconditional bail. Social welfare contact with a young person is always likely to have to include within its ambit issues which arise in addition to formal requirements. At this stage of the process as at any other, however, no young persons should be disadvantaged because of failure to live up to some welfare arrangement which has no direct bearing upon their connection with the criminal justice system.

With these caveats in mind, arrangements encompassed within supervised bail programmes include the monitoring of behaviour at home and in the community by regular visiting, the provision of help and advice, and the consolidation of the props of daily living – somewhere to live, something to do, and so on – which have an impact both upon getting into trouble and upon the ways in which future court appearances might be negotiated. Bail support schemes are worth having if they add something distinctive which youth justice services, in particular, can provide. If bail support means only surveillance and regulation, then the pressure towards thoroughly unacceptable developments, such as electronic monitoring of offenders, becomes harder to resist.

Of course bail support has to include elements of supervision and control. These formal aspects, however, have to be counterbalanced with a genuine interest in the well-being of those made subject to such schemes and a desire to see them succeed within it, and in which the provision of advice and assistance is a cornerstone of effective practice. It is these elements which allow workers to legitimise the very significant and ongoing contact with individuals and their families before any finding of guilt or otherwise has been determined. It increases the positive interest in such schemes by young people themselves, and thus promotes their primary aim of influencing behaviour so as to reduce the level of offending on bail. And where evaluations of such schemes have been carried out (see, for example, Raynor 1995) it is the human contact and the helpful and constructive aspects of available support which dominates the assessment of their operation, in the views of workers and consumers alike.

A systems management analysis of the bail process provides the justification for targeting services at those points where a difference is most likely to be made. As argued consistently in this book, however, if a systems management approach is to work most effectively then it means being clear about and committed to the particular value system of the social work service in seeking to bring about change. The children-first approach, as set out elsewhere, provides the core of such a value system. It means that the first test of services has to be their capacity to protect and promote the best interest of young people and the second, and subsidiary test, their capacity to impact upon their status as offenders. And this in turn means that services have to be provided by skilled and enthusiastic practitioners, capable of using these skills with judgement and discretion and vitalised by a determination to improve the prospects of the young people for whom such services are provided.

In the following case study the factors discussed above appear in practical application. Readers are invited to consider the information provided and to develop a bail proposal which might be put to the court. In doing so, the proposal formulated should be tested for its consistency both with the general principles outlined here and with the specific details of this case.

Case study: Steven

Steven is due to appear before the local Youth Court charged with three offences of house burglary. He is 16-years-old, and this is the fourth time he will have appeared before the courts. For his first offence, committed when he was 12, Steven received a conditional discharge. On his second and third appearances he received Attendance Centre Orders, both of which have been completed. On the last two occasions you have prepared PSRs.

Steven's family circumstances are challenging. He has a very dominating father, Mr Williams, who has always made it clear that he has 'no time for social workers'. His attitude towards Steven has been both fiercely protective and highly critical at the same time. Steven's mother has been even more coldly hostile towards him. In interview she has had little to say and has come across as saturated with dislike. Both parents have made it clear that Steven, then 15, remained at home on sufferance. Yet, Mr Williams has been active on his behalf, attending interviews, negotiating with school, looking for work experience placements and so on.

Steven himself has been taciturn and uncommunicative, even when interviewed on his own. 'He just laughs at you people' said Mrs Williams, although this was a household where humour of any sort seemed in short supply.

This time Steven is not living at home; four weeks ago he was thrown out following a quarrel, and during the weeks that followed he lived rough in woods nearby. During this time he had no money or reliable source of food. The house burglaries took place in the fourth week of this period. Steven checked that house-owners were away, standard items were removed and there was no damage other than that caused in gaining access. Some items were sold and, in this process, Steven was recognised by the police. Remaining items were found in his tent in the woods.

Yesterday, following his arrest, he was taken by the police and held overnight in the cells. You know that when he appears in court later this morning there is a real prospect that the CPS will oppose bail. You have been asked to attend in order to propose some alternative arrangements.

Remand

In cases which are regarded by the police or the courts as too serious to warrant bail, a decision may be taken to deny a young person liberty pending the resolution of the charges brought against her or him. Once again, in terms of systems management and intervention, the decisive points occur both at the police station and at court itself.

At the police station

Here a custody officer will have the responsibility of deciding upon what action to take where she or he believes that bail may not be granted. The grounds for that decision must be one of four set out in Section 38 (1) (a) of the Police and Criminal Evidence Act (PACE). These are:

1. That the young person's name or address cannot be ascertained, or those given are believed to be false.
2. That a young person has to be detained for their own protection or in her or his own interests
3. The belief that the young person will not answer bail, or might interfere with the administration of justice or the investigation of an offence if not detained.
4. Section 28 of the Criminal Justice and Public Order Act 1994 amends the previous fourth criteria (see Cavadino, 1995) so that the police are now able to refuse bail whenever, in their view, there are reasonable grounds for believing that the person would commit an offence on bail.

As set out in more detail in earlier sections, it is the first duty of youth justice workers to ensure that all possibilities of bail have been thoroughly exhausted. Only when that has been established should intervention move to the second stage which, at the police station, relates to the actions which follow once a custody officer has decided that bail must be denied. It should be a systems management priority to ensure that general criteria, drawn up away from the pressures of individual cases, are agreed with the police which confine the range of situations in which they will request local authority accommodation. Where that point has been reached, other than in two particular circumstances set out below, the law requires that 'the arrested juvenile is moved to local authority accommodation' (section 36 (6) PACE).

At this point a number of important systemic decisions have to be made. Remand to local authority accommodation may include specialist remand foster carers or other non-institutional forms of substitute accommodation, and can include returning the young person to live at home. It may mean a residential establishment or even, in limited circumstances, a secure residential establishment. Clearly, best practice would demand that the restriction upon a young person should be no greater than the minimum necessary to ensure compliance with requirements to attend court and meet other more ordinary obligations. Whatever level of accommodation a young person enters the task of youth justice social workers should then be to de-escalate the remand arrangements in any subsequent hearing before the court. The difference which an active approach can make is set out in a report of the Social Services Inspectorate (1993). Not only did inspectors observe significant variations between different departments inspected, they also found different approaches in basic practice matters such as police detention and appropriate adult duties, 'in different parts of the same department'. The report pointed to the value of an active approach to practice in this area, concluding that 'vigorous intervention at the point of arrest could reduce the need for remand of juveniles'. Where remands did take place, the nature and quality of the subsequent experience could also effectively be influenced. The key lies in an active approach which regards each point in the system and each shift in the process as an opportunity to promote as normalising an outcome as possible for the young person involved.

There are two occasions when a custody officer may deny bail and not transfer to local authority accommodation:

- *When 'it is impracticable' to arrange a move.* These circumstances are narrowly defined. Here the law means what it says – impracticable for example because of a sudden heavy fall of snow – rather than inconvenient or needing some effort to arrange, these last two aspects applying equally to police officers and to social service workers who must make arrangements for a young person to be accepted.
- *When, in the case of any juvenile aged from 12 onwards, the custody officer believes that other accommodation, 'would not be adequate to protect the public from serious harm from him.'* Serious harm, in this context, has been defined within the 1991 Criminal Justice Act in relation to sexual or violent offences as, 'death or serious injury, whether physical or psychological, occasioned by further

offences committed by him' (see NAYJ 1996 for a more extended account of this issue, including references to case law). Where a police officer determines that serious harm could not be avoided by transfer to local authority accommodation, the young person is kept overnight in police cells to appear before the court on the next day. As Paul Cavadino (1995: 74) has suggested, it is both undesirable that children now as young as 12 years old should be held in such accommodation, and almost always unnecessary.

This change opens the back door to a breach of the 'impracticable' rule in which inconvenience can be overcome by invocation of the serious harm clause. There is disturbing evidence for this in the operation of pre-1991 Criminal Justice Act practice where, as Cavadino puts it,

> young people of this age were not infrequently held in police custody in circumstances where local authority accommodation was available; and in many such cases bail or a remand to non-secure local authority accommodation was the most likely course when the child appeared in court. There is a real danger that the new change will mean a return to a similar position.

For youth justice workers attempting to influence such a decision two sources of potential strength can be identified. In the first place PACE Codes of Practice (Code C, Note 16B) make it clear that 'neither a juvenile's behaviour nor the nature of the offence with which he is charged' can provide grounds for refusal to transfer to local authority accommodation. The likelihood of future serious harm has to be established. In the second place the decision has to be made within the context of available local authority provision. Authorities such as those cited by the Inspectorate as having a developed and varied pattern of available resources will therefore be most strongly placed to argue that a suitable place can be made available.

At court

A young person who appears before the court already denied bail will find her or himself in immediate difficulty. Those who have been marked out as not even safe enough for local authority accommodation will be even more disadvantaged. Yet at this point a further chance occurs to change the direction of a case and to promote outcomes which decrease rather than escalate the seriousness of a young person's situation. Decision-making has now shifted away from the police station and to the courtroom. Once a young person has appeared before the court, should the case not be brought to a conclusion, then the basis upon which the case might be adjourned has to be determined. Among the options available – other than bail – will be remand to local authority accommodation or, in cases which meet particular criteria, to either a remand centre or prison.

As ever in a systems management approach, access to information and active use of it will be highly significant in attempts to be influential at this stage. It is all the more disturbing therefore to find NACRO (1991) suggesting that, 'in many instances, young people are remanded into local authority accommodation following a first court appearance because there is very little information available to the court about the young person's circumstances and background'. In contrast, an example of the success which can be achieved by an informed and informative scheme dedicated to intervention at this point in the process has been demonstrated in South Wales by the Newport Community Remand Project. This aims to persuade courts to place teenagers on remand with specially prepared and trained foster carers instead of putting them in adult prisons or local authority secure units. Based on a partnership between the local Probation and Social Services, the Home Office and the Children's Society, the project can provide a wide-ranging programme which goes beyond the provision of accommodation to address other areas of concern within a young person's life. That young person has to agree to any arrangements proposed; the project will then provide a written report at the sentencing appearance outlining the progress made during the remand period (see Childright 1995a for a fuller account of the project's operation).

Where the court is unwilling to consider bail or a remand to any form of local authority accommodation, then for male offenders of at least 15 years of age a remand can currently be made to either a remand centre or a prison. These are intended to be transitional arrangements pending the availability of sufficient local authority-provided secure accommodation. At that point the court will be able to impose a condition that individuals be kept in such secure accommodation, a power which the 1994 Criminal Justice and Public Order Act extended to include those aged as young as 12. In the meantime a further five tests must be satisfied, over and above those of age and gender, before a custodial remand can be made. These are:

1. The Court must first consult a probation officer or social worker.
2. The young person must be given the opportunity to be legally aided.
3. Such a remand must be the only means by which the court can be satisfied that the public can be protected from serious harm.
4. The individual must have been charged or convicted of a violent or sexual offence, or an offence punishable by at least 14 years in the case of an adult.
5. As an alternative to (4) the Court can consider such a remand where an individual has a recent history of absconding while remanded in local authority accommodation and has been charged with or convicted of an offence while so remanded.

Each of 1–3, together with either 4 or 5, has to be satisfied before a remand to custody can be made. While this might appear to amount to a considerable level of restriction, in practice this has not proved to be the case. Stipendiary Magistrate for Sussex, Paul Tain (1995), was able to reassure colleagues that the Divisional Court had already determined that a history of absconsion could be achieved in 'a single absconding'. The problem of serious harm to the public could also be imaginatively addressed: 'This category is not quite as restricted as might be thought. Most courts will interpret the danger from the persistent car thief as one which creates a risk of serious harm to the public at large . . . The court has a high degree of interpretative discretion'.

The results are recorded in research conducted by NACRO (1995) which concluded that, 'despite widespread agreement that prison is not a fit place for young teenagers, there has been a dramatic increase in the number of 15 and 16-year-old boys held in prison awaiting trial'. The survey showed that 1478 juveniles were remanded to prison while awaiting trial, an increase of 86 per cent in the 12-month period up to September 1994, compared with an earlier survey in 1992–3. When the number of juveniles in prison awaiting trial on the last day of each month was compared, an even higher rise of 154 per cent was recorded. Just as the number of juveniles on remand has increased so had the length of time they spend in prison.

In common with so much other research in the criminal justice field, which has emphasised the impact of geography upon justice, the NACRO study uncovered striking variations in the use of custodial remands across the country. While this remains a deeply disturbing pattern, it does emphasise the scope for a systems-directed impact upon the process. Different patterns certainly reflect different sentencing cultures, but they are also influenced by resource variation. A Social Services Inspectorate (1994) commented that, 'At the time of the inspection none of the sample SSDs had in place the necessary range of provision to meet the different ages and needs of young people detained, remanded or subject to residence orders'. Even at times of resource starvation, youth justice workers have a responsibility to work actively towards achieving an equal access to the widest range of facilities. When resources differ widely, outcomes will be similarly diverse.

Children remanded away from home

Children remanded to secure accommodation or prison custody will need prompt and regular contact with youth justice services in their local area. Such contact has a series of important purposes. It should ensure that proper attention is afforded to the emotional and physical needs of any young person. It should aim to repair or reduce the damage caused to important community resources, such as accommodation, employment and family relationships. It should begin the management of a de-escalating process in which the remand arrangements are made less restrictive, through presentation of alternatives at subsequent court hearings, promotion of appeals to a judge in chambers and intervention with other agencies able to expedite reconsideration of remand arrangements. Systems management at this point will be more complex and involve a wider scope for negotiation than at less-intrusive points in the decision-making spectrum. The consequences for individual young people, however, are all the more significant and have to be pursued with all necessary vigour.

Throughout the bail and remand process the need for reliable collection of necessary information has to be an ongoing concern of a systems management approach. Cavadino (1995) suggests that this would best be done by joint monitoring arrangements between police and social services. Quite certainly, if arrangements in which both parties have an interest are to be kept under active review, then change is more likely to be forthcoming when confidence in basic data provides an informed basis upon which discussions can proceed. Within youth justice teams themselves, such information will provide the essential foundation for remand management panels in discharging their responsibilities to promote the principle of least-intrusive intervention at the bail and remand stage, and to monitor and gatekeep the use of the resources available in pursuit of that principle.

A recent report commissioned by Barnardos (Buchan *et al.* 1995) investigated the views of young people in Wiltshire, asking them directly how they might be assisted to stay out of trouble. One of the most striking themes in the responses was the extent to which they saw themselves as characterised by 'waiting': waiting for court, waiting for a school placement, waiting for work. A pervasive sense of chaos and stress percolated their everyday lives and was matched by a fatalism that decisions which had major repercussions upon them would be made by other people. In the experience of these young people, systems and services placed them last rather than first. The suggested children-first approach would aim to challenge this experience by placing a proactive pursuit of best interest as the focus of youth justice activity. The feelings which children in Wiltshire report, however, come powerfully to the fore at the next stage of the process, to which this chapter now turns.

Pre-sentence reports (PSR)

It is not the aim or the purpose of this section to provide a detailed account of the knowledge, skill and value-base which is demanded by the task of preparing pre-sentence reports upon young people, nor to investigate the various and complex issues which are a part of even routine practice in this area. Chapter 7 returns in some detail to the most contemporary of these issues. Here, particular attention is provided to those *systemic* issues which arise at the PSR stage.

The first such issue surrounds the basic legal framework governing PSRs. In recent·years, as Criminal Justice Acts have become an almost annual part of the government's legislative programme, so the requirements which surround the commissioning of reports have altered with bewildering speed. The most recent formulation is that of the 1994 Criminal Justice and Public Order Act which requires a report before passing a custodial or community sentence unless 'the court is of the opinion that it is unnecessary to obtain a pre-sentence report'. Where the offender is under 18, the court cannot decide that it is unnecessary to obtain a report unless the offence is triable only on indictment or the court has considered a previous pre-sentence report on the offender. As Cavadino (1995) suggests:

> the change contained in the Act is a retrograde one. The requirement for courts sentencing those under 18 to consider a previous report is a wholly inadequate safeguard; an old report cannot contain up to date information about the young person's possible rapidly changing life, about the precipitating circumstances of the current offence, or about an appropriate community sentence tailored to the requirement of the present case.

While the legislation was passing through parliament, the Magistrates' Association opposed the removal of the mandatory requirement for pre-sentence reports in relation to offenders under 21. It has subsequently issued (Magistrates Association 1995) an advice note to sentencers which concludes that

> research and experience show that the situation and circumstances of young people can change very dramatically over quite short periods of time. This is true both of juveniles and of young adults. The Magistrates' Association has taken the view that there will be few cases in which it would be wise to dispense with PSRs whether for juveniles or young adults, or to rely on previous reports.

From a systems management perspective, therefore, PSRs need to be set within local agreements which reinforce this advice and back it up, if necessary, with routine arrangements to number copies of reports and to have them all returned to youth justice service staff at the end of proceedings.

Thereafter systems agreements need to cover basic arrangements such as negotiating adequate time for preparation. Pre-sentence reports need to draw on a series of sources of evidence; they require, in a systemic sense, that consultation takes place with a range of other relevant services. Parents as well as young people have to be involved within the preparation process. Without adequate time for preparation it is impossible that these tasks can be properly completed and the opportunity for extending influence upon the operation of other important systems will be lost.

Guidelines must also be in place for report-writers, adequate supervision to assist in preparation, and robust gatekeeping procedures designed to address those issues which in a systems-sense are likely to have an impact upon outcomes. As noted above, it is not the purpose of this chapter to deal with all the practice issues with which PSR writers have to deal, and the following are therefore included strictly as *examples* of the sort of issues which systems-sensitive gatekeeping needs to address:

- The 'offence analysis' section of reports ought to provide a broad understanding of what has taken place within the context of that young person's life. It requires a *systemic* analysis which links the behaviour with which the court must deal to the experiences and dealings with others which have shaped that young person's actions. National Standards (Home Office 1995) suggest that such information must be 'directly relevant' to any offence. While this is true in the case of young people particularly, their experiences at the hands of adults, and their treatment within other systems, should always be considered by report-writers as potentially falling within this category.

- Gatekeeping should ensure that reports provide positive as well as critical comments upon a young person and that these positive elements are accentuated. Courts are imbued with what Allen (1991) has called 'the culture of pessimism'. Magistrates are attuned to bad news about the young people who appear before them. Good news has to be shouted louder, in such contexts, if it is to be heard and given proper consideration. Pre-sentence reports are so important because they represent the only document which the court is likely to see in which such information might be included. Yet, the evidence of performance in this regard is not encouraging. The Probation Inspectorate (1993), reporting on their appraisal of a sample of 574 PSRs in May 1993, found that fully 42 per cent failed to say anything positive about the person on whom the report was being written, or identify a single redeeming feature. This is a perversion of the purpose of reports which gatekeeping ought actively to prevent.

- As well as proposing courses of action within reports, gatekeeping needs to ensure that where necessary the adverse impact of unwanted outcomes is also addressed. In Chapter 7, which deals with risk-assessment, an exploration is provided of the way in which courts apply different standards in their investigation of risk in relation to particular sentences. A strange pair of sliding scales seem to operate here. The less-intrusive a form of intervention which the court is asked to consider, the more the outcomes which such courses of action might produce are sternly interrogated and tested. Where courts decide on more intrusive interventions, less consideration is given to the outcomes.

  In a systems management approach, report-writers have to stand in the way of the all-too-easy manner in which adverse effects of punitive actions can be conveniently overlooked in sentencing calculations. Clearly this will always be the case where custody is under consideration but should also include other options, in other circumstances. An Attendance Centre Order, for example, will not be suitable for young people with particular health problems or where the avoidance of influence by others is of primary significance.

- Finally, this brief series of examples now turns to the role which gatekeeping must play in ensuring that reports are free from discrimination. For youth justice practitioners, this means not only continuing vigilance concerning the central issues of gender, race, class, disability and sexuality; it also means ensuring that the life-stage of young people who are the subjects of reports is not ignored or distorted. It would be a considerable advantage, for example, if the term 'offender' could be struck from the vocabulary of youth justice report-writers, and the word 'child' substituted far more often than is currently the case. The other essential elements of discrimination begin when the basic status of the report subject is neglected, yet in the anti-discriminatory orthodoxies it is most often overlooked. Gatekeeping has the responsibility of tackling this issue. In a systems sense it is part of the attempt to influence attitudes and reactions in a way which turns a process from a preoccupation with hyena-caricatured offenders to children who are in trouble.

The case study which follows provides the background to a PSR in which issues of systems management and final outcome are particularly acute. The intended proposal – a conditional discharge – is already known. Readers are invited to consider the information provided and to think of the arguments which might be deployed in support of such a conclusion, drawing on general strategy principles and the details of the particular case.

Case study: Luke

Luke is eleven years old. He appears before the court with three offences of theft, one of actual bodily harm, one of assault on police, two of criminal damage, and one of take and drive away.

This is the first time Luke will be dealt with by the courts. He has, however, an extensive previous history of involvement with the local authority child and family service. His family, more generally, are well-known to social services and probation services. His father is currently in prison.

Luke's mother and father have a long history of violent separation and reunion in which domestic disputes have been witnessed by their children. Luke is the oldest of four, having two younger brothers and a sister. All have been received into local authority accommodation on several occasions. The last time this happened the children returned home separately and in sequence, in order to allow Luke's mother a chance to cope with them. Luke was the last to be returned home and four weeks later the placement broke down. Luke's mother asked for him to be removed saying that he was beyond control, staying out late at night, not going to school and hitting his younger sister. His younger brothers and sister still remain at home.

In the weeks which followed, Luke moved rapidly through a number of different local authority resources. He failed to settle at emergency foster carers and at a small family group home. Matters stabilised at a third residential unit where he formed an attachment to a female member of staff. His history suggests that such attachments have been an important part of his experience. He is said to have been close to an aunt who died when he was eight; he had a close relationship with a teacher at a special school where he had received most of his primary education; and the same sort of relationship has been important in stabilising him at his current address.

Despite this his behaviour remains volatile with outbursts of uncontrollable anger followed by real contrition. This pattern has been a familiar part of his previous history and has led to the involvement of Child Guidance services. Complex plans for Luke's future have been laid out at meetings involving his social worker, residential care staff, a psychologist from Child Guidance, together with contributions from his special school teacher. His mother has been informed of meetings, kept in touch with progress but has chosen not to attend. Plans involve a further placement in a family setting, with a phased hand-over period.

Offences for which Luke appears were nearly all committed in the weeks immediately after his last arrival in local authority accommodation. The three offences of theft relate to minor items removed from the communal area of a local sports centre, in the company of other youths from his first residential unit. The offence of actual bodily harm involves an assault on a local authority care worker at the same establishment. In temper, Luke had tried to push past the staff member in order to leave a room. Her shoulder injury resulted in three days away from work. The police were called to that incident and Luke is said to have assaulted a police officer while being removed from the Unit. Two charges of criminal damage relate firstly to damage to the interior of the police van, and secondly to the wall of the juvenile cell at the police station to which he was conveyed.

The only further charge is one of take and drive away. This happened two weeks after Luke was placed in his current accommodation. Together with two other, older young men he absconded from the Unit. A car was stolen from a nearby street. It was stopped by police about one mile away when the manner in which it was being driven gave rise to suspicion. Luke was driving the vehicle when it was stopped.

In order to be consistent with your team's policies of minimum intervention and systems-management you intend to propose a conditional discharge.

Supervision and breach

This section on supervision in the community concentrates on the question of breach because this is the point where, in a systems-management approach, many of the most critical issues rise most powerfully to the surface. Issues of effectiveness in supervision in the context of a research-based evaluation of face-to-face practice is to be found in Chapter 6. A sensible response at the point of breach will only be possible if proper practices in relation to supervision itself have been instituted and maintained. To be able to address the former requires that the latter will have been achieved.

The background to the approach to breach suggested here has been developed in greater detail elsewhere (Drakeford 1993). Youth justice practitioners have to reject the entirely fallacious argument that 'credibility' with sentencers depends upon the ability to parade failure before them as quickly and as often as possible. Nowhere is the dominant thinking which infuses National Standards more destructive, nor its prescriptions more vacuous than in relation to breach. An action which in any system-orientated understanding should be regarded as a failure is somehow celebrated as proof of seriousness and punitive power. Instead, an approach is suggested here which regards breach as a last, not a first, resort and which has in place a series of system strategies which strengthen the prospects of success and diminish the dangers of failure. The approach is rooted in the same principles of minimum appropriate intervention which, as argued earlier, remains at the heart of successful systems management within youth justice practice as a whole.

Separation of enforcement and help

Breach action occurs when an individual subject to some form of supervision fails to comply with its requirements. The most basic step to be taken, therefore, needs to be a separation of the enforcement criteria from the provision of help. The fewer enforcement rules an organisation operates, the fewer the chances of failure to comply with them. Rules which if broken will lead to breach should therefore be kept to the absolute minimum requirements of contact. Provision of help, by contrast, should be pitched at the highest level which the individual requires and the service is able to pro-

vide. Once a young person has met the basic enforcement standard, however, breach action should never follow failure to take
help.

Providing active supervision

Within the minimum framework of enforceability, the first responsibility of youth justice workers and organisations should be to
provide an active service which seeks out young people. Youth
justice services should provide points of contact where young
people are likely to use them. A spirit is needed which lies at the
opposite end of the spectrum to the sort of redundant practice
which relies, for example, on instructions by standard letter and
where contact is organised entirely to suit the convenience of the
powerful organisation. This means, also and particularly, that when
difficulties occur in contact the content of supervision should be
reassessed to ensure that it is relevant and worthwhile for the
individual. Services have to recapture the notion that supervision
should be 'rewarding' as well as instructive. Steve Rogowski (1995:
46), for example, looking at the development of intermediate treatment practice in recent years, rightly laments the fact that 'com-
pensatory aspects of dealing with young offending have largely
been eclipsed'. Such elements were, he argues, an attempt 'to
compensate for past negative interest, experiences and relationships'. His conclusion draws out the criminal justice advantages of
such activities:

> there is a clear case for re-emphasising the compensatory aspects of the
> old IT schemes – positive interests, experiences and relationships should
> be offered...Although it may be unfashionable to say so, developing an
> interest in outdoor pursuits may well give the 'buzz' young people obtain
> from joy-riding and burglary for example. (p. 48)

The argument suggested here would endorse this emphasis upon
development of the content of supervision which goes beyond the
narrowing concentration of 'offending behaviour'. Supervision
needs to contain elements which grasp the attention and pursue
the interests of young people. Where contact threatens to break
down, the content of supervision should be tested against such
criteria, and alternative methods considered where these might
lead to greater success. Full advantage should be taken in all this

of the ability to count contact with other relevant organisations as fulfilment of enforcement criteria (see National Standards, 1995, para 4: 26; Home Office 1995). Youth justice services, in short, should be dedicated to assisting young people meet the obligations placed on them, rather than placing additional obstacles in their paths.

Maximising flexibility

Thereafter, services should aim to maximise the amount of flexibility which systems can tolerate. Even the 1995 National Standards (4: 27) include a reference to retention of 'the degree of flexibility demanded by the individual's age, stage of development and degree of responsibility for his or her actions' at this point, and reinforce the requirement that enforcement action should '*take full account* of the welfare of the child or young person' (emphasis added). Explanations concerning missed appointments, for example, should not be judged against the criteria which are able to be applied in smoothly run bureaucracies or in personal lives which are organised upon solid foundations of reliable income, a place to live and enough to eat. The 1992 version of National Standards was sensible enough to acknowledge that avoidance of discrimination 'requires more than a willingness to accept all offenders equally or invest an equal amount of time and effort in different cases. The nature and extent of differences in circumstances and need must be properly and actively addressed by all concerned' (Home Office, 1992, p. 32 para 5). The flight from reason of the Home Office in eliminating this section from the 1995 version should not be a signal for a similar desertion by others. Decisions within an enforcement framework have to be tested against such criteria if the disadvantages faced by young people are not to be compounded by actions which fail to take these firmly into consideration.

Finally, therefore, to the role again of gatekeeping. Panels need to be established which would oversee those cases where breach action had become under active consideration. The primary purpose of such a panel would be to ensure that every avenue towards successful conduct of supervision had been thoroughly investigated and strenuously attempted before action could go ahead. In a children-first-led approach it would be axiomatic that no child should be blamed or breached for the failure of others to do their job properly, or provide services which ought to have been provided. Panels should enforce this test rigorously in assessing the nature and conduct of supervision plans which are said to have broken down. Panels would also have the function of ensuring consistency of decision-making across individuals and teams. They would have the responsibility of ensuring that the voices of young people and their parents were actively included within the decision-making process.

The separation of enforcement requirements – which should be minimised – and the provision of help – which should be maximised – is a prescription not just for breach, but for supervision itself. The arrangements of services so as to place the needs of users first, and those of powerful organisations lower down the order, together with the active pursuit of courses of action which meet those needs, are at the heart of defensible and successful practice. Such principles have to be embedded in a systematic way within the services youth justice workers provide.

The case study below illustrates some of the issues which face youth justice workers in the enforcement of supervision orders where compliance might be difficult to achieve. Readers are invited to consider the information provided and to identify those issues which would require a judgement to be made about compliance.

Case study: Julie

Julie has been the subject of a supervision order for two months. She is 17 years old and lives with her partner and their ten-month-old daughter in a caravan outside the town where your team is based. During the time she has been on supervision she has missed six appointments, and has given a number of reasons for these failures. Firstly she lives just inside the three miles distance from the office and therefore doesn't qualify for fare reimbursement when she does come in to see you; secondly her baby has been constantly ill because of dampness in the caravan and has needed the care and attention of both parents; thirdly, the conditions in which they live have aggravated the stress in an already-stormy relationship. Three of the missed appointments have been preceded by serious rows between Julie and her partner.

Custody

All actions taken up to this point have an important bearing on whether or not a young person ends in custody. This final section looks directly at what happens when young people find themselves sentenced to custody. A later section deals with the most recent departures in government policy in relation to custodial sentencing, while here the concentration is upon the general systems management principles which youth justice services and workers should seek to apply at this point within the process. The changing pattern of sentencing of young people was discussed earlier in Chapter 2, illustrating the ways in which the 1990s have witnessed what the Howard League (1997) in its report of the *Troubleshooter* project describes as a 'sea change in policy', producing a rapid rise in juveniles remanded and sentenced into prison. The *Troubleshooter* initiative was conceived at a time when the practice gains of the 1980s and the reforms of the 1991 Criminal Justice Act had resulted in only 25 young people of 15 years of age remaining in prisons in Wales and England. Based at HMYOI Feltham, the project aimed to rescue 15-year-olds from prison custody by providing support and advocacy directly to them and by working cooperatively with other agencies to that end. By the time of the launch of the project, however, the favourable climate in which it had been planned was already in reverse. On 30 June 1991, some 102 15-year-olds were held in prison custody. On the same date in 1993 this had risen to 126 and by 1994 to 167. The number of 15-year-olds held in English and Welsh prisons stood at 224 at the end of May 1996 (Howard League 1997: 5).

Destructive rhetoric and punitive legislation have combined to produce this increasing risk to young people and sharpened the atmosphere in which youth justice practice takes place (O'Mahony and Haines 1993). An approach which has been endorsed by the whole organisation and which aims to change systems rather than individuals is therefore particularly important at this point. This is all the more significant in the case of those young people who also face the additional impact of discrimination, for example because of gender and racial stereotyping. Once again, what follows does not aim to provide a comprehensive practice manual for through- and after-care practice. Rather it is to identify some crucial points in the process to which a systems management approach ought to respond. Consideration is divided into three main sections.

At the point of sentence

Systemic intervention here, then, begins at the pre-sentence report stage. Reports should never propose custody. This is not to say that the possibility of custody should not be *recognised* in reports where this is a clear danger, but reports which do not deal with the consequences of a custodial sentence are likely to add to the risk of this occuring. It will also be important to include direct evidence of discriminatory practice at this point in the system. It is known that young black people are significantly over-represented in the custodial population, and reports written upon them need to draw this fact to the attention of the court because, despite the state of knowledge, actual practice continues to be disfigured by the results of discrimination. The *Troubleshooter* project at HMYOI Feltham, discussed below, for example, found that

> one of the most obvious causes for concern running through the figures is the hugely disproportionate number of Black and Asian young people in custody. This bias is seen most clearly in relation to the Caribbean group and is worse in relation to those of remand status. 68 per cent of the total number of Caribbean clients were referred as remands compared to 45.5% of the European group. (Howard League 1997: 35)

Putting this in perspective, the report notes that while Caribbean 15-year-olds account for 2 per cent of their age group in the primary catchment area of the institution, they make up over 24 per cent of their peer group in Feltham itself.

Punishment and welfare needs

A further systems-related issue which still requires attention at this point in the process lies in the continuing risk of young people with high welfare needs being treated more punitively within the criminal justice system. While the old days of making care orders in criminal proceedings have gone, the mind-set which produced such decisions lives on. Evidence from the Northern Ireland Training Schools (Collins and Kelly 1995: 32) suggests that 'young people with a care background , i.e. care offenders, appear to have an accelerated passage through the justice sentencing process when compared to young people who do not have such a background, i.e. community offenders'. When the characteristics of the two groups were compared, however, analysis indicated that care offenders were less 'delinquent' than community offenders.

The researchers suggest not only that magistrates' decision-making is 'influenced by a young person's care status when deciding on how they should be dealt with for offending' (p. 37), but that this thinking also extended to report-writers. Indeed, not only might writers be influenced in this way but also, the authors conclude 'there remains the danger that in the continuing twin track care and justice system the care system under pressure will prematurely off load its more troublesome young people into "justice" establishments'. These possibilities are not confined to Northern Ireland. The *Troubleshooter* project at an English YOI found that 145 its 15-year-old clients, or 31 per cent of the total, had been the subject of a care order or had been accommodated by social services at some time (Howard League 1997: 3).

Systems need to ensure that such dangers are guarded against whenever reports are being prepared in such circumstances.

Future use of reports

Report-writers must also be aware that once a custodial sentence has been imposed, that report will accompany the young person on her or his career in custody. Information provided for use in one context – that is the courts – may well be unintentionally distorted if applied in another, for example, custodial institution. Writers should be alert to such dangers in their construction of reports. Gatekeeping panels, for example, should have this as one of their areas of consideration in cases where custody is clearly a possibility. Risk of self-harm and other relevant additional information should be made available to institutions independently of the PSR following a post-sentence interview.

Finally, whenever a custodial sentence is imposed services ought to have a process which leads to active consideration of an appeal. Appeal strategies were amongst the successful systems management techniques of the 1980s and need to be reconfirmed and readapted to current circumstances. Arrangements for bail during the remand period leading to appeal should have been considered in advance when danger of custody appears real. These can then be put immediately to the sentencing court or to a Judge in Chambers. Reconsideration of programmes proposed to the original court should form part of any lead-up to appeal hearings.

Appeals

Appeal strategies are, by their nature, adversarial and place individual staff members in situations of conflict with courts. For this reason it is especially important that they are conducted on a policy basis which has the support of the organisation as a whole, and that the organisation takes the responsibility for ensuring that all staff are acting in accordance with its intended response at this point in the process.

It may be that a number of the system-specific points outlined above appear relatively straightforward and part of mainstream practice. However, the Howard League *Troubleshooter* initiative, noted above, found that problems in most basic areas had resulted in young people unnecessarily being placed in custody. In 'many' cases, the report notes, the work of the project was confined to 'contacting the Youth Justice team and notifying them that a young person from their area was in custody' (p. 7). The need to advise youth justice services of such a fundamental fact arose, in the analysis of the report, from the finding that young people were increasingly being remanded or sentenced by adult courts:

> The Crown Courts' increasing involvement as a sentencing forum for 15-year-olds was marked over the currency of the project. The adult magistrates court accounts for a disturbingly large number of remands at over 20% of the total. Many clients were remanded by adult Saturday morning courts lacking a specialist knowledge of the law relating to juveniles or the services available to them in terms of bail support. (p. 32).

On a significant number of cases, in such circumstances, the youth justice team had neither been represented in court nor informed of the result. Attention to basic system-sensitive points in the court process, therefore, continues to be regularly and rigorously required.

When custody is being served

Once young people were received in custody, *Troubleshooter* found a similarly disturbing failure to observe basic rules and good practice principles. The report cites instances of illegal remands to prison custody, for example through failure to abide by statutory criteria or mis-application of bail procedures. There were also examples of illegal sentences to prison custody involving young people sentenced at the age of 15 for offences in respect of which guilty pleas had been entered, or findings of guilt established, when they were 14. Accurate knowledge and speedy intervention by youth justice services are requirements where appeals have to be launched or time owed on remand has to be claimed back in calculating length of time to be spent in custody.

In order to move closer towards such a service, systemic action by youth justice services following sentence should include the following elements:

• Systems should exist to allow as full a level of contact as possible with sentenced young people. Letter and telephone contact should be used where face-to-face visiting is impracticable.

• Systems should ensure that contact with families of young people forms an ongoing part of practice during a custodial sentence. The provision of basic support and information services for families is amongst the most fragmented part of the criminal justice process. Youth justice workers are by far the best placed individuals to ensure that accurate knowledge and understanding are communicated at a time when this will be most important, and that families are helped to deal with the powerful feelings and emotions which such a sentence is very likely to engender.

• Information provided to institutions should be followed up to ascertain the steps which are being taken to ensure the safety and well-being of individual young people. The involvement of child protection staff in cases where such concerns arise should be a standard part of a Social Services Department response to custodial sentencing. Such a procedure is likely to be controversial and, in getting such a system established, to involve considerable conflict and bad feeling. From a children-first perspective, however, the justification would be clear. Youth justice services in their duties towards young people in custody should ensure that the interests of such individuals are protected as fully as in any other context.

Where instances of abuse arise, the role of youth justice workers is to challenge, not to sanitise, and the vehicle for challenge should be the civil rights which the 1989 Children Act provides to all young people. The next chapter will deal with the agenda which faces youth justice services in extending a systems approach to work with other major organisations. Here, the first boundary which has to be negotiated is an internal one – that of persuading other arms of the same Social Services Department to respond as fully to a referral arising from abuse in custody as in any other context. From a children-first perspective this represents a real challenge to services to live up to those standards to which they are already publicly committed.

On release

Release from a youth custody institution is by no means confined to those who have served a custodial sentence. Rather, as the *Troubleshooter* project has demonstrated, efforts to obtain follow-up information about the 15-year-olds who had been remanded in custody prior to sentence, found that 115 or 42 per cent received a sentence of imprisonment at the conclusion of their court proceedings, while the remaining 156 young people (58 per cent) were either acquitted, discharged or were given a community sentence (Howard League 1997: 36). Many of this majority of young people, emerging without the courts feeling obliged to impose a custodial sentence, will need services from youth justice workers in order to reassemble their lives and to fulfil any non-custodial penalty which has to be completed.

The possibility of fruitful work on release will depend very largely upon the extent to which the foundations for that work have been laid by contact at earlier parts of the process (Haines 1996). Once again, the *Troubleshooter* experience suggested that social services organisations are not always well-placed to lay down such foundations. Instances are cited of failure to take responsibility, for example in border disputes when young people are known to more than one social services area, or breakdowns in communication between for example the child and family and youth justice dimensions of the same local authority. More disturbingly still, the report suggests that in the harsh climate of the 1990s 'hard pressed social services departments reduced the priority of, and resources for the demonised group of "young offenders"' (Howard League 1997: 35).

There are sufficient problems inherent in post-release work without adding unnecessarily to them in this way. The period of post-release supervision is likely to be short, and the idea that this period is an integral part of the original sentence is unlikely to be welcomed. The skills of youth justice workers are sharply tested in such circumstances. From a systems management approach the most important point to ensure is that the consequences of difficulty in responding to this challenge do not fall unfairly upon young people. The 'taking the fight to them' approach suggested in relation to supervision and breach is all the more necessary in the post-release context where young people will need to be actively persuaded that it is worth their while investing some time and energy in contact. Systems are needed which allow workers sufficient time and resources to provide services which are relevant and rewarding for young people who are likely to be both disaffected and difficult to reach. Prior investment in building contact with individuals and their families needs to be met now by a system response which recognises the vulnerability of young people at this stage in the process, and which regards work with them as an investment in the management of any further contact which they may have with the criminal justice process.

This chapter has looked at the ways in which the systems management approach outlined in Chapter 2 can be infused with the philosophical approach outlined in Chapter 3, and the resulting approach applied to the most significant systemic points which face contemporary youth justice services. In all of these aspects, fruitful practice involves engagement with other agencies – police, courts, prisons and so on – in an attempt to influence outcomes. The chapter which now follows considers ways in which the same approach can be developed in relation to other significant services which lie outside criminal justice itself, but where the results of their dealings with young people are replete with criminal justice consequences.

5

Managing Other Significant Systems

The preceding chapters of this book have attempted to describe and analyse the real achievements, as well as deficits, which emerge from the coherent youth justice approach accomplished during the 1980s. Against this background, worthwhile practice at the end of the 1990s has to adapt that model to the changing needs and circumstances of young people. This chapter looks at an area for practice development which, in the argument of this book, should have found a stronger place in the conduct of social work within youth justice throughout this period, and the absence of which has contributed significantly to the problems faced currently both by young people in trouble and by workers seeking constructively to address their difficulties. In principle our starting point is close to that of Carlen (1996: 48) who argues that, 'in the rush to renounce rehabilitation, few supporters of the justice model seemed to realise that the 1970s attack on welfare in juvenile (criminal) justice was the thin end of the wedge as far as welfare in general was concerned'. In practice this chapter begins from the position outlined by the lead organisations in youth justice who, in their 1995 discussion paper (AMA 1995: 4), suggested that

> local authority policies also bear upon young offenders; a rise in school exclusions, a reduction in youth work or a reduction of other services for children in need can be expected to increase the crime rate...All legislation, not merely criminal justice legislation needs to be sufficiently scrutinised at a governmental level for its effect upon the lives of young people and their future behaviour.

The arguments which follow are also based upon a clear appreciation of the ways in which young people come to the attention of social welfare agencies in a relatively arbitrary fashion but with relatively specific consequences. The needs of young people who emerge for attention in the criminal justice system are, research suggests, broadly the same as those of their peers receiving attention within education, medical and social services systems (Malek 1991; NHS Health Advisory Service 1995). As Coppock (1996: 56) suggests, however, once identified in a particular area,

> Each system assigns its own diagnostic label or definition derived from the historical vagaries and precedents of its particular professional knowledge base. Consequently a child or young person could be given the label of 'emotionally and behaviourally disturbed' (education – 'special needs'); 'beyond parental control' (social services); 'conduct disorder' (health – psychiatry) or 'young offender' (criminal justice). Such research not only demonstrates the arbitrariness of the processes by which 'disturbed' and 'disturbing' behaviour in children and young people is defined by parents and professionals but also reveals how the diagnostic label applied is contingent upon the first point of contact, identification and referral. Thus, the defining process is as much a cause of concern as the definitions themselves.

Youth justice and other welfare systems: four problems

It should be clear from this brief introduction that a youth justice strategy which aims to produce an impact upon offending cannot profitably confine itself to offending alone; intervention in other systems will be essential if the rights of young people are to be protected and their future prospects enhanced. Yet, one of the explicit purposes of the justice model lay in the willing sacrifice of over-intrusive welfare-motivated infringement in the lives of young people appearing before the courts in exchange for a more proportionate approach to sentencing. Amongst the criticisms which might be made of this strategy, four are particularly important for our purposes here:

1. In its least useful guises the justice approach exhibits

    a convenient adherence to the idea that individual moral responsibility exists within a vacuum somehow detached from the circumstances in

which people might find themselves and an equally co
that this equality of moral responsibility disappears on
has been committed. (Drakeford and Vanstone, 1996a)

Clearly, in the case of young people, the idea of m
criminal responsibility has to be modified to take acc   t of
their age and understanding. Yet the emphasis upon personal
responsibility upon which justice models rely has had the effect
of diminishing the significance attached to these distinctions, as
Chapter 1 suggested. Within the particular context of the present chapter these two characteristics combine to produce a
further serious fault in legitimising the view that the social
circumstances of young people in trouble lie beyond the
scope of state-sponsored intervention. If young people who
commit offences are largely responsible for their own plight –
as the poor are for their own poverty or the homeless for their
lack of shelter – then, as Jeffs and Smith (1996) have argued,
the upshot is swiftly 'a theory which simultaneously blames the
victim and bolsters an unwarranted collective smugness
amongst the prosperous'. It certainly means that punishment
and coercion rather than help and assistance have become
their just deserts.

2. The model never quite worked as some of its supporters had
anticipated. In particular, the systems approach continuously
oversimplified the motivations of other powerful groups of
actors within and alongside its boundaries.

In the case of the criminal justice system, in particular, Raynor (1996) has persuasively argued the importance of attitude
change, independent of legislative or organisational amendments, in altering outcomes. In the context of youth justice
and in the argument of this book, policy-makers and practitioners have undervalued the extent to which the powers of
persuasion, as well as determined advocacy, have needed to be
employed with sentencers in pursuit of systemic aims. This
deficit proved particularly problematic in dealing with lightly-
convicted but socially-troubled young people where sentencers
remained stubbornly attracted to the utility of putting right the
problems which had been identified in their lives.

In practice this led to a twin-horned dilemma. On the
one hand youth court workers might attempt to eliminate, or

minimise, the inclusion of such material in their reports on the grounds that it was not relevant to offending. Such an approach proved fraught with difficulty. It was often problematic in its own terms because information about difficulties in circumstances of health, housing or family life often was directly relevant to offending, and because such information might in any case come to the attention of the court from other less manageable sources such as school reports, defence solicitors or parents and young people themselves. On the other hand, when such material was included in reports it was likely to invoke a something-must-be-done response from magistrates, and that something was highly likely to include consideration of a statutory Supervision Order.

Indeed, the purist refusal to contemplate services which might contain the taint of welfare paradoxically increased the risk of unnecessarily intrusive criminal sanctions at the least necessary end of the conviction spectrum. The more a youth justice service made it clear that it no longer provided welfare assistance, the less inclined were magistrates to be persuaded that informal or voluntary help with identified difficulties would accompany measures such as conditional discharges. Instead, a formal Supervision Order would at least guarantee that intervention of some sort would follow.

3. In linking precipitating causes with offending, magistrates may have been closer to a working appreciation of the link between social difficulties and the risk of criminal prosecution than the justice model itself.

    Like them, and like Hudson (1993), crime is not viewed here as simply 'the outcome of individual's reasoned decision-making' devoid of a structural context. Neglect of the conditions in which crime is created and the devaluation of the social context in which young people live their lives has been the hallmark of more than 15 years of Conservative administration. It is an indication of the extent to which youth justice practice has been stripped of content that the case has to be reasserted for workers seeking to support trouble-free behaviour amongst young people to, of necessity, direct their attention to those social systems which support such possibilities.

4. The model led to the neglect of some of the most vulnerable young people, who found that at a time when welfare services

generally were being withdrawn from them here was another potential source of assistance which had turned sour.

The 'not-my-problem' school of youth justice practice was, of course, not one which justice-enthusiasts set out to establish or would condone. Yet in too many instances this is the message which young people and their families on the receiving end of youth justice social work most powerfully experienced. Social work with young people caught up in the criminal justice system is a demanding and wearing occupation in which persistence, resilience and optimism remain core characteristics for any worker determined to remain useful to those for whom a service is being provided. Equally, there is little doubt that for some less resilient and committed workers, the legitimised concentration upon 'offending behaviour' provided a convenient escape route from some of the fatigue of dealing with real people, in the complexities of their real lives. In its place, and its most exaggerated form, it has enshrined a macho insistence on tackling, confronting and acting upon deviancy in place of proper concern with the human needs, rights and potentials of the children and young people entrusted to its care. In doing so, as argued elsewhere, the reduction of social work in the criminal justice system to

> a series of formulaic confrontations also prepares the ground for those political forces anxious to de-professionalise the public services and replace thoughtful and critical practice with a new, poorly paid, lightly skilled and automatically obedient workforce. (Drakeford and Vanstone 1996a).

Work with adult probation clients has demonstrated that the qualities most valued in their contact with workers include respect and trust, the capacity to be listened to without being condemned, and the provision of relevant help (Bailey and Ward 1993; Pritchard *et al.* 1992). Such qualities apply all the more powerfully in contact with individuals who through age and structural location are inherently less powerful than those with whom they are in contact. Young people are constantly in such situations across a range of major institutions with which they are in contact. Youth justice workers have a particular responsibility, therefore, to assist those whose fates within court processes and systems are contingent upon the ways in which they prosper, or fail to thrive, within other major institutions.

Shaping a systems approach for today

This chapter aims to suggest ways in which the many advantages of a systems approach can be adapted to promote such possibilities. In essence this means recapturing some of the ground which the justice movement voluntarily and deliberately vacated, but with the intention of avoiding previously discredited ways of acting upon it. For many practitioners whose training and practice has all taken place within the past ten years, of course, this may involve less a 'recapture' than some learning of entirely new territory. The point which requires emphasis here is that while the *application* of a systems approach may need to alter, the *aims* of intervention remain the same while the chance of achieving fruitful *outcomes* will be enhanced.

The first chapter of this book provided an account of young people's lives in contemporary Britain which suggested that the transitions from childhood to adulthood had become more extended and more often fractured than those generally experienced by their parents. The major props which support a trouble-free lifestyle have all become less reliable, and for many of the most vulnerable young people have turned from anchors around which a productive and rewarding future might be fashioned into depth-charges pulling them below the surface of survival and threatening an explosion of chaos in already-troubled waters. The major purpose of this chapter is to suggest that youth justice social workers have a duty to intervene in such circumstances, to do what is possible to turn the remaining assets of social welfare services to the benefit of young people in trouble, and to do so in a systemic fashion. Of course an emphasis upon the 'less comfortable and accessible task of addressing structural issues with clients' (Cochrane 1989) is not easily translatable into practice. Yet, it can and must be done.

The case study which follows illustrates many of the issues with which this chapter is concerned. It is placed here to allow the reader to consider the information it contains in relation to the sections which follow. The reader is invited to think of ways in which intervention in the wider systems which surround Robert might have an impact upon the report which must be prepared, the outcome which might be secured at his court appearance, and his future prospects more generally.

Case study: Robert

Robert S. is aged 15. He lives with his parents in a privately-rented flat in a run-down area near the centre of a large city. He has appeared in court for the third time since his fourteenth birthday, when on each occasion he has been charged with theft from cars. This is the first occasion on which reports have been requested. The adjourned hearing will take place in three-weeks time.

On visiting the flat you find it to be in a very poor state of repair. A roof leaks and there are bare electricity wires at head height in the hallway ceiling. Robert's mother suffers from angina and has extended periods in which her mobility is severely reduced. His father tells you that he has suffered from mental health problems and has recently been discharged from a period of in-patient treatment at the local mental hospital. During this period Robert went to stay with his grandmother who lives on a council estate about five miles away, on the edge of the city. Since discharge, Mr S. has had difficulty in re-establishing his benefit entitlement and the family have had no Giro this week. Mr S.'s manner makes interviewing difficult. He is a large man who moves unpredictably around the small living room in which you have been shown to speak to Robert.

Robert is not attending school. He was, he says, 'expelled' from his last school for 'barking all the time in class'. This took place nearly three months ago and he has not been to school since. His mother says that she has asked for him to be transferred to another school, but Robert says he won't go and there has, in any case, been no reply from the education authority.

In the conditions of the interview you make little progress in discussing the offences with him, other than establishing that each incident had taken place in the immediate locality where workers and other visitors to the city centre routinely parked their cars for the day.

You decide to interview him again, away from his home, in a few days time. In the meantime you will make inquiries about the wider family circumstances which have come to light in this visit.

Basic principles

The remainder of this chapter turns to the particular strands of social welfare explored in the opening pages of this book. Running through these individual considerations, however, are a series of linking principles which, in the argument of this book, ought to support and permeate a remodelled systems approach to youth justice social work. These include:

- A resource strategy which recognises the beneficial impact which single changes in systems can bring about in the lives of multiple individuals. A policy decision to align the 'in-need' provisions of the 1989 Children Act and the 'vulnerable' definitions of the 1985 Housing Act, for example, would do more for the general well-being of young people with accommodation problems in a local authority area than the continual struggle to solve the individual crises of youth justice clients.
- A sensitivity to the particular importance of timing systems-intervention when working with young people. Youth justice has been very successful in concentrating investment at key points of a young person's appearances before the court and basing that concentration upon a systems analysis. Thus, for example, heavy involvement in preparing, obtaining and delivering a package of services for a young person at risk of a custodial sentence will still be resource-positive when compared to the efforts which would have to be made in repairing the damage done by that sentence to the social and personal circumstances of the individual.
- An emphasis upon the importance of bringing about attitude change towards young people as a technique in systems management. Attitudes towards young people by providers are often the first and most powerful stumbling block in obtaining access to the services which they control. In the case of young people in trouble, in particular, these negative associations extend to areas of provision to which young people have a general right of access, such as education, as well as those for which particular needs have to be established. Youth justice workers have a unique opportunity to combat the demonisation of the human beings with whom work is undertaken. As an occupation, social work is founded upon the premise that attitudes and actions are open to influence and to change. A systems approach which matches contemporary circumstances must retain a commitment to placing greater emphasis upon attempting to change the attitudes of powerful players, and all the more so

within a context which appears so often to turn its fire upon the powerless.

- A greater prioritising of interagency work that is genuinely cooperative and where values are shared, and being prepared to be assertive when these are not. Youth justice services have a more creditable record than their adult probation counterparts in developing partnerships with others in order to create services for young people. A systems approach which is in tune with the times, however, may need to pay more attention to this way of proceeding.

- An understanding of the importance of local factors. Systems approaches within youth justice have been developed within a national system of laws and administration. When large-scale initiatives are made difficult by government then local initiatives become all the more important; and as part of local government, youth justice services are well-placed to attune themselves to the more fruitful soil of local cultures and ways of doing things.

- Finally, an emphasis upon the need to 'normalise' services for young people, both generally and, in the case of those with whom youth justice workers are in contact, specifically. This is not an argument for intervention in other systems which is rooted in making young people in trouble into some separate group, needing always to be provided with different or separate services. Indeed, those responses to youth crime which pathologise those involved within it and claim to provide technical solutions to their difficulties need to be treated with suspicion. The history of child welfare services is disgraced by its vulnerability to regimes which sacrifice decency and humanity in the pursuit of claimed cures. Baldwin and Barker (1995: 43), for example, in their consideration of the Pindown enquiry, noted the ways in which 'many questionable treatment programmes have remained widespread both in the USA and Australia. In particular, unevaluated "dynamic" techniques of confrontation, isolation, shaming and humiliation have continued to characterise many treatments'. As Coppock (1996: 58) suggests, 'it has long been acknowledged within critical psychology and psychiatry that it is easy to dress-up control and call it "therapy"'.

Youth justice practice has a similar and continuing vulnerability to developments in which 'treatment' disguises the sacrifice of rights and respect on the grounds that this will be in the

long-term best interests of its peculiar subjects. The corollary of
this argument is that provision for young people generally has
to be improved, and that the task of youth justice workers is to
help its clients to obtain their share in the rights which are
available to all. Of course this is a long-term goal. In the short-
term it may be that specialist projects provide at least some help
to particular groups or individuals. It cannot be a sustainable
solution, however, to turn every young person in need of a basic
income, a worthwhile job or a reasonable place to live into some
sort of 'special case'. Normalisation of such provision for young
people generally, and for those in trouble specifically, has to be
the touchstone against which actions ought to be tested. The
principle of normalisation is one to which this book returns in
more detail in Chapter 6.

In parallel with the services considered in Chapter 1, the account
which now follows concentrates primarily upon those major systems – family, income maintenance, education, training and
employment, housing and health – which form the essential context within which young people live their lives. The role which is
played by the family, friends and neighbourhood networks in the
successful upbringing of young people has been only perversely
recognised in official policies of central government and, in some
areas at least, has all but disappeared from actual practice of social
work agencies. The treatment of parents within contemporary
criminal justice will stand here as an example of broader ways in
which work with informal support systems needs to be redirected
and reinvigorated if youth justice workers are to be able to help
young people obtain the maximum benefit from such sources.

Parental responsibility

For as long as records exist, politicians have identified the parents
of young people in trouble as a source of their children's antisocial
behaviour. The power to place real sanctions upon them, however,
if of far more recent origin. In modern times the 1982 Criminal
Justice Act introduced measures which were said, in the preceding
White Paper *Young Offenders*, to be useful to 'reinforce parental
authority' in the control of adolescent family members (Home

Office 1980). The proposals were widely attacked by both sentencers and workers and, in practice, the powers were almost never
used.

These difficulties did not prevent further legislative efforts less
than a decade later. The Criminal Justice Act of 1991 contained
three distinct powers which operated to identify parents more
closely with the criminal activity of their children. The powers
requiring parents to attend court with their children, and making
parents responsible for payment of fines, were strengthening of
measures which already existed under previous statutes. The third
and most important change was the introduction, in Section 58, of
a completely new duty upon magistrates to bind over the parents of
a child under 16 so as to 'take proper care and exercise proper
control over the child' (s58(2)(b)).

The rationale for this approach to parental responsibility was set
out clearly by the then Minister of State at the Home Office, John
Patten, who declared the parents of young offenders to be individuals, 'who could cope, but simply choose not to... these are
families which have failed not through misfortune or misjudge-
ment, but through wilful neglect by parents of their responsibilities'
(Hansard vol. 149, col. 767). More generally, from the perspective
of right wing governments, an interventionist state tramples on
parental responsibilities in ways which are politically unacceptable.
The socially hollowed and economically diminished state sought for
during the Thatcher years, had as its corollary the replacement of
spheres of public and State activity by private and family activity.

Recent evidence concerning the practical use of 1991 Act powers
suggests that their use has become sporadic and, to a large extent,
tempered by the absence of any practical steps which courts can
take to enforce Binding Over Orders which might be imposed
(though, see Drakeford 1996 for an alternative perspective). In
many ways, though, the level of application is less significant than
the attitude of mind which is betrayed in the introduction of such
powers and in the understanding of them outlined above. The
punitive ethos towards parents contained within the Act produces
a powerful impact which, in practice, undermines rather than
reinforces the ability of parents to offer necessary help to their
children, and the easy targets which struggling families provide
has resulted in rapid further extensions of the 1991 Act approach.
Increasingly coercive powers to intervene in the lives of parents of

young offenders have, for example, been introduced in the 1994 Criminal Justice and Public Order Act. The new powers pose a major danger of casting the net of the criminal justice system over a new and wider group, drawing whole families, parents and children within its jaws. Nor are such developments at and end.

The Labour government elected in May 1997 had, while in opposition, regularly endorsed the need to place greater obligations upon parents of young people in trouble. Commenting on a leaked copy of the highly critical Audit Commission Report (1996) concerning the operation of the youth justice system, Labour's home affairs spokesman, Alun Michael, was quick to endorse the possibility: 'Given that the burden of crime has increased so massively over recent years, it is right that a share of that should come from those who contribute to it' (*Guardian* 19 August 1996). In November 1996 the shadow Home Secretary, Jack Straw, published a Labour Party document called simply *Parenting* which quoted research to demonstrate a claimed link between 'the character of parental supervision' and later delinquency. Amongst a list of policy proposals, the document included curfews for under-10-year-olds and 'parental responsibility orders' for the courts.

In government, these themes have continued. The incoming administration of 1 May 1997 faced a set of public services which had been progressively squeezed or eliminated altogether. Unable or unwilling to reconstruct these 'middle-range' services – youth provision, out-of-school activity and so on – Ministers inevitably found themselves in the position of making use of 'emergency services' such as those for dealing with serious or persistent delinquents at the earliest stage of intervention. Thus the parental control order proposed in a Green Paper produced in the dying days of the previous government was confirmed in a restatement of the 'parental responsibility order' of its successor.

Parenting and systems management

From a systems management perspective, youth justice workers have a clear investment in finding ways of persuading the Courts not to use these new powers. What will be needed are alternative means of addressing the problems which parents of adolescent offenders face which will be useful to them, capable of being carried out in a manner consistent with social work values, delivered in a spirit of partnership, and still capable of being used within the criminal justice system as a way of influencing sentencers. All this suggests a reinforcement of productive parenting which would be far from the sense of embitterment and erosion which appear to have been the result of recent policies.

A starting point for such a development will have to be a reinvestment in areas of work which in some youth justice teams have ceased to find a place in everyday practice. Where a justice approach has been narrowly interpreted as meaning only work with a young person about their offending, then even the immediate social circumstances of that individual have taken on a diminished significance. Withdrawal from family work has sometimes been the result. The model suggested in this chapter is very different. An example of the sort of informal systems intervention which might be put in its place is to be found in a proposal for a social action groupwork programme for parents of young people in trouble (see Drakeford 1994). Without repeating the detail of that suggestion, the proposal envisaged a voluntary group-work programme in which parents of young people who appear before the courts could meet to discuss issues of common concern, receive help in obtaining information and in working on strategies for dealing with difficulties. From a systems management perspective, such a group would provide the courts with a means of addressing deficiencies or difficulties in parenting without the attachment of a criminal justice sanction. For parents themselves, a social action group could provide a forum in which experiences could be shared and through which a collective power might be mobilised to overcome problems and resist the pressures of negative labelling and scapegoating.

The attractiveness of parental responsibility to vote-hungry politicians means that the developments traced above are likely to produce a continuing impact upon youth justice workers. In line with the case set out in the preceding chapters for systems management techniques to promote the possibility of doing good in the lives of those who use youth justice services, this chapter argues for the same principles to be applied to work with systems outside the justice system itself. A reinvestment in family work and in working with parents where this will assist them to promote their childrens' interests are examples of intervention within informal systems designed to achieve such ends. The same approach can be extended to work with other informal networks of friends and neighbourhood support systems, helping to draw together and reinforce those sources of assistance which young people in trouble so badly need.

This ecological approach to work with other systems extends to intervention in the more formal forums to which this chapter now turns. The complexity of modern societies means that for us all, reliance on a range of services is a requirement of daily life. Individuals who find themselves on the margins of managing have an additional and acute series of interests in ensuring that these support services operate effectively to their own advantage. Yet, in practice, such an outcome is often very difficult to achieve. In the basic areas of money, education, work and health which now follow, this chapter argues for the part which youth justice social workers should play in achieving best outcomes for their users in these arenas.

Income

The growth in poverty, its unequal impact upon particular groups, and its deliberate employment as a tool of social policy where young people are concerned were all important themes of Chapter 1. It is no part of the argument set out here that primary poverty can be conquered by social workers but, while the stark facts of poverty dominate the lives of so many young people, it has to form a central part of any repertoire for placing their lives on a footing which does not include offending. Quite certainly, despite evidence that social workers find the pervasive nature of poverty amongst the most daunting aspects of their working lives (see, for example, North *et al.* 1992: Northumbria Probation Service, 1994), when service users themselves are asked it is assistance in just such basic areas which is most valued and appreciated (see, for example, Stockley, Canter and Bishop 1993).

Severe hardship payments

At this point, just one aspect of income maintenance for young people will have to stand for all the wider knowledge now possessed concerning this aspect of the social circumstances of young people. Many of the individuals with whom youth justice workers come into contact have difficulties in finding a footing within the labour market. The withdrawal of benefits from 16 and 17-year-olds led to such a public increase in distress amongst young people that a particular route back into benefit – the Severe Hardship provision – was introduced to provide some fall-back assistance for those most in need. The system is far from generous, difficult to use and provides only temporary assistance. A recent report published by the Children's Society (1995) outlined a series of case studies in which vulnerable teenagers were initially refused benefits to which they were entitled. Once advised many did receive severe hardship payment, but in the meantime some survived by borrowing from friends or relatives while others took to begging or stealing. The report found problems with the 'three-stop' procedure where young people have to visit three offices before a claim can be processed. Over 60 per cent said it was either difficult or impossible to complete this in one day. As most teenage claimants do not have access to private transport, their journey between offices could amount to many additional miles by scarce public provision.

For those able to negotiate these considerable hurdles, severe hardship payments do nevertheless provide one means of obtaining relief from the worst effects of poverty. Assistance and advocacy from social welfare workers contributed to growing numbers of young people able to obtain this new right. In a sane social policy system, evidence of fuller take-up of entitlement would be regarded as success. In recent years, however, this approach has been turned upon its head. When take-up of a particular benefit improves, government has reacted by castigating those who promote entitlement as putting pressure upon claimants, criticising those who administer the system as too ready to concede claims, and characterising the benefit itself as too generous. So it has been with severe hardship payments. The rate of application and of successful claims of this benefit of last resort has grown throughout the period in which it has been in operation. In the first six months, from September 1988 to February 1989, 4058 applications were made of which 2827 were successful. By September 1993 to February 1994, the number of claims made had risen to 65 888 and 57 952 of these had resulted in a payment being made (NCH 1996).

This rise in claims, and in successful outcomes, had taken place entirely within rules set by the government and administered accordingly. Yet, on 1 April 1996 changes came into force 'to reflect the Government's opinion that young people who are offered suitable training should both accept it and complete it' (Childright 1995b). These changes are said to be designed to ensure that only genuine claims are successful. In practice, of course, they make the process of claiming more difficult for all. The changes are especially relevant to youth justice workers because they place new powers in the hands of benefit officers to investigate claims made by young people about their family circumstances, on the transparent basis that their own testimony is not to be believed. Unskilled and partial intrusion into fraught family circumstances can only risk making difficulties more intractable. Youth justice workers are able to intervene to support young people and to prevent these unnecessary and harmful investigations. They need to do so.

Welfare to work

The problems faced by 16 and 17-year-olds are in the process of being extended to their older contemporaries. The 'Welfare to Work' programmes of the current government represent a move away from a Manifesto commitment in which the Labour Party proposed that 18–24-year-olds not taking part would not be able to rely on *full* benefit payment, to a situation where *all* benefit is to be denied to any non-participant (Department for Education and Employment 1997). Many of the difficulties which compulsory workfare has produced for 16 and 17-year-olds are likely to be reproduced in the process. Youth justice workers, probation officers and others working with young people who for reasons of criminal record if nothing else find themselves least attractive to potential employers, will find an additional urgency in the need for a sustained and systematic approach to rescuing young people's rights to a basic income, and this has to be a key task for social workers and their agencies. In the brief space available here, three strands in a systems approach to poverty amongst young people can be suggested.

- *Services themselves are major holders of resources and are part of wider organisations – local councils – which remain major players in the economies of their localities*. The decisions which services and authorities make about the deployment of their own spending and purchasing power ought to be tested against the impact which such determinations have upon the circumstances of vulnerable young people and their families. Working in impoverished communities, youth justice personnel see at first hand the impact which decisions about employment strategies, location of offices, purchase of goods and services all make upon local economies. A systems approach to poverty would contribute to spending and service-delivery decisions which invest such resources, as much as possible, in those places which would benefit from them the most.

- *A second element lies in a refocusing of work in the basic business of welfare rights*. There is an obligation upon all workers who have daily contact with young people caught up in the justice system to maintain an up-to-date and accurate understanding of the remaining ways in which the benefit system can help some young people. Within youth justice the strength of teamworking has been one of its substantial assets. Shared responsibility for remaining in touch with the changing patterns of welfare provision can provide additional benefits, although this is not a substitute for the responsibilities which individual workers hold to be properly informed and capable of providing accurate advice to users.

The process of doing so is tedious, the information is mindnumbing, the application of that information is subject to the whim of a system which relies increasingly on discretion exercised within a framework of coercion and hostility, and even successful outcomes are pitifully mean in the rewards which follow. Yet, for individual young people even that pittance can make the difference between survival and submergence. In a systems sense it is vital that intervention does not proceed from a naive belief in their basic helpfulness, or in a way which places a premium upon the maintenance of 'good relations' between one worker and another or one bureaucracy and another. Rather, and in a renewed spirit of determined advocacy, a fresh emphasis on direct intervention within state income maintenance provision must take the hostility of those systems as its starting point, and direct its efforts on behalf of young people in a way which is dedicated to the protection

of their interests and prepared for the confrontation which
might follow.

- *A systems approach to improving the income circumstances of youth
  justice clients would need to lift its sights to encompass the natural
  enterprise and efforts of which such young people are capable.* There
  is no absence of such qualities in the individuals with whom
  youth justice services are in contact. Rather, the communities
  in which they live are characterised by an ingenuity and resour-
  cefulness in the face of poverty which would put to shame the
  elegant theorists of underclassism for whom the absence of a
  wine waiter would represent a major challenge to self-reliance.
  The idea that an incoming tide of economic prosperity will
  eventually reach the shores of such communities is a cruel
  deception upon those condemned to wait upon that unlikely
  eventuality. In its place local and self-help initiatives have produced practical ideas such as credit-unions, debt-redemption
  work, cooperative buying schemes, LETS schemes, self-build
  initiatives and cooperative employment arrangements. Young
  people have a real part to play in these economies but, as in
  the other transitions which were discussed earlier, they are likely
  to need assistance in making successful links with those who take
  a lead in their development. The broker role which social workers have traditionally occupied (Drakeford 1993) will be of
  particular importance in bringing this about.

Poverty and crime are intrinsically linked; to bring about
improvement in the former will produce a positive impact upon
the latter. That is why youth justice workers have to play their part.

Housing

Of all the major social services, housing has suffered the greatest
cutbacks during the Conservative years since 1979. The collapse of
public provision produced a fall in expenditure from 4.1 per cent
to 1.6 per cent of GDP between 1976/7 and 1988/9 (Lowe 1993).
For young people, as the opening chapter of this book set out, the
transition from original family to independent accommodation has
been affected by general trends such as the decline of private
renting and the sale of public housing, as well as particular devel-

opments brought about by the ill-fitting nature of Children Act and Housing Act provision and the impact of wider shifts in social policy towards young people. Thus, just as 16 and 17-year-olds were to blame for their own unemployment – and therefore denied benefit by the 1988 Social Security changes – so their homelessness was also largely a matter of choice. Kay (1994: 5) quotes Prime Minister Thatcher in June 1988:

> There are a number of young people who choose voluntarily to leave home. I do not think we can be expected, no matter how many they are, to provide units for them... these young people already have a home to live in, belonging to their parents.

The presentation of naked ideology as simple common sense has been one of the consistent features of government policy-making over the past 15 years. Mrs Thatcher's assertion that young people were able to remain unproblematically at home both wilfully mis-understood the real situation faced in some households, and neglected the policy pressures which her government had pro-duced in order to make other courses of action more difficult. As Gill Jones (1995: 1) suggests, 'now, in the mid-1990s, there is more talk about preventing young people from leaving home than cele-brating a major event in the transition to adulthood. Leaving home is seen as inherently problematic'. Even for well-supported and relatively prosperous young people, as she shows, leaving home is more of a process than a simple end in itself. Help with material goods (old carpets, passed-on fridges and so on), continued use of services at home (using the washing machine), and a bolt-hole in times of difficulty or distress all bolster the chances of successfully making such a transition.

The young people with whom youth justice workers come into contact often stand at the opposite end of the spectrum from those able to draw upon such sustained and reasonably-resourced net-works of support. Rather, they find themselves at the sharp end of ever-deteriorating social rights and services. A recent report of the National Council of Voluntary Child Care Organisations (1995) highlighted the adverse impact of changes in homelessness legisla-tion. Rejecting the depiction of homelessness applicants as queue-jumping, pregnant single women, leaving home on a whim in order to take advantage of an over-generous system, the report pointed to the damage which the further erosion of the right to a decent dependable place to live would produce upon families. It concluded that, 'these changes could result in insecure and possibly poor standard housing for homeless children' creating 'an unsettled and stressful lifestyle with damaging effects on health, education and social development'.

Chapter 1 considered the impact which the 1996 cuts in housing benefit entitlement would produce upon young people. The combination of benefit reduction, limitation in the type of accommodation for which benefit can be claimed, and payment of benefit in arrears means that the most vulnerable young people will find themselves, again, at the losing end of these market-dominated changes. In the case of youth justice clients, particularly, such accommodation difficulties gain in importance because of the very direct links which living circumstances can produce upon their treatment within the operation of the courts. As the last chapter demonstrated, there is substantial evidence, for example, to show just how significant are the very earliest accommodation decisions within the arrest, charge and bail process in shaping final sentences.

Housing and the social services department

Absence of sufficient and suitable accommodation for young people continues to be one of the most pressing and recurrent themes in daily practice. In a systemic sense it is the contention of this book that senior officers within Social Services Departments have an undischarged obligation to campaign within their own authorities for the implementation of Children Act responsibilities in relation to young people in need of decent, affordable and safe accommodation. Changes in systems are difficult to bring about but are far more effective, for far more young people, than the constant battles to cobble together individual solutions in circumstances of continuing crisis.

Changing policy at such organisational level provides only a long-term solution to very pressing difficulties. The following example of work in the housing field which came from the individual efforts of a group of grass-roots workers suggests some more immediate ways in which workers might be able to act to the advantage of their clients. The Llamau Housing Society in Cardiff was founded by three probation officers specialising in work with young people. It sprang from frustration at the lack of resources available for such individuals and the way in which that disadvantage was compounded by the manner in which courts regard and deal with young people without a stable base. The purpose of the society is to provide supported accommodation for young people in the 16–21 age range where the absence of decent and affordable accommodation underlies other problems, particularly offending or risk of offending. The philosophy which motivates the society centres around a commitment to the belief that a decent and affordable place to live should be an elementary right in any civilised society. Within that framework it aims for equal opportunity in selection and full participation in the progress of individuals through the project by those individuals themselves.

The details of how the society was turned from an idea into a reality have been set out elsewhere (see Drakeford and Vanstone 1996b). The point to emphasise here is that the project has succeeded because a group of workers combined their efforts to influence the offending careers of some deeply disadvantaged young people in a recognition that the needs of those individuals could best be served by collective action which made a difference to the system. The demands of daily practice, especially when dealing with the crisis-ridden problems of accommodation, do make it difficult for sights to be lifted above the particular and to see how those issues might be addressed on a more general basis. The message about which this chapter hopes to convince the reader is that such efforts are worthwhile and deserve to be attempted more often.

Education

In Britain, the state not only provides an education system, it places a duty upon every adult citizen with children of school age to educate those children. Access to education is a key to social inclusion in many different ways. It prepares individuals for participation in the productive economic system and enables them to develop their skills so that their future prosperity can be enhanced. It also provides children and young people with access to participation in the wider lives of their contemporaries: in sport, culture and social activities, for example. Youth justice workers have long been aware of the impact which difficulties in education can produce upon young people who appear before the courts. This section concentrates upon one such aspect – the growing evidence of very large numbers of young people who are now excluded from this form of public provision altogether. The introduction of quasi-market forces into education marks out particular pupils as likely to detract from the image of individual schools through published league tables of attendance or examination success (see, for example, Imich 1994; Bourne *et al.* 1994; Smith and Noble 1995). Young people who appear before the courts are particularly vulnerable in such circumstances.

There are a number of sources of evidence of rocketing school exclusion. The University of Plymouth, for example, reported the results of its research in 1996 as set out in Table 5.1.

The characteristics of those excluded within the Plymouth research may be summarised in this way: young people were drawn from families experiencing other social problems, particularly poverty; exclusion falls upon boys not girls, by a ratio of 5:1; the peak age for exclusion is 15 but numbers are also increasing at primary level. Detailed Plymouth figures show that in one LEA, 12 of the 134 primary age exclusions were for children of infant age.

The extent to which exclusion decisions have come to be driven by market considerations is revealed in research conducted by MORI, who were concerned to investigate the cause of rising exclusion. Their findings are set out in Table 5.2.

When school decisions about exclusion are shaped by fear of market failure, the impact of these determinations does not fall equally upon all groups within the pupil population. The Advisory Centre for Education reports that in September and October 1991

Table 5.1 Permanent exclusions, 1990–96

Year	All exclusions	Primary only
1990–91	2 910	378
1991–92	3 833	537
1992–93	**8 636**	**1 215**
1993–94	11 181 (**11 013**)	1 297 (**1 253**)
1994–95	11 084 (12 458)	1 365 (1 445)
1995–96	12 500 (13 581)	1 600 (1 872)

Sources: **highlighted estimates** are from the University of Portsmouth survey; 1990–92 figures are DfE 1992; 1993–94 are Parsons *et al.* 1995; 1994–95 are DfEE, 1996, and figures in brackets are Parsons, 1996; 1995–1996 are DfEE, 1997, and figures in brackets are Parsons, 1996. Hayden, C. (1997) *Children Excluded From Primary School: debates, evidence, responses* (Buckingham, Open University Press).

Table 5.2 Reasons for the increase in exclusions

Reason	First choice (%)	Second choice (%)
Increased competition between schools	42	55
Pressure on school timetables	22	33
Poorer discipline	8	14
Loss of LEA influence over schools	6	17
Introduction of truant tables	3	16
None of these	12	–
Don't know/no answer	7	–

Source: T. Hyams-Parish (1995) *Banished to the Exclusion Zone – a Guide to School Exclusions and the Law* (Children's Legal Centre, University of Essex).

half of the calls to its offices concerned Afro-Caribbean pupils, and just under half were about pupils with special education needs. OFSTED figures in 1993 showed that in one London school 34 of 79 exclusions during the autumn term involved children of African-Caribbean origin although they formed only 12.5 per cent of the total pupil population. The Department for Education's own figures show that between 12 and 15-per-cent of those children permanently excluded from school during 1990–92 had Special Educational Needs statements. These figures do not include those in the process of being statemented nor those unofficially at home while the process is being negotiated. The integrationist policies of the 1981 Education Act are being rolled back by the competitive approach embodied within subsequent education reforms. Children with special needs come to be perceived as a drain on school resources and exclusion is one way in which that drain can be removed.

Young offenders and school exclusion

For many schools, young people in trouble with the courts clearly represent the acute end of market failure. Youth justice services have a particular interest in ensuring that the worst excesses of market-driven rejection do not produce a disproportionate impact upon court-based decision-making. Earlier research has amply demonstrated how school reports can damage young people in the eyes of sentencers (see Ball 1983; McLaughlin 1989; NACRO 1994) for reasons which have nothing to do with their court appearances. In the case of exclusions, systemic intervention is required to ensure that schools are following the procedures laid down by their own rule-books. The Advisory Centre for Education comments on the irony in which 'schools which seek to sanction pupils for breaches of the school code of conduct may try to do so without paying due attention to the law of the land'. ACE case histories reveal a whole catalogue of illegal procedures and poor practice, especially in the use of 'informal' exclusions. One-third of all callers in January and February 1992 had been asked by the headteacher to take their child away from school without any recourse to the protections which formal procedures provide.

At the sharpest end of practice, the *Troubleshooter* project discussed in the last chapter reports the following information in relation to 15-year-old young people remanded or sentenced to custody. The project dealt with 650 children altogether, collecting information about education in 431 of these cases. Only 89 or 20.5 per cent, from a group which were all of compulsory school age, had been attending a mainstream school immediately prior to their being sent to prison. The remaining 342 youngsters had been excluded from mainstream schooling or were defined as long-term non-attenders at the time of entry into the prison system Of the excluded and non-attender group, 132 or 38.6 per cent were Black or Asian and only 19.3 per cent of Caribbean clients were attending mainstream school compared to 21.7 per cent for the European, 23.5 per cent for the Asian and 27.8 per cent for the African groups (Howard League 1997: 31).

Youth justice services, provided very often by the same local authority, have a vested interest in ensuring that exclusions are conducted with full regard for proper process. When young people have been excluded from one establishment they continue to have a right to education. Figures show, however, that once excluded from one school, the chances of reintegration into mainstream education are very low. In the particular case of those young people with whom youth justice workers are in contact, the absence of education can have additional problematic consequences, as courts deal with individuals more harshly for social rather than criminal failure. At this point, also, a systemic solution is required, either by improving arrangements through which re-entry into a different school is provided or, where that would not be in the best interests of the individual child, by some other means of alternative education.

The point to be stressed here is that these are *systemic* requirements. Hours and hours of worker time are taken up when
attempting to resolve the escalating pattern of school difficulties
on a case-by-case basis. Time invested in changing systems which
then provide improved and normalised access for all young people
in these circumstances will be repaid many times over, both in
terms of the organisation's own resources and in terms of outcome
for the young people concerned.

When a young person is excluded from school, direct costs (for
example withdrawal of school meals) and indirect costs (for example
on future employment opportunities) follow. This chapter now
turns to the period in a young person's life in which the successes
or failures of education have their first and most direct impact.

Employment and training

The experience of work amongst young people presents a paradox. Lavelette *et al.* (1995) suggest that 'between one third and one
half of school students in their last two years of compulsory schooling will be in some form of paid labour at any given time'. The Low
Pay Unit, extrapolating from a study undertaken in Birmingham,
suggests that as many as two million children may be working in
Britain (Pond and Searle 1991) and concludes that 'what cannot be
denied is that... most children, as they approach the statutory
minimum school leaving age, have had experience of paid employment'. It is only on leaving school and attempting to secure a full
place in the employed workforce that a shortage of work for young
people becomes acute.

proper jobs

Chapter 1 considered the ways in which the labour market for
young people in the 1990s had come to be characterised by falling
relative pay, a declining number of full-time permanent jobs and
high unemployment. Bradley (1994), in his review of the period,
concluded that 'one of the most notable features is the rapid decline
in the number of school-leavers entering employment from school.
For instance, this falls from approximately 50 per cent in 1979 to
less than 10 per cent in 1992'. Chapter 1 considered evidence

concerning those young people who find themselves out of work and out of benefit on the one hand, and those who find themselves in so-called 'proper' jobs on the other. Although nationally there has been a fall in youth unemployment the TUC (1996b) claims this has more to do with demographic change than job creation, as well as the impact of continuous changes in the government's definition of unemployment. There are fewer young people today and more of them remain in education. More than 168 000 people under 20 were registered as unemployed in March 1995, of which almost 125 000 had been out of work for a year or more. While unemployment generally has been falling during the mid-1990s this is not a universal picture. In some parts of the country youth unemployment has increased against the national trend, the TUC research establishing that 'nationally, youth unemployment has risen in 219 of 635 parliamentary constituencies outside Northern Ireland'.

Pricing yourself in

For those young people in work, the chances of being among the lowest paid are disproportionately high, concentrated as they are in low-wage sectors. For male full-time employees, the lowest-paid 10 per cent earn £2.60 an hour or less while lowest-paid females earn £2.64 or less according to the TUC (1996b) figures. The Low Pay Unit, in a follow-up to a major report conducted in Wales (Edwards 1994, 1996) found that during a randomly selected week at the Merthyr Tydfil Job Centre, in an area of acute unemployment and possessed of the highest poverty indicator score of any local authority area in Wales, there were a total of 106 jobs available. One in four did not specify a rate of pay. Less than £4.00 an hour was offered in 40 per cent of cases and 25 per cent were part-time jobs of less than 20 hours a week. In the neighbouring borough of Abergavenny a total of 110 jobs were available in the same week. A fixed rate of pay was not on offer in 57 per cent of cases, nor were the number of hours to be worked specified. In 3 per cent of cases jobs were offered at zero hour contracts.

Training

This chapter intends to concentrate upon those substitute forms of employment which, in variations upon the form of Youth

Training Schemes, had according to Bradley (1994: 31) 'attained a dominant position in terms of school-leaver recruitment in the mid-1980s'. In Bradley's figures, 'over the period 1978–93 at least 5.5 million youths have had some experience of YOP, YTS or YT and millions of pounds of public money have been spent on these programmes. For instance in 1978–79, £156.3 million (in 1990 prices) was spent on YOP, equivalent to £1200 per trainee, rising to a peak of £1287 million in 1989–90, or £3000 per trainee.'

Within this pattern, the experience of young people who are known to youth justice workers is likely to be particularly disadvantaged. Furlong (1993: 25), in an extended investigation of the ways in which young people move from school to work, concluded that the Youth Training Scheme (YTS) had become the repository for those who had failed to enter 'proper' jobs or who had chosen not to stay on in education. As such it provided 'an institutional framework in which educational disadvantages are translated into labour market disadvantages'. Within the YTS, provision had become stratified to 'ensure that qualified trainees enter schemes which offer a realistic route to a permanent job, while the unqualified enter "sink schemes" (Roberts and Parcell 1989) which offer little prospect of employment'. This finding, in particular, has been confirmed in a number of other studies. Bradley (1994: 38), for example, illustrates the way in which different systems combine to contribute to this outcome: 'the Careers Service effectively operated as an initial screening device of YTS applicants, after which the best schemes "creamed" the best youths from the applicant queue'. This role became more formalised under subsequent versions of the YTS. The Manpower Services Commission had devised a system in which Mode-A schemes placed the better able young people directly with employers, leaving Mode-B schemes to work with trainees suffering from different kinds of social disadvantage. It now bemoaned the way in which this bifurcation was translated into the experience of users: 'it is most unfortunate that Mode A and Mode B have become equated... with first- and second-class provision and the trainees taking part with first- and second-class young people' (MSC 1985: 26, quoted in Bradley p.40).

Bradley's conclusion emphasises the way in which different systems, some equipped with the explicit aim of promoting the best interests of individual young people, all came to march to the beat of the most dominant ideological drum: 'first, there is a clear trend, started under YOP, for YTS provision to be segmented, which has been facilitated by the Careers Service acting as a gatekeeper for the programme. Second, additionally and employed status places also helped to reinforce the segmentation.'

Looking beyond the period of training itself, Furlong found that participation within the Youth Training Scheme, as well as being unrewarding in itself, carried no residual advantages: 'ex-trainees were no more likely to find jobs than those who had refused to join the scheme'. The 39 young people studied by Crane and Coles (1995: 10 – see Chapter 1) had taken part in a combined total of almost 90 training schemes, leading to a 'proper job' in only one case. The authors found that the young people they studied had their 'aspirations...deflated by early encounters with the local labour market...and the demeaning pantomime of being conscripted into scheme after scheme'.

In Furlong's analysis two particularly bleak conclusions follow. Firstly he concludes, 'The Youth Training Scheme... provides an institutional context whereby young people come to be regarded as unemployable...those who fail to enter a job straight after YTS are regarded as "double failures", as people who failed to find work on leaving school and who failed again after YTS'. Thereafter, he reminds us, young people have attained 'their own position within the social structure which is a better predictor of their future life chances than the social position of their parents'.

Youth justice and employment

Youth justice workers find themselves very often dealing with young people for whom the 'promise' of a place within a worthwhile Youth Training Scheme has a hollow ring. Most will experience the dissonance between what Mizen (1993: 38) calls the government's setting of 'the level of training allowance and young people's own moral economy regarding its "fairness"'. Many of those who participate will do so as reluctant conscripts. Yet, at the point of collision between a young person's life and the criminal justice system, the calculation of cost and reward in participation will have a series of new and crucial elements. Even in a 'justice' culture, courts base part of their sentencing calculations upon the extent to which young people appear to have positive future prospects. A 'job' will be an important building brick in describing such a future. Youth justice systems, therefore, have a legitimate interest in the formation and operation of schemes which have something genuine to offer young people in these circumstances and which are able to respond quickly and flexibly to a justice-driven timetable.

Such arrangements are not easy to bring about and the commercialisation of provision through the Training and Enterprise Councils has added to these difficulties. Yet, with sufficient investment of time and energy it is still possible to achieve something of value. The Neway scheme in Cardiff, for example, began as one of the original NACRO Youth Opportunities Programme initiatives, heavily supported by its parent organisation and by the local Probation Service. Through a constantly turbulent history in which one of its basic constituent partners was always shifting, the scheme has continued to provide a quality service for some of the most disadvantaged and ill-equipped young people. Participation in the scheme carries a basic message from those responsible that young people are valued as individuals, that their personal predicaments and requirements are important and that the basic limitations of the youth training framework are recognised and not subject to pretence. Within those limitations the boundaries are always pressed to look for whatever small pieces of added value – in terms of training, work experience, job opportunities or extra cash – can be squeezed to the advantage of those taking part. The scheme has long since ceased to deal just with young people in trouble with the law; it takes referrals from a wide range of organisations across the city. The young people with whom youth justice workers are concerned take their place within a scheme which is as 'normalised' as possible.

The employment prospects for so many young people in contemporary Britain are bleak. For those who appear before the courts, the consequences of being in this position can be doubly disadvantageous as a less favourable outcome in criminal proceedings is added to the burden of unemployment. While schemes such as the Neway example quoted above are always struggling at the margins of larger social forces, this is a struggle which youth justice workers have to join.

Health

The health circumstances of young people are an inevitable matter of concern in any society in which their future well-being is taken seriously. There is general evidence, however, that the professional agendas in this area – smoking, drug use, unwanted pregnancy – are not shared by young people themselves who report issues such as skin and weight problems as being of more immediate concern (Jacobson and Wilkinson 1994). This disjuncture is reflected in an uncomfortable quality which characterises a significant range of contacts between young people and health professionals. Nearly 50 per cent of teenagers in a large sample surveyed in school reported often feeling uncomfortable with GP consultations. A recent research project in Cardiff concluded that, 'doctors in the study gave less consulting time to teenagers than to patients of any other age group. The difference was nearly 20 per cent' (Jacobson and Pill 1997: 59).

Against this general background, the young people who come to the attention of social welfare workers for other reasons emerge as the least likely to seek health advice (Morris 1985; Jacobson and Wilkinson 1994). In the case of young people who come before the courts, health circumstances have both a direct bearing upon their criminal justice fates and, in the argument of this chapter, a wider impact upon their chances of avoiding trouble in the future. Directly, health has to be taken into account in proposing certain courses of action – Attendance Centre Orders, for example – and in explaining others, such as the effects of alcohol and drugs upon behaviour.

This section begins by summarising some of the most recent information which is available concerning the actions and attitudes of young people generally in different aspects of health-related behaviour before going on, within each section, to consider some of the ways in which health matters are of especial relevance to youth justice clients and workers.

Drugs and alcohol

One of the largest surveys of young people and health issues ever carried out in the United Kingdom is that by Patrick Miller and

Martin Plant of the alcohol and health research group at Edinburgh University. Set out below are some of their main findings derived from the responses of 7722 pupils aged 15 and 16, at 60 state schools and 10 independent schools.

Within that study 42 per cent of 15 and 16-year-olds had tried illegal drugs, mostly cannabis. Virtually all (94 per cent) had consumed alcohol, and 36 per cent had smoked cigarettes in the month before the survey took place.

Considered in more detail, the figures show that 38 per cent of the boys reported themselves as having tried cannabis, with significantly higher levels reported in Scotland where 60 per cent of boys and 47 per cent of girls said that they had used it. A fifth of the pupils, of both sexes, had used glues and solvents, and 12 per cent of the girls and 17 per cent of boys had tried LSD or other hallucinogens. Use of ecstasy was reported by 7 per cent of girls and 9 per cent of boys, while 2 per cent of both sexes had used crack, and 1.5 per cent had tried heroin.

In terms of alcohol use, 78 per cent of the pupils said that they had been intoxicated at least once, with 11 per cent of girls and 15 per cent of boys saying that they had consumed alcohol on nine or more occasions in the preceding month.

The general conclusion of the report's authors is that there has been a sharp rise in the number of young people experimenting with all types of drugs since 1989.

These findings may be amplified and contextualised by a series of other studies. As far as drink is concerned, Balding (1993) suggests that up to 86 per cent of 14 to 15-year-olds will have tried alcohol, while Sharp (1994) places 90 per cent of those who have attained 16 years of age in the same category. While most studies suggest that most young people are moderate users of alcohol, Fossey *et al.* (1996: 58) found that a 'substantial minority' of young people of both sexes were drinking heavily.

In the case of illegal drugs and solvents, Graham and Bowling (1995) provide evidence that one in two males and one in three females in the 14–25-year-old age range will have experimented with drugs, and that 33 per cent of such young men, and 20 per cent of the young women will be regular users of cannabis. Although the use of hard drugs is increasing (see, for example, Measham *et al.* 1994), the proportion of young people self-reporting such use is small. Furlong and Cartmel (1997: 77), for example, quote evidence of 1 per cent of 15 to 24-year-olds report-ing use of heroin or cocaine.

Drugs, alcohol and justice

Drug and alcohol use are amongst the most difficult questions which youth justice workers have to negotiate, and there is no clear-cut or consistent relationship between the potential harm of a drug and its legal status. Use of drugs by young people is in any case not simply, or even perhaps primarily, a function of its legality. Rather, as Plant and Plant (1992) suggest, the coincidence of most illicit drug use with adolescence suggests that such activity is best understood as part of normal curiosity, the impact of peer pressure and a growing wish to engage in adult or risky behaviour. When such traits meet phenomena such as the rave culture (see Merchant and MacDonald 1994 for a full account of this in relation to ecstasy and rave), then a response which relies upon a combination of moralising, awful warning and social authoritarianism threatens to be at best ineffective and more likely counterproductive. This is not, of course, to deny that misuse of drugs and alcohol are not serious matters and ones which cause immense harm and distress to those whose lives become dominated by them. It is to suggest that the chances of engaging with young people, and influencing their behaviour, are diminished by responses which are not valid-ated by their own experience and are enhanced by approaches which provide reliable and accurate information and advice which avoids the taint of moralising.

In working with young people who are in trouble with the law, some of these general points come into sharper focus. Baldwin (1995: 73), for example, reports that 'alcohol-related offending by juveniles and young adults has increased in Scotland in the 1980s and 1990s...there is growing national concern in Scotland that this pattern is an aggregated product of related trends in housing, unemployment and crime'. In a cross-cultural comparison of youthful drinking in Scotland and France, he reaches the import-ant conclusion that crime levels are influenced not so much by behaviour itself as by the cultural contexts in which it takes place. Thus, 'the behaviour of young drinkers in France has been con-fined to indoor public locations, for example, bars and cafes', while in Scotland 'there is evidence of more use of outdoor public locations (e.g. street, parks) by young drinkers in Scotland'. The result is that 'these topographical variations exert subtle effects on police behaviour and subsequent criminal statistics'. Thereafter, 'although public drunkenness has remained an indictable offence in both cultures, the policy response by police has been markedly different'.

Youth justice staff have two systems-management-related tasks to undertake when working with young people whose criminal activities are connected with drugs and alcohol. One is the basic matter of ensuring that such young people obtain access to services where they need them. The market-driven National Health Service produces, as all markets do, an out-turn of losers as well as winners. There is evidence that patients who are cost-intensive – by having conditions with are chronic and unlikely to respond swiftly to treatment – or whose behaviour is difficult, find themselves at particular difficulty in securing medical services (see, for example, the Community Health Council survey of 1994). The second is to challenge the stereotypes of 'user' and 'pusher' which dominates the way such activity is portrayed by other major actors within the system. The real nature of drug culture amongst young people is far more complex and often very different (see, for example, Parker and Measham 1994; Roberts *et al.* 1995). The educative role which youth justice workers have to play within systems is sharply to the fore in this instance.

Sex

A similarly significant shift in teenage health matters is to be found in self-reported evidence of sexual activity. The 1994 National Survey of Sexual Attitudes and Lifestyles found, for example, that amongst women aged 55–59 at the time of the interview the average age of first intercourse was 21, while in the 16–24 year age range it was 17. The average age at first intercourse for men aged 55–59 was 20, while for those aged 16–19 it was 17. Amongst young women aged 16–19 who are sexually active, nearly 19 per cent reported having had sex before the age of 16, compared to 1 per cent of those aged 55–59. Amongst men the comparable figures are 28 per cent and 6 per cent. This pattern of change has been traced across the century as a whole, for example by Humphries (1991) and Breakwell (1992).

For young people generally, contemporary society holds out an extended range of possibilities and related risks which are relevant to sexual health. At the same time, information and discussion in this area seems persistently difficult to sustain. Barbara Walker (1997: 52) draws this bleak conclusion from her direct investigation of young people's own accounts of constructing an adult sexual identity:

> Young people learn very little about sex from school, the media (and this in spite of periodic concern about the amount of sex in films and on television), their families, doctors, the clergy, their work mates, and – despite suggestions to the contrary – their friends. Learning about sex is a solitary, fraught and haphazard pursuit.

Young people who come to the attention of youth justice workers face additional difficulties still. They are preponderantly young men and, as such, according to Walker and others (for example Askey and Ross 1988; Holland *et al.* 1993) find discussion of sexual matters especially problematic. They are also likely to include a higher proportion of those who have particular experiences such as sexual abuse within their own homes or while in the care of public authorities. Such individuals remain vulnerable to the predatory attentions of others, and in their collision with the criminal justice system they find themselves caught up in a series of self-reinforcing jeopardies. They will be dealt with by a system which clings to a conservative version of public morality, in which the contemporary behaviour of young people is likely to appear aberrant rather than orthodox within its own cultural context. Young women in particular will remain exposed to the enduring impact of the old 'moral danger' concept which leads to the criminal justice system being used to address behavioural issues which have no direct bearing upon offending. Young men, particularly those whose own sexuality leads to behaviour which is outside the criminal law, may be vulnerable to similar confusions. Yet the same system can also commit young people to institutions where they will be more, rather than less, open to exploitation and abuse.

These can be difficult issues for individual workers to negotiate. They call forth powerful reactions which need to be tested for prejudice and discrimination by all critical practitioners. Thereafter, it is the job of youth social workers to normalise the behaviour of young people as much as possible, assisting courts to understand actions which might lie well outside the experience of sentencers, and to separate the reactions to social behaviour from those criminal matters which are properly the concern of the court.

Mental health

According to Wilson (1995), of the ten million young people between the ages of 14 and 24 in England and Wales:

> most prevalence figures now indicate that around 20 per cent have some kind of mental health problem. This amounts to approximately two million children under the age of 16 in England and Wales. About two per cent, that is about 40 000 children, have mental health problems that are severe enough as to be seriously disabling – problems which are persistent, extreme in the ways in which they present themselves, and which cause great distress to the young people themselves and to their families.

Analysis of statistics provided by the Department of Health has revealed a 65 per cent increase in admissions over the five-year period 1985–1990 for those aged 10 to 14, and a 42 per cent increase for under-10-year-olds (Rickford 1995, 1993a, 1993b).

In 1994 the Young Minds organisation mounted a year-long campaign designed to heighten awareness of the wide range of factors which have an impact upon the mental health of children. The precipitating conditions which the campaign identified contain a number which fall disproportionately upon the young people with whom youth justice workers are in contact, including family discord and poverty. At their most severe, mental health problems lead to admission to psychiatric institutions. Table 5.3 illustrates the extent to which such difficulties amongst young people have increased at a time when admissions for older people have fallen.

Furlong and Cartmel (1997: 67) rightly provide a note of caution in the interpretation of these figures, pointing out that some of the increase at least might be linked to social changes, 'as people have become more likely to seek professional help for psychological problems and doctors have become more predisposed to diagnos

Table 5.3 NHS psychiatric admissions in England and Wales

Age	Admissions per thousand of the population			
	1978	*1986*	*1991/92*	*change 1986/92*
under 10	12	12	24	+50%
10–14	33	36	47	+24%
15–19	168	143	160	+11%
20–74	2822	2867	2578	–11%

Source: Taken from NCH Action for Children *FactFile 1995*, derived from Department of Health, 1994.

ing psychological malaise'. Moreover, the value-free claims of the apparently rational and 'scientific' medical world mask the ways in which definitions of behaviour are dominated by the most powerful groups. In the field of mental health, particularly, these definitions need always to be regarded as contestable, rather than definitive, if children's interests are to be actively safeguarded – if only because as Coppock (1996: 57) suggests, 'the implications of being "treated" in one system or another can be far reaching as each system offers different legal rights to children and young people . . . [and] the mental health system offers children and young people least protection from such abuses.'

Even so, the hard facts of increased suicide amongst young 15–9-year-old males since the mid-1970s (Woodroffe *et al.* 1993), for example, have to be a matter of real and legitimate concern to youth social workers because of the ways in which such risks are exacerbated by contact with the criminal justice system. Some young people facing difficulties with mental health will come to the attention of a social welfare worker for the first time when their behaviour brings them into the ambit of the criminal justice system. More often, the child will be already known to other workers in other systems. The tasks which youth justice systems have to undertake are three-fold: firstly, to ensure that individuals are not escalated through the courses of action available to the courts because of their health difficulties; secondly, to guard against the problem of 'trans-institutionalisation' (Malek 1993) in which 'bad' behaviour becomes redefined as 'mad' – an outcome which Malek (1991) attributes to diminishing resources in other social welfare sectors; and, thirdly, to promote the rights of individuals who are genuinely in need of health services on the same basis as they would be available to other young people who are not in trouble.

Mental health and justice practic

There is good practice evidence from the Probation Service in the development of schemes which divert mentally disordered offenders from the formal processes of the law – see for example the Public Interest Case Assessment work reported in Stone (1989), the work of Orme and Pritchard (1996), and Drakeford and Vanstone's (1996b) account of the Mid-Glamorgan diversion scheme. A number of these initiatives reveal the additional impact of discrimination upon particular groups of defendants, including black people and those without settled accommodation. Burney and Pearson (1995: 307), for example, conclude the account of a diversionary scheme in Islington with the suggestion:

> So that while the 'violent' black mentally disordered offender is hardly a big problem in numerical terms, this represents a tight concentration of high-profile social problems. Perhaps it is out of such acorns that the mighty oaks of stereotypical judgements grow.

While numbers of young people with such difficulties may preclude specific schemes for their particular needs, the principles of diversion remain at least as strong as for those of adults. Indeed, the effort required may be greater. Wilson (1995) reports that

> a national review of mental health services for children and adolescents, commissioned by the Department of Health and published last year, found that services are generally unplanned and historically determined, that their distribution is patchy, that their work is variable in quality and composition, and that the work they do seems unrelated in strength or diversity to local need.

Youth justice services therefore need to develop systemic ways of intervening in the processes through which mental health difficulties become elided into notions of 'dangerousness' and 'seriousness'. This is necessary because of the ways in which, within the criminal justice system, such concepts will result in more intrusive sentencing than would otherwise have occurred. Equally, as noted above, systemic steps need to be in place to avoid the dangers of young people being denied access to services they need – as access to youth justice services become more tightly managed – and being dealt with instead through the very substantial and intrusive powers which exist within mental health services. Finally, work in the field of mental health also demands that particular attention be directed to the cultural component of discrimination. In Wales, for example, there is disturbing evidence of the way in which Welsh-speaking service-users have their mental state assessed by English-speaking professionals (see, for example, Davies 1994). Discriminatory outcomes in the conjunction of ethnicity, mental health issues and the operation of the criminal justice system is something which youth justice workers have a particular responsibility to guard against.

Conclusion

Young people in trouble with the law find their prospects within that system fundamentally affected by the state in which their rights to other services are preserved and promoted. This chapter has argued that young people in trouble are vulnerable to having their rights in other systems undermined and disregarded. The disadvantage experienced in this way is then translated into, and amplified within, the criminal justice system. Youth justice workers thus have a series of important reasons for involving themselves in these other systems, both general – in terms of system outcomes – and particular – in terms of the impact upon individuals. Such involvement, however, is best aimed at altering the behaviour of such other systems, rather than attempting to negotiate individual solutions for each recurrent difficulty. This requires that youth justice services invest time and energy in the sorts of schemes, projects and processes outlined in parts of this chapter. In this way, not only will individual workers be assisted in avoiding the harm which enmeshment in the criminal justice system brings young people, but the prospect of doing good in damaged lives will be enhanced as well.

6

Effective Work with Young Offenders

Direct work with young people on criminal court orders is likely to form a continuing aspect of youth justice practice. This chapter is concerned to provide students and practitioners with a framework, based on control theory, within which an understanding of the research into effective, and not so effective, principles of working with young offenders can be developed.

The need for effective youth justice practice

Despite the political rhetoric about progress and the supposed wealth-sharing and broadening of general improvements to the quality of life, there is considerable evidence to suggest that larger numbers of families and communities are moving in the opposite direction (Hutton 1995; Lash and Urry 1987). One aspect of modern societies that affects quality-of-life issues is crime, and crime in general is on the increase.[1] It is known from victim studies (see, for example, Mayhew et al. 1993) that crime has a differential impact on communities (tending to be worse in poorer areas), but victim studies also show that fear of crime has a more widespread impact on the lives of people than direct experiences of crime. The seemingly limited ability of governments to have an impact on large-scale economic factors (such as unemployment, wage levels, mortgage rates and so on), coupled with their inability to deal with crime, has tended to mean that modern nation-states have responded more to popular beliefs about crime than the crime problem itself. This response has tended to take two basic forms: (i) reassurance – that government is doing all it can, and (ii) an increasingly punitive shift in government policy towards identified offenders (see, for example, Haines 1995).

The hallmarks of these responses, and particularly the second, have been very clear in recent developments in England and Wales, although the increasingly punitive shift in the treatment of identified offenders is a more widespread phenomenon not restricted to this country alone (Bottoms 1995a). The implications of this are that there is no evidence to suggest that a more understanding and less condemnatory response towards young offenders can be expected in the foreseeable future, whatever the politics of the government of the day may be. Youth justice workers are, therefore, increasingly likely to find themselves working in a system that is ever more hostile towards young people and young offenders in particular. For this reason, if no other, it is absolutely essential that youth justice practice in the future builds upon the principles and practices of systems management techniques. The ability to exercise a degree of control over the entry of young people into the (what is likely to be an ever more punitive) criminal justice system will prove to be an important and highly-valued characteristic of youth justice practice. Keeping young people out of the criminal justice system has been an important feature of 1980s juvenile justice. In the argument of this book it will be an even more important strategy for the future and systems management techniques will provide the best chance of making this strategy a reality.

Some young offenders will, however, penetrate the criminal justice system. Here again systems management techniques will be essential in strategies of doing less harm and in avoiding the excesses of 'popular' political punitive policies. Some of this can be achieved by maximising courts' use of the least restrictive option, but if youth justice workers are to be successful in avoiding institutional or custodial sentences then there must be credible community alternatives (properly targeted to maximise system management benefits). By the term credible, however, something quite specific is meant.

The development of community sentences since the mid-1980s and especially post-CJA 1991 has been heavily influenced by the Home Office. The major device the Home Office has used to exert a degree of control over the community supervision of offenders is National Standards (see Chapter 7 for a fuller discussion of National Standards). Opinions regarding these are mixed: the Home Office is clearly committed to them; some practitioners believe that they have established helpful minimum standards and that they provide a good basic framework; while research is less positive, indicating that National Standards tend to reduce professional practice to administrative compliance with procedural controls (Haines and O'Mahony 1995). Whatever one's opinions are, there can be no doubt that the Home Office views them as an effective tool for influencing local practice and that this influence has been brought to bear on two main factors: (i) to maximise economy and efficiency within the criminal justice system, and (ii) to enhance the degree of control within community sentences.[2]

Both maximising economy and efficiency, and enhancing control, are intimately related to recent developments in nation-states outlined above (Haines 1995). Public sector politics in England and Wales have been immersed in the rhetoric of the three E's (economy, efficiency and effectiveness) since Margaret Thatcher launched the Financial Management Initiative in the early 1980s (Gray and Jenkins 1986). In practice, however, preoccupation with the first two of these has meant that under-attention has been paid to questions of effectiveness.

Credibility in community sentences, therefore, does not mean advocating an extension of previous methods and practices as exemplified by National Standards. Credibility is not to be measured in the accountancy of economy and efficiency, nor is it to be achieved through the acceptance and delivery of increasingly interventionist and controlling community sentences. There is no evidence to suggest that economy and efficiency have any necessary relationship to professional service provision – and professionalism is a highly-valued characteristic. And there is no evidence to suggest that more controlling community sentences are effective (however one measures this) – and effectiveness is crucial. The term credibility is used here, therefore, to mean community sentences which are (i) effective in reducing offending, and (ii) effective in ameliorating the distress and deprivation experienced by many young people. This definition of effectiveness is that which underpinned the whole of Chapter 5 where it was argued that the best way of reducing offending is to tackle the difficulties which promote it.

This chapter, therefore, will examine questions of effectiveness and review the relevant research about effective methods of intervention related to offending behaviour. This exercise is undertaken because it is absolutely essential that youth justice workers are equipped with effective professional techniques in their face-to-face work with young offenders (and this is a noted weakness of 1980s juvenile justice), and we seek to provide practical, but research based, examples of positive professional practice. It is important, however, for professionals to have a greater understanding of the research on which their practice is based, and how research can be used to justify and support policies and practices that are not universally acceptable. This review begins, therefore, with an examination of the research which underpins at least in part some significant aspects of recent approaches to the treatment of offenders (and potential offenders) which are more controlling or negative, this is what is known as 'criminal careers' research. Attention then turns to overtly punitive custodial responses towards young offenders and we review the research on the effectiveness of boot camps. The remainder of the chapter is then concerned to explore a variety of treatment methods which hold out some promise of success, and which may form the basis of future effective strategies for direct work with young offenders.

Table 6.3 at the end of this chapter summarises the key features of effective intervention programmes which may be used in training or as an aide memoire. The technical detail is also included because it is essential for students and practitioners to understand the messages and the nuances of research, as such knowledge supports the activities that characterise professional practice. Knowledge of complex methodologies and findings is essential to the extent that it provides hard information which may be used to support arguments youth justice professionals might wish to make in places where these arguments might be difficult to win.

Criminal careers research and early intervention

Criminal careers research has a long and distinguished pedigree at home and abroad. For many people, politicians, academics, professionals, journalists and the general public, there is an inherent logic to the findings of criminal careers research which gives it an appeal and a recognition over and above that commonly experienced for most research – 'nipping offending in the bud', for example, makes sense to many people. The essence of criminal careers research, its premises and promises, are cogently summarised by David Farrington, a leading UK proponent, thus:

> The criminal career approach is essentially concerned with human development over time. However, criminal behaviour does not generally appear without warning; it is commonly preceded by childhood antisocial behaviour (such as bullying, lying, truanting, and cruelty to animals) and followed by adult antisocial behaviour (such as spouse assault, child abuse and neglect, excessive drinking, and sexual promiscuity). The word 'antisocial', of course, involves a value judgement; but it seems likely that there would be general agreement amongst most members of western democracies that these kinds of acts were antipathetic to the smooth running of western society.
>
> It is argued that offending is part of a larger syndrome of antisocial behaviour that arises in childhood and tends to persist into adulthood. There seems to be continuity over time, since the antisocial child tends to become the antisocial teenager and then the antisocial adult, just as the antisocial adult then tends to produce another antisocial child. (Farrington 1994: 511)

This approach involves, therefore, not so much the study of crime as the study of criminals. Basic to this is the notion that certain people exhibit high levels of antisocial behaviour and that this is somehow part of their nature which can be studied as it commonly develops over a lifetime (including its manifestations in child rearing practices and the effects of this). Criminal careers research also suggests that these antisocial people tend to be those members of society who commit crime (that is, acts officially designated as offences by criminal statute) and, perhaps more importantly, it is believed that these antisocial behaviours provide indicators which allow us to identify potential offenders (at a relatively young age) and those most likely to be offenders at any age.

The apparent attraction of this research is to be found in the simplicity of its basic argument and because it leads quite naturally to a set of distinctive practical actions (at least for some). If antisocial people commit crime and if these antisocial indicators can be identified and measured, and moreover if these factors can be identifed in the very young as likely to predispose individuals to lives of crime, then a number of options follow:

1. Intervention can be organised in the lives of the very young to correct this antisocial behaviour.
2. In the case of those for whom intervention does not appear to work, steps can be taken to remove them from society and thereby prevent them from going on to commit offences.

There is inevitably a tenuous relationship between research and policy or practice. But criminal careers research has been particularly influential. That the seeds of criminal behaviour are sown in the very young and that criminal behaviour is a developmental process is an increasingly powerful belief. The idea that we can, and indeed should, intervene early to 'nip offending in the bud' is an increasingly popular political response to crime and criminals that is directly bolstered by this belief which is rooted in the findings of criminal careers research.[3] But how reliable is the criminal careers research? To what extent should it be used to inform our approach to the treatment of offenders, and potential offenders? Criminal careers research can be used to justify excessively interventionist approaches towards the young, and harsh deterrent approaches to those of a slightly older age.[4] To justify excessive or deterrent approaches we need to be confident in our beliefs. It will be argued here that criminal careers research does not warrant this degree of confidence, and that it suffers from two basic problems: (i) methodological, and (ii) concerning matters of interpretation.

Methodological problems

Research methodology in general is becoming ever more sophisticated, and advances in statistical analysis facilitate increasingly complex analyses. There is a danger in this development, however, that the enhanced levels of our sophistication cloud the fundamental bases on which research is undertaken. Like most fields, criminal careers research tends to be undertaken with a characteristic methodological approach. There are of course variations in methodology between studies, but the longitudinal study is generally regarded as the most reliable for criminal careers research (allowing the identification of causes of criminal behaviour). It is worthwhile, therefore, to look at the most basic aspect of typical criminal careers research methodology – the sampling frame.

Because criminologists tend to be pre-occupied with criminals, criminal careers researchers typically focus their studies on social strata within the population where official criminal statistics show that most offenders are grouped, and to form their research samples from within this group (that is, sampling from the most deprived strata and not the increasingly well-off areas). There are serious methodological problems with this research strategy:

- The samples are often quite small – and sometimes too small to justify the significance attached to the results of sophisticated statistical manipulation.
- Criminal careers research dates very quickly; a study which began, say, 30 or more years ago may now be revealing its most interesting results, but how relevant these results are for today is questionable. For example, how useful is data about the experience of early childhood and adolescence in the 1950s or 1960s for an understanding of today's youth?
- Focusing the research sample in a particular strata of the general population that is known to exhibit certain characteristics is, of course, likely to produce research results that confirm the presence and prevalence of those characteristics.
- Inferring from the presence of those characteristics (that is, antisocial behaviour) that they are causally related to criminal behaviour cannot be substantiated without knowing the prevalence of antisocial and criminal behaviour within other social strata. Criminal behaviour cannot be understood without reference to those people who do not offend because there may be a characteristic shared in common by offenders that is also shared more widely within the population

For example, one of the risk factors shown to be a highly correlated indicator of persistence within the course of a 'criminal career' is unemployment. Firstly, unemployment is a social problem and not just an individual one[5], thus there is a tendency within criminal careers research to individualise problems that have a social cause and then to link these individualised problems with criminal behaviour.

Secondly, unemployment is a characteristic of multiply-deprived communities, so is crime and a wide range of other factors. But criminal careers research by its own admission is meant to be about criminals and not crime. Criminal behaviour is found in a wide range of groups within the general population, thus criminal careers research in choosing to focus on crime by selecting high-crime or 'problem' areas as targets for research has created at best a partial picture of offenders. The way in which such research has selected a sub-population and studied it in detail has only been possible because of the blurring between crime and criminals.

Problems of interpretation

Criminal careers research has a problem associated with the interpretation of findings, in arguing that certain individuals exhibit certain antisocial behaviours and characteristics which (while they may differ in significance over the lifespan of an individual) are highly correlated with criminal behaviour. This argument is sustained by studying groups of individuals at several times during their lives, identifying these antisocial behaviours and characteristics and measuring criminal activity, and then performing statistical analyses of these findings to demonstrate correlations. Criminal careers researchers tend then to conclude that antisocial behaviour is highly correlated with the onset and prevalence of offending – and that these correlations can be traced over time. This, however, is just one conclusion that can be reached from an analysis of such data.

To a large extent the criminal careers research methodology involves studying individuals and their behaviour at different times during their lives in the context of the social situation these individuals find themselves in at each of these periods in time. The research typically finds a high degree of correlation between various factors and criminal behaviour, and the thesis rests on the basis of these correlations over time. That is, the correlations are interpreted to mean that offending is related to an individual's antisocial behaviour both developmentally, and at particular points in time.

There is an alternative interpretation of the criminal careers research findings, however, which is, incidentally, sensitive to the criticisms outlined above. Criminal careers researchers have typically set out to test a hypothesis, i.e. that individual characteristics, over the lifespan, are correlated with offending behaviour. In the search to prove this hypothesis alternative explanations of their research findings have not generally been explored. However, an equally plausible interpretation of their findings is that offending is related to a range of situational factors rather than individual characteristics. Thus if, for example, unemployment is one of the factors which is highly correlated with offending, and employment is highly correlated with desistance then perhaps it is the employment status that ought to be the target and not the individual.

It is not academic pedantry to question the basis and conclusions of criminal careers research in this way, as these are serious matters, and more so when so much of the recent political and policy approach appears to be based on these findings. What evidence is there, therefore, to support this critique of criminal careers research? There is a dearth of research which has set out to directly critically assess the hypotheses or results of criminal careers research. One study, however, has reinterpreted such research in terms of an alternate model for understanding offending behaviour as described below.

Social context of offending

Sampson and Laub (1993) based their work on a re-analysis of the original research data into the 'onset and development of offending behaviour over the lifespan' collected by Sheldon and Eleanor Glueck (1964, 1974). The Gluecks' work, the debate in criminology it sparked and the criticisms made of it, are far too extensive to review in detail here (see, Glueck and Glueck 1964, 1974; Sampson and Laub 1993). In short, the Gluecks' research demonstrated the relationship between age and crime, and how youth delinquency was indicative of adult offending. Their primary explanation of the onset of delinquency was rooted in family relationships and dynamics. Early childhood family experiences, it was contended, were related both to delinquency in youth and offending in adulthood, that is early life experiences shaped an individual's future life-course to a significant degree.

For Sampson and Laub, the Gluecks' explanations of delinquency were too heavily reliant on the emphasis of early family experiences (and the psychological paradigm this involved), and gave too little recognition to the possibilities for change and the potential influence of situational factors over the lifespan. Based on their re-analysis, Sampson and Laub produced a more complex explanation of the onset and persistence of offending behaviour as summarised in Figure 6.1.

As the figure is clearly quite complex some explanation is necessary. Firstly it is important to note how the model eschews explanations of delinquency and so on that are rooted in psychological models of individual pathology. Instead, Sampson and Laub's summary comprises three main themes:

> The first is that structural context is mediated by informal family and social controls, which in turn explain delinquency in childhood and adolescence. The second theme is that there is strong continuity in antisocial behaviour running from childhood through adulthood across a variety of life domains. The third theme is that informal social capital in adulthood explains changes in criminal behaviour over the life span, regardless of prior individual differences in criminal propensity. (Sampson and Laub 1993: 243)

Thus the emphasis in this research is on 'individuals' and not 'variables' (as in the criminal careers research), and the focus of attention is shifted on to the implications for an individual's development of various social factors, and the ongoing relationship between subsequent behaviour and the likely implications of that behaviour for future events. These implications are, however, avowedly 'social'; that is, punitive or incarcerative criminal justice responses can and do damage social ties in such a way as to promote rather than diminish offending behaviour.

In this way Sampson and Laub's re-analysis of the Gluecks' data provides some support for this chapter's critique of criminal careers research, by (i) de-pathologising individuals, and (ii) demonstrating the importance of situational factors for delinquent development and continued offending. This situational theme is extremely important (as Chapter 5 demonstrated), and is examined in more detail below. Before doing so, however, the negative implications of punitive exclusionary criminal justice sanctions need to be examined.

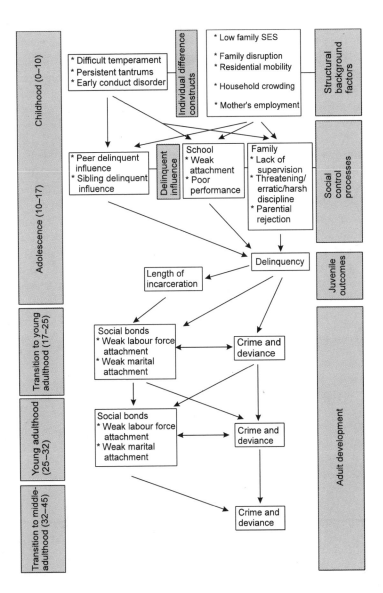

Figure 6.1 Dynamic theoretical model of crime, deviance and informal social control over the life-course
Source: Based on Sampson and Laub (1993: 244–5).

Boot camps and the institutional treatment of children

A recent Europe-wide survey of trends in the treatment of young people in trouble and in need concluded that for both categories of children there was a discernible shift away from institutional forms of treatment (including custody) towards dealing with youth in the community (McCarney 1996). While it is undoubtedly true that in England and Wales in the 1980s and early-1990s community-based forms of treatment for young offenders were in the ascendant, both politically and in practice, the mid-1990s has seen a significant reversal of this trend. The last Conservative Home Secretary not only proclaimed that 'prison works', but his government developed plans to build new forms of custodial institution, Secure Training Centres, for very young children. The new Labour Home Secretary, Jack Straw, has confirmed his government's intention to go ahead with the opening of the first such Centre. It is regrettable that England and Wales seem so out of step with the rest of Europe and that so much of our political response to crime and offenders is influenced by the United States.

The United States, as Chapter 1 suggested, is a country with the highest per capita imprisonment rate in the world (and this is growing); it is a country in which electioneering politicians vie with each other in the extent of their support for the death penalty; it is a country in which they execute young people; it is a country in which public expenditure on prisons is outstripping health and education. Rationally, one might think, there is little to learn from such a country. Domestically, in England and Wales, politicians would have us believe that the reason for their support of the United States' get-tough stance on crime and criminals is because the US crime rate is declining – in fact this belief is based on flawed criminal statistics.[6] Nevertheless there are things which can be drawn from the United States' criminal justice practice, and from the recent experience with 'boot camps'[7] – although, perhaps inevitably, this is more of a lesson in what not to do rather than what should be done.

The United States has experimented with boot camps since the early 1980s, and their use has expanded to over half the States (National Institute of Justice 1994). There is no national boot camp 'model'; there are boot camps for adults and juveniles, men and

women, boys and girls; and there are variations in the regimes
between different boot camps (see below). What all boot camps
have in common, however, is a significant emphasis within the
regime on harsh military-style structure, rules and discipline. The
National Institute of Justice, a research and development agency of
the US government, traces the origins of boot camps to the crisis of
prison overcrowding in the States (and the associated escalating
costs of imprisonment), and to the inherent appeal of 'intermediate' sanctions. The appeal of boot camps, it has been argued, is
vested in the way in which they satisfy the concerns which give rise
to intermediate sanctions or, to put it another way, in their ability to
be 'all things to all people'. That is, boot camps protect the public,
reduce institutional overcrowding, save money, punish offenders,
deter future crime and rehabilitate offenders (National Institute of
Justice 1994).

It is important, however, to draw a distinction between rhetoric
and reality. Even within the United States there is recognition that
boot camps have a certain political, media and public appeal, and
that the reality of a single measure that promises to deliver
successfully on so many goals is likely to be disappointing in implementation:

> Understandably, perhaps, proponents may find it easier to get support
> for boot camps by sticking with the rhetoric.
> To find out whether boot camps really work, however, their
> claims must be measured against the reality. (National Institute of Justice
> 1994)

Despite having been around for over a decade in the US, there is
relatively little research on their effectiveness. In a report on the
most comprehensive review so far undertaken, MacKenzie *et al.*
(1995) begin by making reference to the rhetorical appeal of boot
camps, and continue with an indication of the wide variation in
regimes; including the extent to which they include rehabilitative
or educative programmes, and how these factors may influence
measures of effectiveness:

> Since their inception in 1983, boot camp prisons...have enjoyed con-
> siderable popular support. The programs have been enthusiastically
> embraced because they are designed to save scarce correctional dollars
> by reducing time served in institutions while simultaneously providing

adequate *punishment* by virtue of the quasi-military environment, strict schedule, and daily work assignment... In contrast to other intermediate sanctions, they are perceived as alternative sanctions with 'teeth' – an imperative in the current political climate...

Boot camp prisons are distinguished from other correctional programs by their emphasis on physical labor, exercise, and a military-style atmosphere... Most are designed for young offenders convicted of nonviolent crimes who do not have a prior history of imprisonment...

Many boot camp prisons also offer greater access to rehabilitative programming, such as drug treatment/education or academic education, than would be available in a traditional prison... In large part, however, the appeal of such programs stems from their promise of providing an attractive intermediate sanction within severely overcrowded correctional systems...

Although all of the boot camp prisons use military basic training as a model, they differ considerably in other respects... One of the largest differences among programs is the amount of time in the daily schedule that is devoted to work, drill, and physical training versus such treatment-type activities as counselling, drug treatment, or academic education... Another large difference among programs is in the type of community supervision provided for program graduates... With this in mind, one might well expect the impact of the programs on inmates to differ as a function of heterogeneity in type of offenders selected, program rigor, daily schedule of activities, and community supervision intensity. (MacKenzie *et al.* 1995: 1–3, original emphasis)

MacKenzie *et al.* (1995) then report on their study of the effectiveness of boot camps in reducing recidivism. The research was conducted in eight States and recidivism rates for boot camp 'completers' were compared with up to three 'control' groups (boot camp dropouts, prison parolees and probationers). On the basis of their analysis MacKenzie *et al.* drew some fairly unequivocal conclusions: they postulated that if the military-style components common to all regimes were instrumental in reducing recidivism, then a consistent pattern of results would be obtained for all the boot camps in the study. Such a consistent outcome was not found. On this basis it was concluded (*ibid.* p. 351) that *military-style structure, drill and discipline do not of themselves reduce recidivism.*

There were differences of results between boot camps and 'control' groups, however, and these can helpfully be explored. Firstly, no evidence was found in four States (half of the sample) that boot camps had *any* impact on programme completers. For two of these four States this conclusion was based on the absence of significant recidivism rates between boot camp and control group samples; and in the other two States this conclusion was based on 'sampling effects' (that is, there were no significant recidivism differences between boot camp completers and boot camp dropouts).

The results for three of the remaining boot camps did show lower than estimated recidivism rates, but the research could not isolate the specific programme components responsible for this result. What the research did demonstrate, however, was that these 'successful' programmes all shared certain factors or characteristics in common that were not equally shared with other boot camps. Boot camps with lower than estimated recidivism rates:

- only accepted offenders who would otherwise have gone to prison;
- only accepted offenders on a voluntary basis (the alternative being prison);
- had a higher percentage of offenders dismissed from programmes prior to completion (that is those who did not comply with the regime were more likely to be excluded);
- had longer programmes or sentences (over 120 days);
- had a higher level of emphasis on treatment and education within the regime; and
- provided a more intensive form of community supervision post-release.

'Successful' boot camps, therefore, tended to select offenders who were more likely to be receptive and cooperative (excluding those who proved not to be), and they provided more help or assistance to offenders during sentence and on release. Both of these sets of factors, MacKenzie *et al.* concluded, were likely to account for the more successful result. This conclusion was supported by the findings from the only boot camp which produced worse recidivism results than control group samples, i.e. in the boot camp where there was an almost total absence of treatment-oriented activity in the regime and minimal supervision post-release – an amplification of offending behaviour resulted. Getting tough, it seems, produced more hardened criminals.

MacKenzie *et al.* suggested that their results were not very surprising given previous research which showed the benefits of certain 'treatment' programmes, and the negative results obtained from other programmes designed to promote fear or to shock offenders. If the military-style components of boot camps have been shown to have no positive impact on offenders, then there can be no justification for such programme elements. Moreover, if as the research indicates it is the treatment-oriented aspects of regimes which show some benefit (including those aspects of the treatment which take place in the community), then there is nothing in the research to justify any custodial programme and many more reasons to promote community-based treatment of offenders.

Indications from the Home Office are that custodial programmes for children in England and Wales will have a significant emphasis placed on education and training. But if it is the education and training which are the important or desirable programme components then why are these not being provided in the community? The provision of education and training is not a justification for establishing and dispensing new forms of custodial sentences. These concerns were made clear by magistrates when they were surveyed about their opinions on the establishment of Secure Training Centres (O'Mahony and Haines 1993). Such measures are never likely successfully to punish conformity into the heads of young people, and the apparent political gains to be made from get-tough policies can never justify such approaches.

Research has consistently demonstrated the negative effects of punishment-oriented institutional programmes. Community-based measures, however, particularly those which operate within a normalising principle, have produced much more positive results. The remainder of this chapter now explores such approaches.

The community-based treatment of offenders and issues of effectiveness

Within the criminological literature there is a distinction between *instrumental* and *normative* measures. Instrumental measures are primarily punishment or deterrence-based, with no attempt at treatment or rehabilitation, and the aim is simply to punish or censure – often publicly. Normative measures are treatment-based or rehabilitative in orientation, attempting to restore the offender into the community in some way. Instrumental sanctions tend to be institutionally-based (that is, custody), but in more recent times there have been a number of developments of instrumental community-based measures (for example electronic monitoring). Conversely, normative measures tend to be community-based, but 'treatment' can take place within an institution; which might be a physical building with restricted access or a group in a community setting run along institutional lines (that is, no involvement of individuals or groups outside the treatment group). Within the breadth of normative sanctions it is possible to make a distinction (broadly) between two types of programme: (i) those which focus on 'criminogenic' need and target intervention on changing offending behaviour directly, and (ii) those which are more community-focused and which aim to change the relationship between the 'offender' and their social situation in such a way as to diminish offending behaviour. These general distinctions within the overall category of normative treatments (set out in Table 6.1) are important because they have implications for issues of effectiveness.

Control theory

It is helpful in considering the overall classification of programme characteristics and effectiveness outlined in Table 6.1 to think in terms of control theory (Hirschi 1969; Lilly *et al.* 1989; see also Tittle 1996). Most criminology is concerned with identified offenders, and much of the criminological enterprise is concerned with explaining or trying to explain why some people offend. In other words much criminology takes conformity for granted and assumes the 'problem' is one of explaining deviance. Control theory reverses the problem and questions the assumption of the natural order of conformity. In other words it does not try to explain deviance, or why people offend, but asks the question – why do people conform?

Table 6.1 Categories of normative treatment

	A: *Criminogenic focus*	B: *Situational focus*
1: Institutionally-based	1+A Poor effectiveness prognosis	1+B Limited effectiveness prognosis
2: Community-based	2+A Weak effectiveness prognosis	2+B Strongest effectiveness prognosis

According to control theory, deviance or offending behaviour occurs when an individual's *bonds to society*, or to groups or individuals within society, become weak or broken:

> The more weakened the groups to which [the individual] belongs, the less he depends on them, the more he consequently depends only on himself and recognises no other rules of conduct than what are founded on his private interests. (Durkheim 1951, quoted in Hirschi 1969: 18)

In other words, in its simplest form, control theory suggests that people conform because they have good reason to; and where there are no or few good reasons to conform then deviance or offending can occur. To understand the mechanisms involved in this process of conformity the nature of an individuals' *bonds* and the concept of *society* need to be explored in a little more detail.

Coming as it did at a time when psychological models predicated on individual factors, dominated explanations of human behaviour, Hirschi's use of the social bond was the source of some confusion. For Hirschi, however, the social bond is avowedly sociological in nature, that is a dynamic social product made and remade continually through social interaction. Thus control theory locates personal control through social control and shifts the burden of control on to the social system as well as the individual. This, according to control theory, does not mean that society should act in a necessarily condemnatory manner or with exclusionary measures, but 'that regulation of the individual must come through integration into the social order rather than through social isolation or punishment' (Lilly *et al.* 1989: 113).

Conformity, therefore, is socially-produced and constructed behaviour; it is the product of a range of ongoing social processes which maintain an individual's social bonds, and where the nature of the bond has four key elements:

1. *Attachment* of the individual to others. An emotional connection and sensitivity to the opinions, feelings and expectations of others, whereby the individual internalises the norms of society through sustained interaction.
2. *Commitment* to internalised norms. A rational decision based on accumulated investments and the interest or dividends an individual gains through remaining committed to 'shared' norms,

coupled with an assessment of the losses that would result if the norms were broken.

3. *Involvement* with others. The constructive use of time, either through work or leisure, that reduces the opportunity to be deviant and gives practical meaning to the more cognitive elements of the bond.

4. *Belief* in the norms of society. A term used more sociologically than psychologically to indicate an assent to certain norms or values rather than deeply-held convictions.

Once again, the concept of society as it is used in control theory is more sociological than psychological, and includes a whole range of social relationships ranging from individual interaction with family and friends, through to schools, the workplace, leisure groups and the local community, but also including macro-level institutions such as political parties or the state. An individual may be bonded with any or all of these aspects of 'society' to a greater or lesser extent, and the precise meaning of these bonds for the individual may vary, but according to control theory the nexus of an individual's bonds to society (in whatever form these take) are central to conforming behaviour.

Control theory is not without its critics (Box 1981: 153), but it does provide a framework within which it can be better understood why certain approaches to the treatment of offenders are more likely to be effective than others. Firstly, control theory sharpens the fallacy of punishment as a deterrent to criminal behaviour, as punishment (in general, but particularly where this involves removal of an individual from their social context, that is *1A* and *1B* in Table 6.1) damages the social bond and directly inhibits the maintenance of processes which produce conformity. Secondly, control theory helps us to understand why treatments focused on 'criminogenic need' (that is *2A* in Table 6.1) have a limited prognosis of success, because such programmes rarely address aspects of the bond but seek to inhibit criminal behaviour without paying sufficient attention to incentives to conform. And lastly, control theory helps to explain the relative success of community-based situational interventions (that is *2B* in Table 6.1) precisely because such programmes have the best chance of establishing and building upon an individual's bonds to society.

Control theory of course may look good on paper, but to what extent is it supported by empirical evidence? In fact there is a long historical theme within the research literature which supports the central ideas of control theory.

Establishing community ties and the importance of social situations

In the early 1970s the Home Office published a study which examined the impact on teenage boys' offending behaviour of different hostel regimes (Sinclair 1971). This research found wide variations in offending patterns across the different regimes while the boys remained in the hostel environment, but no similar pattern of variation once the boys returned to the community. In fact there was no evident relationship between hostel performance and subsequent behaviour; some boys, for example, performed well in the hostel environment itself, but relatively badly on release. For Sinclair this emphasised the importance of immediate environmental factors for behaviour rather than an individual's past history (Sinclair 1971: 137).

Another study which clearly shows the importance of situational factors for an individual's behaviour concerned the effects on re-offending of a modified borstal regime (Bottoms and McClintock 1973). This research was based on a sophisticated reconviction predictor and the outcomes for boys who underwent either the modified borstal regime or a traditional regime. The results showed that both groups of boys had subsequent reconviction rates squarely within the predicted range, that is there were no measurable differences between the two institutional regimes (Bottoms and McClintock 1973: 275). This finding supports our general statement about institutionally-based programmes above, but of further significance are the more detailed results of the research. While traditional or modified borstal regimes appeared to have no impact on re-offending, an assessment of post-release social problem scores were highly correlated with subsequent offending. Those young boys with high post-borstal levels of social problems had statistically significantly higher than predicted reconviction rates, while those with the lowest social problem scores had lower than predicted reconviction rates (*ibid.*: 379). Thus, the research demonstrated that the nature of the social situation that borstal releasees were living in for the year following their release had a significant and measurable affect on the likelihood of their offending. Association with deviant peer groups, a lack of constructive leisure activities, and low levels of family involvement were factors more likely to lead to re-offending (*ibid.*: 368).

The findings for borstal boys are supported in the case of adults by research into the Massachusetts State Department of Corrections' reintegrative programme (LeClair 1984, 1985). Based on research which demonstrated the negative impact of imprisonment and the general failure of traditional rehabilitative programmes, the reintegrative programme was designed to minimise disruption of social ties on imprisonment and to facilitate, develop and reinforce positive community links (LeClair 1985: 442).

An overall evaluation of the Massachusetts reintegrative programme is not available, but recidivism rates have been provided for three aspects of the programme: furlough participants (that is, those who participated in structured home leave), those released from pre-release centres, and security classification on release (which may be seen as an indicator of the type and regime of the prison). Comparative recidivism rates for prisoners who participated in these elements of the programme are provided in Table 6.2.

These results clearly indicate positive benefits accruing from participation in elements of the reintegrative programme; recidivism rates for those prisoners who participated in more community-oriented activities designed to build links with the outside were significantly lower. The Massachusetts findings reinforce, therefore, the importance of situational factors and social bonds for subsequent behaviour.

Table 6.2 Average recidivism rates for reintegrative programme participants and non-participants

		Recidivism rates for participants (%)	Recidivism rates for non-participants (%)
Home furlough		12	29
Pre-release centres		14	25
Security classification	Max	30	n/a
	Medium	23	n/a
	Min	17	n/a

There are difficulties, however, in accepting at face value the significance of research results for adults and transposing these onto juveniles. Processes of social integration that are likely to be relevant for juveniles are not necessarily the same as for adults.[8] A central theme of this book is that due recognition must be given to: (i) the special status of children as individuals who have few legal or social 'rights' and who must, therefore, be afforded an element of protection, and (ii) that children do not have the cognitive maturity of adults and therefore require special understanding. For these reasons the detail of reintegrative programmes designed for adults is not dealt with here, although this does not mean that research into adults should be discounted: the principle that reintegrative regimes are more beneficial and more likely to lead to a reduction in offending is transferable. But for the details of what such programmes might look like in the case of younger people it in necessary to concentrate upon research which has focused explicitly on this age-group.

Meta-analysis: lessons for practice

Meta-analysis is a recently developed technique for analysing large numbers of research studies. It involves conducting sophisticated statistical tests on the results obtained from empirical research studies to determine whether any overall conclusions about the efficacy of interventions in reducing offending can be discerned. Lipsey (1992) has carried out such tests on a sample of over 400 (mostly American, but also Canadian and British) research studies into the effects of various treatments on delinquency. Lipsey's analysis and findings are quite complex and it is not proposed to summarise all of his results here, but one set of results stood out and we will concentrate on these.

From all of the variables analysed by Lipsey (and there were 15 overall categories directly related to treatment issues), the factor with the strongest relationship to outcomes was the type of treatment an individual received. These effects were both positive and negative:

> There is striking consistency in both the juvenile justice and non-juvenile justice treatments. In both cases, the more structured and focused treat-

ments (e.g., behavioural, skill-oriented) and multimodal treatments seem to be more effective than the less structured and [less] focused approaches (e.g., counseling)...

Further, a couple of treatment categories appear to produce negative effects – most notably, deterrence treatments. (Lipsey 1992: 123–4)

Lipsey's meta-analysis, therefore, provides clear support for the harmful effects of punitive approaches towards the treatment of juveniles: a conclusion which other meta-analyses have also drawn. Gendreau (1983), for example, found that when behaviour modification techniques are 'imposed' upon offenders they are ineffective. Furthermore, Gendreau found that when programmes of intervention focus on antisocial behaviour (that which others have called 'criminogenic need') these too are ineffective and can result in an amplification of deviance due to an overemphasis on such behaviour to the neglect of more positive behaviour. This echoes what was said above (see Table 6.1) and earlier comments about the professional sterility of new orthodoxy practice (see Chapter 2).

When Lipsey is talking about structured and focused treatments, therefore, he does not mean programmes of intervention that focus on offending behaviour, nor does he mean programmes that are managed within a strict administrative or bureaucratic set of requirements about reporting and so on (as one might see reflected in the National Standards approach). Structured and focused treatments in this context means: (i) programmes which have clear aims; (ii) where these aims are primarily about promoting positive behaviour; and (iii) where there are clear steps for achieving these objectives, including treatment types which enhance an individuals' capacity to realise these positive objectives. Where such programmes have been successfully implemented, Lipsey's meta-analysis demonstrates reductions in offending of between 20 and 40 per cent that are directly attributable to the 'treatment' (as opposed to other factors, for example maturation).

The results of Lipsey's research are extremely important and provide significant support for the general thrust of our arguments, but it would not be wholly appropriate to simply transpose these findings into the British context. There are two issues to consider here: (i) the general message that punitive deterrence-based practices are harmful and that positive results can be achieved from community-based treatments, and (ii) the precise nature of these community-based treatments. There is no problem with the first of these issues; the notion that some treatments are effective while others are detrimental is clear progress on previous 'nothing works' statements, and is the product of detailed and sophisticated research. The second issue requires some further consideration.

Institutionally-based treatment programmes

Although Lipsey's meta-analysis included some Canadian and British research, it was predominantly based on American studies. The difficulty here, therefore, is whether it is appropriate to transpose the results from research which are based on a particular country's practices into other countries with different cultures. The answer to this problem is a qualified yes. The types of interventions commonly found in the North American context straddle the categories of treatment identified as *1B* and *2B* in Table 6.1 above. In other words, the North American response to the treatment of delinquents tends to be heavily programme-based, where such programmes tend to emphasise closed 'institutional' regimes and where less emphasis is placed on broader situational factors. While there are important institutional aspects to effective programmes, situational matters must also receive attention. Much of the thrust of this chapter has comprised evidence which: (i) demonstrates the negative effects of punitive deterrence-based approaches, (ii) depathologises individuals and re-articulates the problems of delinquency as social problems, and (iii) emphasises the importance of situational factors for behaviour. The material presented so far supports this general stance on these matters, but account must also be taken of the research which shows positive benefits accruing from institutionally-based treatment programmes.

Effective institutional programmes

Within the Lipsey (1992) and Gendreau (1983) studies reported above (see also, Lipsey 1995), much is made of the significance of pro-social modelling coupled with cognitive/behavioural therapies in treatment programmes. In the UK context there has been a considerable amount of interest in cognitive offender therapies in recent years (Knott 1995; Lucas *et al.* 1992; Raynor *et al.* 1996; Weaver and Bensted 1992). The basis of cognitive treatment programmes is the idea that some individuals lack certain personal characteristics and possess others which tend to mean that they respond to situations by committing offences rather than being able to see more positive alternative courses of action. Cognitive therapy, therefore, comprises a programme of treatment whereby an individual's cognitive skills are improved such that they have a greater ability to appraise situations and respond more positively to them. The mechanism for delivering cognitive therapy is almost exclusively a lengthy and closed highly-structured groupwork programme (Ross 1988). In North America, quite impressive success rates are claimed for such programmes with re-offending rates of around 20 per cent of programme participants and 70 per cent for control groups, but the results of UK-based programmes have been more modest (see Knott 1995).

In an Australian context, Christopher Trotter (1993) reports on an experiment in the use of an 'integrated supervision model' – based partly on cognitive models. This experiment involved training Community Corrections Officers in the principles of effective supervision which were identified from the research (including that of Gendreau 1983 above) and defined in the following terms:

1. the use of pro-social modelling and reinforcement;
2. the use of problem-solving (that is, cognitive skills training);
3. the use of empathy; and
4. focusing on high-risk offenders.

Fundamental to the integrated supervision model, therefore, were two of the basic ingredients of effective offender interventions – pro-social modelling and cognitive skills therapy. The offenders who participated in the experimental group programme achieved lower breach rates than those in the control group (and on breach tended to receive lower rates of imprisonment), and they demonstrated lower recidivism rates. However, the results of this Australian experiment are further interesting because they demonstrate: (i) that community-based professionals working with offenders can be successfully trained in effective treatment methods, (ii) the importance of this training for establishing coherent and effective treatment programmes (that is, what is generally known as 'programme integrity', see Hollin 1995), and (iii) that properly trained officers deliver coherent treatment programmes which are successful in reducing re-offending (Trotter 1993).

The importance of these research results in demonstrating that positive community-based interventions can be effective is not to be underestimated. But the difficulty with these results concerns (i) the fact that they have been delivered to older offenders, (ii) the extent to which they have been delivered in lengthy and closed highly-structured programmes, and (iii) the level of attention paid to broader situational issues in individuals' lives.

It is not appropriate simply to transfer effective adult-oriented treatment programmes to juveniles and it is essential that treatment programmes are sensitive to the age of participants. A lengthy, closed and highly-structured programme may be appropriate for adults, but it is much more difficult to engage juveniles in such a process, especially those of a much younger age. It would be quite wrong to deliver inappropriate programmes to juveniles which then result in failure (or a lack of success), and then to blame this on the juveniles. It may be possible to modify cognitive therapies in such a way as to sensitise delivery methods to the age of the offender, but some adaptation of adult-oriented programmes is necessary. Part of this adaptation will concern the extent to which community-based treatments for juveniles take place in closed groupwork sessions and the extent to which these programmes are institutional in character (see Table 6.1 above). Part of this adaptation will concern the degree of attention paid to broader situational factors – indeed Robert Ross, the leading proponent of cognitive offender therapy, argues for the importance of dealing with situational issues alongside structured cognitive programmes.

The present state of research-based knowledge does not allow for a full resolution of these issues. In part this is because research reports rarely, if ever, describe in sufficiently comprehensive detail the actual content of community-based programmes; and in part it is because much learning must be done in practice. Research can, however, provide some pointers for the direction in which practice may usefully be developed.

Reconciling institutional and community-based programmes?

In establishing a framework of offender treatments in Table 6.1 above, a distinction was drawn between institutionally-based and community-based programmes – identifying the latter category as the more beneficial. One of the problems with some of the research reported above, therefore, is the extent to which treatment programmes that are conducted in the community in fact replicate the institutional environment (and, by implication, are less likely to be effective). One of the best-known studies on the differences in outcomes from institutionally vs community-based programmes is based on the 'Massachusetts de- institutionalisation experiment' for juvenile offenders (Coates *et al.* 1978, and Coates 1981).

The Massachusetts research found that while there were some identifiable benefits from institutionally-based treatments, these gains were mainly evident while individuals remained in the closed setting (young people tended to comply with the rules of institutional regimes). Of much more significance for subsequent reductions in offending was the quality of the individuals' social experiences on return to the community (cf. Bottoms and McClintock 1973). And in terms of community-based programmes themselves, the Massachusetts research found that regimes with a greater extent and quality of community linkages yielded lower recidivism rates than the more closed or institutional regimes (Coates 1981: 91).

Miller and Ohlin (1985) have summarised the overall findings of the Massachusetts juvenile research in the following manner:

> Perhaps the most important finding of this study, however, pertained to the short-term impact of most forms of [institutional] treatment. Although the results documented positive changes in youth... these changes correlated less highly with recidivism than the experiences of youth before adjudication and after release from the programs to unsupervised living in the community. It thus appears that youth correctional programs will have limited short-term effects unless they engage the relationships and problems a youth must deal with when free of correctional supervision. In short, community-based programs must be more fully integrated into the everyday life of the community and should allow for greater continuity between the more intensive and isolated group therapy programs and those which deal with problems arising in programs with more extensive contacts and relationships of youth in the community. (Miller and Ohlin 1985: 26)

Two related issues arise from the Massachusetts research. The first concerns the nature of community ties, and the second is related to the extent to which community-based programmes replicate institutional environments or are truly community-based. Coates defines the 'extent' of community ties as the, 'frequency and duration of interaction with people in the community' (Coates 1981: 89).

And the 'quality' of community relationships is defined in terms of treatment programme participants' access to community resources, participation in decisions about their interaction in the community, participation in decisions about what and how behaviour is punished or rewarded, and their sense of fairness as to how they are treated in the community (*ibid.*: 90). For Coates, therefore, simply transposing an institutional regime or programme into smaller settings, closer to local communities but with no material change to the treatment programme, is not what effective community-based treatments should be like. A truly community-based programme aims to increase the extent and quality of community relationships in a purposeful manner such that there is a greater sense of continuity between 'the more intensive and closed group-work aspects of treatment programmes and those aspects of programmes which deal with problems of youth in the community' (cf. Miller and Ohlin 1985).

Thus, the Massachusetts research does not necessarily preclude an element of more closed treatment processes (such as work on cognitive skills) as a part of overall treatment programmes, but it does suggest that these should not be the emphasis of treatment programmes and proper regard must be paid to situational factors and issues of community relationships.

Further empirical support for this position was obtained from the results of the Intermediate Treatment Evaluation Project (ITEP) (Bottoms 1995). Among other things, this research demonstrated that certain types of heavy-end intermediate treatment (IT) programmes were relatively more effective than custody, ordinary supervision (which tended to be less structured, cf. Lipsey 1992), and other forms of heavy-end IT. The more successful projects tended to be delivered through an 'IT Centre' which had an identifiable philosophy which integrated an anti-offending stance with a pro-social modelling approach. Offenders who participated in these projects reported significantly lower personal and social problem levels 12 months after treatment. The results of the ITEP are not entirely unequivocal, partly because, perhaps, the supervision of offenders on IT in this country has tended to be rather limited, retaining a focus on criminogenic interventions (that is, the offending curriculum) and not developing the use of more positive reinforcement programmes. But there is, nevertheless, sufficient material in the results of the ITEP to indicate the importance of a pro-social philosophy for projects which also pay attention to offenders' wider social experiences.

What might effective community-based programmes of offender intervention look like?

This has been a long and at times complex journey through the research into the effectiveness of community-based criminal justice sanctions for young offenders. Contrary to the pessimism of the 'nothing works' doctrine, it has been shown that some things do work in terms of successfully integrating young people into community structures and reducing offending, as well as showing that some things definitely do not work and can be counterproductive. By way of a conclusion to this chapter, therefore, a synopsis is provided below in Table 6.3 which summarises the characteristics of community-based programmes of intervention that the research evidence indicates as most effective.

Table 6.3 A synopsis of the characteristics of effective community-based offender intervention programmes

Modality	Characteristics of effective programmes	Things which do not work (or which are less effective)
Location I	In the community and as integrated as possible with local family, school, and other support structures	Institutional programmes (including community-based programmes which replicate an institutional environment)
Location II	An identifiable centre or project which forms a focus for the programme	Programmes which lack a sense of identity
Philosophy	A pro-social ethos. An anti-offending stance coupled with empathy for the individual	Vindictive, punitive, blaming attitude towards young people
General approach	Constructive and aimed at giving individual good reasons to conform through investment	Deterrent approaches which try to frighten or achieve conformity through punishment

Table 6.3 *continued*

Modality	Characteristics of effective programmes	Things which do not work (or which are less effective)
Programme content I	Should be positive and encourage/develop desirable behaviours	A negative emphasis on offending behaviour (criminogenic need)
Programme content II	Structured group or individual work to develop cognitive/social skills	Structured work which tends to stigmatise
Programme content III	Structured individual work which aims to tackle problems individuals experience in their daily lives	Ignoring reality of social experience of young people
Programme content IV	Structured individual work which aims to develop and improve social ties	Unstructured or unfocused individual work
Regime	Flexible and responsive approaches which put boundaries around individual consistent with other elements above and below	Bureaucratic or administrative requirements unrelated to programme content
Appropriateness I	Programme should be tailored to the characteristics and needs of individual	A lack of necessary consideration for the individual
Appropriateness II	Intensity of programme should reflect the seriousness of offending and risk presented by individual	Overly interventionist programmes for less serious offending, and insufficiently responsive programmes for more serious offenders presenting greater risk
Programme integrity I	A consistent message or ethos should be presented by all staff and should pervade all aspects of the programme	Giving mixed messages
Programme integrity II	A complete programme (individually tailored) should be delivered consistent with all of the above	Do not select buffet-style from range of programme elements and characteristics

7

Some Contemporary Concerns

Much of this book has been taken up with considering the central principles of youth justice practice as laid down in the 1980s, and updating and adapting them to the contemporary context. Yet there are features of the current landscape which were simply missing when many of these basic principles were being developed. From the new phenomena, those have been selected which seem to be already having an impact upon the daily business of practice, and which seem likely to continue to do so in the future. These issues are: National Standards, risk assessment, restorative justice and young people and criminal responsibility.

National standards and management control

Ten years ago no-one thought that the government would issue documents which specified in some detail how social workers and probation officers should write court reports and supervise offenders, but National Standards (Home Office[1] 1992, 1995) are here and they appear to be a fairly fixed feature of the modern criminal justice system. There are eight separate Standards covering different areas of practice: the preparation of PSRs, Probation Orders, Supervision Orders, Community Service Orders, Combination Orders, Bail Information schemes, Management of Hostels and the supervision of offenders before and after release from custody. In the government's terms:

> The aims of these National Standards are to strengthen the supervision of offenders in the community, providing punishment and a disciplined

programme for offenders, building on the skill and experience of practitioners and service managers:

by setting clear **requirements** for supervision, understood by all concerned

by enabling service practitioners' **professional judgement** to be exercised within a framework of **accountability**

by encouraging the adoption of **good practice** including the development of local practice guidelines (which should be in line with the requirements set by the standards)

by ensuring that supervision is delivered fairly, **consistently** and **without improper discrimination**

by setting a priority on the **protection of the public** from re-offending (and from fear of crime)

by establishing the importance of considering the **effect of crime on victims**

by ensuring the public can have confidence that supervision in the community is an **effective punishment** and a means to help offenders become responsible members of the community. (original emphasis, Home Office 1995: 2)

Thus the Standards contain mainly procedural requirements in respect of such things as the speed and frequency with which certain tasks should be completed by the supervising officer (that is timescales for completing PSRs, contact between supervising officer and supervisee and so on), the manner in which social workers or probation officers should undertake certain tasks (such as the content of court reports, the challenging nature of supervision and so on), and how non-compliance by supervisees should be dealt with (for example breach proceedings and so forth).

The previous government clearly favoured National Standards and invested a great deal of significance in them. The present Home Office Ministers show no signs of departing from that enthusiasm. Those working within the government inspectorates also appear to highly value National Standards as, *inter alia*, they evidently preoccupy inspectors and the reports they compile (HMIP 1994; SSI 1994). In local agencies, too, both senior and middle managers appear to value the extent to which National Standards add a hitherto absent clarity to the function of a managers' role (that function is now, in large part, to manage the Standards into practice). And at the level of youth justice practitioners, or front-line service providers, reaction to National Standards has been one which generally welcomes them for the clarity they bring to the role and expectations of practitioners.

For the most part therefore (although not universally – see, for example, Stone 1995) – there has been little questioning of the Standards in any way, and debates in the field tend to concern not whether National Standards are a good or a bad thing and whether practitioners should aim to work within them or not, but how compliance can be improved. The effect has been to diminish or even destroy a necessary discussion concerning some fundamental issues which need to be aired and debated, especially as these Standards seem to be here to stay. Three basic issues can be identified: (i) the purpose of National Standards, (ii) their legitimacy, and (iii) managerialist control vs professional activity. Consideration of each of these questions now follows and this section then concludes with some suggestions as to how the Standards might be approached in practice.

The real purpose of National Standards

First of all, it is absolutely essential to be clear about the purpose of the National Standards. Just as Home Office Circular 30/1992 'Young People and the Youth Court' was the government's managerialist attempt at controlling the manner in which local agencies implemented the CJA 1991 (see Chapter 3), so too National Standards represent the government's managerialist attempts to control the activities of local agency managers and the practices of frontline service providers. The bottom line is that National Standards are about control.

The exercise of control by government and its departments over the activities of local agencies is not inherently a bad thing. It is not a bad thing, for example, if this control is exercised responsibly, but there are dangers. Control can veer off into a cosy consensus between government and local agencies that does little or nothing to promote the interests of the wider population (Peters 1986). Or control can sink into the cynical political manipulation of local agencies by politicians seeking to do no more than promote their private and party interests.

Those who doubt the potential dangers of ceding control over the details of local practice into the hands of politicians need only look at the differences between the 1992 and 1995 Standards to see the impact of different political thinking on the content of the document. For example, new in the 1995 Standards is the explicit notion that community sentences should be actively punitive. The facility to manipulate policy and practice offered by such managerial control mechanisms is almost irresistible to politicians, but it is anathema to professional organisations and services which are dedicated to public service.

Mechanisms of control, like National Standards, that link central with local government in ways which are devoid of checks and balances, and where the power differential between parties is deeply skewed are, or should be, matters of great concern to us all.

The legitimacy of National Standards

On what basis can and does government develop National Standards? This is an important question and it goes right to the heart of the issue of control. The United Kingdom does not possess a codified legal system (as in many other European countries), nor does it have a written constitution (in the manner of the USA), but established conventions do exist concerning the respective roles of the various parts of the state which are more or less binding. In short, the government can make whatever laws it sees fit – the so-called principle of 'parliamentary sovereignty' – but the government has no power to instruct others about how the law must be implemented. This separation of powers is what establishes the independence of the judiciary and the police, and it applies equally to the activities of local authorities in the discharge of their statutory duties, responsibilities and powers. Government, therefore, has no legitimate power to tell a local authority or any of its employees how a law must be implemented.

It is generally accepted, however, that government has a legitimate interest in the activities of various state agencies because it provides the funds necessary for these agencies to operate. Traditionally, on the basis of this legitimate interest, government has provided advice and guidance to local agencies on how aspects of particular pieces of legislation may be implemented and systems have been developed to check local action in this respect (mainly through various Inspectorates, but also more recently through the National Audit Office and the Audit Commission). If a local agency is failing to implement legislation effectively then it will most likely receive advice from government, further failure can result in certain circumstances in financial penalties and ultimately (again in certain circumstances) with the government stepping in to run services. Advice from government is quite common, a stiffer response is very rare.

In the UK, therefore, the government makes the law and while it has no power to tell local agencies how the law must be implemented, it has a legitimate interest in local action which allows the government to give advice and guidance. It is on this basis that the Home Office has produced National Standards for the Supervision of Offenders in the Community (Home Office 1992, 1995).

In the Introductions to these Standards, however, the Home Office appears to invest them with a compulsory quality. Under the heading of 'what is the status of the Standards?' the Home Office says that local agencies 'are expected to follow the guidance and requirements in the standards' (Home Office 1992: 1), and the 1995 Standard contains the following emboldened statement:

> Where, in exceptional circumstances, a judgement is taken to depart from a requirement of the standard, this should be authorised by the appropriate line manager and the reasons for it should be clearly recorded and justified. (Home Office 1995: 1)

To talk, in a document supposedly giving guidance, of the *requirements* of the Standard, to talk in terms of an *expectation* of compliance, and to talk of non-compliance only in *exceptional circumstances* moves National Standards out of the realm of the government's legitimate interest and crosses the boundary of the separation of powers between government and local agency. Guidance is no longer guidance when compliance becomes expected. The constitutional limits on the ability of government to compel local agencies has been overstepped.

Managerialist control vs professional activity

There is an interesting developmental sequence to community sentences in modern penal systems. Eighteenth century community sentences tended to be fairly short and sharp – a public whipping or an hour in the pillory or head stocks (Ignatieff 1989). Whatever else, these punishments were over and done with quickly and did not rely on any active ongoing participation on the part of the offender. In the twentieth century, however, community sentences became more demanding for offenders as compliance with these sentences increasingly meant routine, long-term adherence to a series of bureaucratic behavioural control mechanisms, reporting requirements and so on. More recently, while these offender-control mechanisms have remained in place,[2] a whole new set of supervisor-control mechanisms have been established. The bureaucratisation of community sentences has involved an increasing level of specificity in the determination of precisely what a community sentence should involve. There is thus a necessity for a greater level of prescription in the construction of community sentences and in the mechanisms of managing those responsible for the conduct of the community sentences.

Quite apart from the constitutional importance of limiting the government's extent of legitimate interest in local action, there is an agenda hidden within the National Standards approach which must be brought out into the open; this concerns the extent to which the Standards represent attempts by government departments to control the activities of managers and practitioners in local agencies, achieved at a direct cost to the professionalism of local agency staff. Professional activity by its very nature involves reasonable levels of discretion and individual action predicated on judgements made in the context of individual situations and circumstances. National Standards are aimed at producing the same response in a series of given situations, such that practice becomes predictable and consistent within a framework established by those who have no necessary professional expertise and who are distant from the point of service provision.

Quite apart, therefore, from National Standards establishing a set of minimum professional standards for the supervision of offenders in the community, they actually diminish professionalism. What the Standards actually establish is a set of minimum *procedural* standards for the management of community-based supervision: procedures which specify how long certain tasks should take, how frequently certain activities should occur and so on. The maximisation of such procedural controls can only be obtained at the diminution of professional decision-making.

Professional practice and National Standards

This unpromising background inevitably prompts the question as to how a defensible professional practice can be sustained within a National Standards context. The essential approach which in the spirit of this book needs to be adopted in relation to Standards is one which uses the utility to the person under supervision as its touchstone. As this section has already demonstrated, National Standards have been designed to serve the interests of centralised authority. At the same time, their unquestioned acceptance by local agencies has been much facilitated by the ways in which the Standards promote the prioritisation of working practices which serve their own organisational interests. What is required, in the approach proposed here, is to seek out and rescue from the Standards those elements which allow for the basic interests of children to be pursued and promoted.

To begin with, the Standards do provide a statement of service which users can expect to receive. The single most serious criticism which this book has levelled against youth justice practice lies in the sanctioning of a disengagement from the real difficulties which young people face and which provide the precipitating conditions in which crime takes place. In the past, the most acute form of disengagement was to be found in failure to provide even a basic level of contact with young people and their families through which difficulties might be identified and addressed. National Standards offer the basic benefit of allowing such a situation to be rectified because they do offer a guaranteed level of service to which young people are entitled.

The spirit of the Standards, of course, does not encourage such a positive view of the content of contact, and contact itself is not a guarantee of either the ethical basis or practical calibre of conduct. Imagination and creativity are required to extract from the Standards every ounce of flexibility and assistance which can be wrung out of them. The 1992 version, as suggested above, was a good deal more amenable in this regard than the version produced in the dog days of 1995. Where the later version simply omits rather than amends material from the earlier, there is no reason why the advice already available should not continue to be used. Thus, while the 1995 Standards fail to deal at all with issues of discrimination and equal opportunity, the advice of three years earlier can be relied upon. If the 1995 document is to be relied upon alone, then full advantage must still be drawn from whatever latitude can be dredged from its text. Chapter 4 in its discussion of breach, provides examples of both such possibilities.

A fuller mechanism for drawing out whatever positive possibilities can be obtained from National Standards can be found in those organisations which have produced Local Standards of their own. Youth justice practitioners in 13 inner-London boroughs, for example, have produced just such a document (see Pitts *et al.* 1996) which aims to take account of issues such as race, gender and class injustice in a statement of principle and practice standards. More locally, the youth justice service in Swansea has negotiated a Local Standards statement with magistrates and other interested groups which seeks to provide a service to young people which combines guaranteed levels of contact and supervision with a positive intent to use that contact in order to respond positively to the needs of the young people concerned.

When the demands of the Standards prove unamenable to even the most determined attempts to humanise them, youth justice workers are fortunate in having a clear enough hierarchy of obligation by which their practice can be guided and defended. Whatever the dogmatic bluster with which National Standards surround themselves, their legal status remains that of *advice*. Youth justice practice must be more fundamentally framed by its *statutory obligations* as enshrined in the 1933 Children and Young Persons Act and the 1989 Children Act. The welfare of the child remains the paramount test. Whenever, therefore, a conflict arises between the requirements of the Standards and the needs of children, it is clearly a children-first test which should be applied.

Risk assessment

Risk assessment is a phenomenon of the 1990s which has already reached a level of penetration into the discourse of the times, carrying it well beyond the professional enclaves in which youth justice workers operate and into the public domain. No matter of controversy in the social welfare field is now complete without some solemn reference to the quality of risk assessment already undertaken or the need for improved performance in the future.

Risk assessment is a panacea: it excuses everything that has happened in the past, it solves all the problems of tomorrow. Thus even the Home Secretary of the time called on to explain the chaining up of women prisoners during the act of giving birth or receiving treatment for terminal illness, was able to claim that shackles were justified because a 'full risk assessment' had preceded their use (*Guardian* 12 January 1996). Andy Clayton, medical director of the Southern Derbyshire Mental Health NHS Trust, looking ahead from the murder by a released mental health patient, of that patient's own mother and younger half brother, sought to reassure the public by claiming that 'strengthened risk assessment procedures' were already in place (*Guardian* 7 March 1996).

It is not the purpose of this book to look in detail at the postmodernist condition which can, without shame or irony, attach such certainty to the business of risk. Rather, a particular set of arguments will be advanced looking at the dangers of attempting unthinkingly to transfer actuarial methods into the field of human behaviour, and suggesting a way of applying risk assessment in the youth court which is consistent with the major themes of the general approach to youth justice which this book has attempted to develop.

It is worth beginning by noting the intimate connection between the rise of risk assessment rhetoric and the demonisation of young people with which this book began. Hazel Kemshall (1995), setting out to identify the precipitating factors which in her view underpin the rapid growth of interest in this area, cites six 'dangerous events' as creating the climate in which ideas of risk and dangerousness have come to dominate discussion of social welfare policies. Three of these six events specifically concentrated upon young offenders.

It is our contention that the application of checklists and scoring systems which purport to predict the risk of future offending or some other predetermined 'danger' are, at best, to be treated with scepticism. In two articles published in the *Probation Journal*, Kemshall (1995, 1996) highlights a series of caveats which need to be borne in mind when drawn into the risk assessment arena. These include:

- The danger of regarding risk assessment as a neutral, value-free technical operation. In fact it is an enterprise determined by the political and economic context within which it takes place. 'Risk' is not a shared or unproblematic concept in which everyone might be expected to take a common view. Even within the Probation Service she found that 'beliefs and definitions of risk' showed a high level of response variation within and between teams and grades...it is already clear that there is no consensus' (p. 2). In such circumstances, of course, ideas of risk and dangerousness are most strongly shaped and defined by the most powerful interest groups within society.

- The danger represented by reliance on data which has the appearance of reliability and 'science', but which turns out on closer inspection to be far less rigorous. Records of previous convictions from the Criminal Records Office, for example, are far from infallible, yet play a very significant part in almost all predictive approaches.
- The difficulty which such methods encounter in encompassing qualitative as well as quantitative information.
- The danger which arises from the 'potential for the concept of risk to be used as a mechanism of social regulation, justifying the extension of community surveillance and dis-proportionately affecting some groups of the population' (p. 68).
- 'Play it safe' regulations which elicit cautious practice and which do not, in any case, guarantee risk-free practice.
- 'Hindsight bias' which shapes practice on the basis of enquiries into disasters, rather than learning from successes.
- The over-use of negative indicators by management.

Kemshall comes to the conclusion that

> risk assessment is always going to be a judgement-call informed by knowledge, even if that knowledge is acquired through practice wisdom and is understated by those operating it and undervalued by those managing them...Prescription and regulation cannot respond to diversity and fluctuation and the risk business is definitely about these. (*ibid.*: 7)

It is a measure of just how powerful the call for formulaic risk assessment has become that she nevertheless provides a checklist for predictive calculation, albeit one which includes a disclaimer to the effect that: 'Hazel Kemshall and the University of Birmingham wish to confirm that the model of risk assessment suggested in this article is merely one possible method of assessing the risk of an offender and no guarantees can be given that such a model is infallible. Those officers using the model must consider each individual case on its merits' (p. 72).

Readers who are interested to discover checklists which purport to provide a way of charting future behaviour will have a choice of material from which to improve their understanding. These include Ward (1987), Humphrey *et al.* (1992), Wilkinson (1994) and Webb (1996).

Our final reason for avoiding this approach, particularly in youth justice, lies in its tendency to institutionalise and exaggerate existing forms of discrimination. Thus it is known that black defendants are more likely to be sentenced to custody earlier in their criminal careers than their white contemporaries. If reconviction predictors then attach a significant weight to custodial sentences as an indication of future bad behaviour – as they do – then black defendants might find themselves ruled out of certain core courses of action available to the courts – such as probation orders – on the grounds that they represent too great a risk of reconviction.

More directly in the case of young people, Stenson and Factor (1994: 4) report the results of an extended ethnographic case study of a local area shared by a large number of 'young and predominantly affluent, Jewish people' and a smaller number of African-Caribbean young people and where separate youth worker initiatives emerged to provide services for each group. Their account is worth tracing in a little detail.

Stenson and Factor begin by noting the widespread use of 'risk' as a magnet, drawing a range of professional workers to focus upon particular groups of young people 'in relation to a variety of dangers. These include the development of criminal careers, drug abuse, sexual health and other problems. *However, within this list of inter-related risks, those associated with offending are highlighted and professional intervention focused accordingly*' (p. 1, emphasis added).

Within the offending context, those authors distinguish two groups of young people who emerge in popular and policy discourse about risk and offending: '"troublesome" youth, at risk from sliding into routine criminal offending, and more affluent young people, seen principally as vulnerable to victimisation' (p. 2). Within the particular circumstances of their field-work this division was clearly apparent:

despite overlaps in values and practice between the Jewish youth workers and those working with the African-Caribbean young people, their
work was conditioned by a wider backcloth of policy goals, cultural
assumptions and working practices of other agencies and involved parties... This backcloth crystallised a differentiated view of the status of the
Jewish and non-Jewish – particularly African-Caribbean – youth...
Broadly, the African-Caribbean young people were viewed as 'at risk'
as actual or potential 'offenders'. On the other hand the Jewish young
people were viewed as 'at risk' as actual or potential 'victims'.

The shifting and negotiable character of risk is thus starkly demonstrated, as is the powerful potential for this negotiability to
be used in a way which adds to the discrimination faced by
some groups, while rewarding others with more socially acceptable
roles.

It is for these reasons that the focus of risk assessment suggestions here will be upon ways which help prevent these greater risks
from occurring – or at least being exaggerated still further by
youth justice workers. These suggestions begin from a belief that
the profession should resist the pressures to act as though unique
individuals, and especially those who are still in the process of
growing and changing, can be reduced to a series of formulae
which will, in any meaningful sense, provide a reliable guide to
their future conduct. Instead, attention needs to be redirected
away from the individual to those circumstances in which risk is
created and which, by the attention of determined workers, may be
lessened. The 'checklist' provided below is, as a result, rather
different from those with which risk assessment has come to be
associated.

Risk behaviour is situation-specific, that is to say it is a reaction to
particular circumstances which may alter if the circumstances
which precipitate that reaction can be altered first. This is particularly true for young people who, because of their stage in the life-
cycle, are less likely to have control over important elements in
their own circumstances – where they live, how to spend their time
and so on – and are therefore more vulnerable to having their
behaviour shaped by events and contexts outside their own control.
Risk assessment should attend to these contextual and precipitating
factors as to the individual characteristics of the young person.
Examples of such precipitating conditions are set out below. The
list is illustrative, not exhaustive.

1. Check if risk of offending is being influenced by factors which are not the responsibility of the young person – for example 'breaking into' buildings which have been left derelict and unattended, or theft from shops which place goods deliberately on display where they increase temptation.
2. Check if risk of offending has been influenced by the actions of adults from whom the young person is owed a duty of care – for example that minority of families which lacks the resilience to provide adequately for the needs of young people, particularly in conditions of poverty and disadvantage, or those cases of direct harm from abuse of young people by adults who have a duty of care towards them.
3. Check if risk of offending has been influenced by the actions of public services by whom the young person is owed a duty of care – for example the impact on offending of the withdrawal of benefit from 16/17-year-olds, or the rise of school exclusions.

As well as checking on factors which might have precipitated offending, it will also be important to see if these elements have been subject to positive change since the offending took place – or if they might be changed in a way which could assist in lessening future risk. Examples would include:

4. Check contextual factors which might have improved in a young person's situation since offences were committed – change of address, school, employment and so forth.
5. Check contextual factors which could be changed in order to lessen risk of offending – schooling, introduction to leisure, mobilising wider family support, referral to specialist services, provision of pocket money or benefits.

Finally, some precipitating events are very specific and as such may be either non-recurring or open to direct intervention. Thus it is important to:

6. Check risk as produced by specific contexts or behaviours which might be altered – offences committed only when drinking, in response to specific family events such as moving between separated parents, at times of particular stress such as school exams, and other disruptions.

Risk behaviour is also shaped by the responses which are made to it. The ways in which other people and systems react have an impact upon the likelihood of such behaviour decreasing, staying the same, or increasing. The problem which youth justice workers often face is that courts, responding to calls for punishment and toughness, appear attracted to simple solutions which are more likely to aggravate risk behaviour, rather than more complex and less clear-cut courses of action which are more likely to reduce risk, or at least not lead to its increase. Working within the system it is sometimes difficult not to be co-opted into its dominant value system, and to fall in with, rather than attempt to counteract, the culture of pessimism which leads to perverse outcomes. The checklist below focuses upon *responses* to risk behaviour and suggests questions which youth justice workers might use to help reduce rather than increase the chances of outcomes which aggravate risk behaviour.

1. Check what risk you pose to the young person yourself. Social workers, as earlier discussions of systems management and the rise of the 'new orthodoxy' have made clear, pose risks to young people which such individuals themselves are often ill-equipped to recognise. Here are just a few:

    - Workers can be too anxious to 'help', too quickly attuned to the difficulties of a situation and still, if not careful, likely to respond by tying the help required to a criminal justice sanction. The high price which such help too often entails does not need to be repeated here – nor the fact that this is a danger which attaches more to some groups, particularly young women, than others. Perhaps this sort of practice is over and the dangers no longer exist, although the evidence is that such an assertion is over-optimistic.
    - Poor practitioners are too often badly prepared and not well enough informed. There is no excuse for this sort of practice but there is, unfortunately, considerable evidence that social workers and probation officers who find the nitty-gritty of the jobs they do unpalatable, solve that problem by not bothering about it too much. Now, in our view, effective social work practice means a willingness to grasp and learn much tedious and mind-numbing detail about the remaining services of the welfare state – and then to keep up with these details as they constantly change. To take just one

example: a Midlands Probation Service conducted a survey of information contained in pre-sentence reports concerning the financial circumstances of defendants. It found a large reservoir of ignorance and misinformation about the benefit system and the impact this had upon people appearing before the courts. Worse still, however, this lack of knowledge did not stand in the way of probation officers providing information or advice to courts. As a result, individual circumstances were badly misrepresented and courses of action suggested which directly increased the difficulties which had contributed to offending in the first place. Where similar deficiencies characterise youth justice practice, they too act to increase the risks which vulnerable young people already face.

- Social work in the criminal justice system means battling on behalf of young people in forums which are deliberately and explicitly adversarial. Social workers are not at their best in these arenas. Our motivation and training combine to make us seekers after consensus rather than conductors in conflict, believers in misunderstanding rather than deliberate power struggles as the basis for what goes wrong in peoples lives. This means that young people can be put at risk in situations where workers are deliberately charged with protecting their interests. Chapter 4 dealt in some detail with the role of the Appropriate Adult. Writing a recent court report one of the authors was sent a Crown Prosecution document in which the police drew attention, on a number of occasions, to the presence of the Appropriate Adult *observer*. Now, quite certainly, the person concerned should not have been simply a passive observer but an active presence, prepared to intervene in the interview process if it were to be conducted in an oppressive manner. The failure to be so is emblematic of a wider difficulty which social workers experience in uncomfortable settings. The risks which then occur within explicitly adversarial systems such a criminal justice are carried by those whose interests ought to have been more vigorously pursued and defended.

2. Check what risk is posed to the young person by the organisation you represent:

- At their worst Social Services Departments are organisations bereft of confidence, characterised by siege mentality in which avoiding scandal is achieved through a chronic managerialism in which the good social worker is caricatured as the one who does nothing but meticulously records that fact. In Youth Justice this works itself out in the folk horror that the organisation will be criticised by some judge or politician for having committed that most serious sin of suggesting something they happen not to like. In terms of risk to young people, it means that this feeds itself through to individual workers who respond to new and uncertain demands by playing safe. And playing safe in risk assessment, for example, means entering the seriousness auction which characterises our court system, in which every player bids up seriousness higher and higher in order not to be left accused of being 'unrealistic'. These risks are all the higher when individual workers feel that their organisations are likely to leave them high and dry when taking risks on clients' behalf

- Resource instability is the second way in which social welfare organisations can place young people at risk, and is so evident in the constant preoccupation with the reorganisation and redeployment of staff and facilities. While some of this is beyond the control of local departments, by no means all of it has to be so. Staff who are demoralised by not knowing where they will be tomorrow provide a diminished service to clients.

  Even more culpable, perhaps, is the changing basket of services which are on offer at all: projects which open and then close; initiatives which are begun and then not supported. What happens to a young person in the criminal justice system is so basically affected by whether or not there is a motor project, or a bail support scheme, or even a simple activities project and so on. Resource instability increases at the border zones between services, so that 16 and 17 year olds continue to give rise to real concerns as social services and probation services debate where responsibility lies. Risk is increased when resources are unstable and it is young people who carry that risk most directly.

- Resource instability is linked most closely with resource starvation, and local authorities are undoubtedly badly caught in this trap. Yet authorities and departments do make choices and the choices they make can increase or decrease the risk which young people face. Accommodation for young people under supervision is amongst the most worrying problems for practitioners. Lack of suitable accommodation increases the risk for young people at all stages of youth justice work, from pre-court to supervision.

Youth justice workers are purveyors of systems management. When systems fail to deliver necessary goods and put young people at risk, a duty exists not to allow the consequences of that failure unheedingly to descend onto them.

3. Check what risk is posed to the young person by other adults by whom s/he is owed a duty of care:

Of the five risk areas being considered here, this is the one which requires least emphasis. In our experience the families of young people in trouble are generally as concerned, caring and keen to pursue the best interests of that young person as any other of their fellow citizens. Yet all youth justice workers will have dealings where, through despair and disadvantage, families run out of the resilience which is a basic requirement in attending to the needs of young people in their teenage years. Neglect and indifference are not the general experience of working with the families of young people in trouble, but where they do exist they plainly add to the risks which that young person faces. In the worst cases straightforward abuse will have been the experience of some young people at the hands of adults who will have had a duty of care towards them.

Such young people have rights due to them from public authorities. Social workers are employed by a government which is a signatory to the United Nations Convention on the Rights of the Child, and by departments which have duties under the 1989 Children Act. These are at least as important as obligations under criminal justice legislation and, given the damage sustained by some young people, can be a lot more so. The risk highlighted here is that in the forum in which youth justice workers find themselves, these experiences will add to the disadvantages young people already face. Quite certainly they will do so unless workers are prepared to point these things out on their behalf.

4. Check what risk is posed to the young person by other services by whom s/he is owed a duty of care.

Young people who come to the attention of youth justice workers are surrounded by other systems, both those within Social Services Departments and beyond. As set out more fully in earlier chapters, the history of the past 15 years is that these systems have increasingly become sources of indifference or hostility to these young people, rather than of positive assistance. To give just one example: at its worst the education system has long been one where the only thing worse than some young people not being at school was one of them actually turning up. Now a new market-driven culture has overlaid and underpinned these existing reservations. In the new system such problematic pupils carry direct costs, and the result has been an escalating explosion in school suspensions and exclusions over the past five years. Once again the risk falls unevenly. Now boys more than girls are at risk, and black young men more than white, and Afro-Caribbean young men most of all.

The young people with whom youth justice workers are in contact carry these risks into the system which the same workers represent. It increases the difficulties which they are likely to face. 'Show me a persistent truant and I'll show you a potential criminal' said John Patton, a Conservative Home Office Minister with a reputation which laid claims to liberalism. Courts act on such assertions and treat young people who have lost an education, or any of the other social assets, as though they are to be held responsible for that loss, and as though they have nothing much else to be bothered about losing either.

5. Check what risk is posed to the young person by the operation of the criminal justice system itself. Here are just three of the ways in which young people are put at risk by the Court system:

- Magistrates are surrounded by what Professor John Pitts (1995) calls the 'persistent pre-pubescent predators from purgatory' view of young people. They see only their failures and are inevitably influenced by the small number of repeat offenders who come their way: 'One sees some families so often one feels almost on Christmas card terms with them', one magistrate suggested, when interviewed about courts dealings with parents. The result is the seriousness escalation referred to earlier, when competition breaks out to take the most serious view possible of what has taken place.

- Secondly, seriousness escalation is promoted by the way an adversarial system goes about its business. When a young person appears before the courts, the behaviour which has brought them there is ripped out of context and highlighted as though that were the only thing which is of importance in that individual's life and circumstances. This process is not only de-contextualising, it is dehumanising as well. It legitimates such developments as the hyenas advert which the government ran about car thieves in which young people were literally portrayed as animals. The risks which young people face in such a climate and in such a process are enormous. Youth justice workers are amongst the best bulwarks against these dangers when, in a real risk assessment they move positively to counteract these possibilities, putting a young person into context, explaining their behaviour in relation to all the other aspects of their lives.

- Finally, the criminal justice system operates on the basis of differential accountability. Some courses of action available to the courts are subject to far greater scrutiny than others, and some outcomes are far more visible than others. In the great 1991 Act divisions, it is community sentences which bear the brunt of scrutiny. Other courses of action such as custody are too often embarked upon as though they were risk and cost-free.

In summary, risk assessments need to be conducted with the image of a spiral in mind. Risk behaviour is preceded by events, circumstances and actions by which that behaviour is precipitated, and followed by events, circumstances and actions by which that behaviour is maintained, escalated or diminished. Escalation twists the spiral upwards and increases the rate and intensity of risk behaviour, diminution twists the spiral downwards and reduces the rate and intensity of risk behaviour.

The contribution which youth justice workers make to the sentencing process is to shine a light onto the before and after of a young person's actions, and to suggest ways to the court in which precipitating factors might be amended and responses tempered so as to lower future risks. This is what risk assessment should be all about.

Finally, in this section we set out some checks which could be used to assess the impact which risk assessments are intended to make. Risk assessment ought to be:

- set out in language which has been tested for the effect it may produce upon sentencers – make sure the report not only says what it means to say, but says it in a way which assists intended, not unintended, messages to be conveyed;
- clearly balanced by positive information about the young person;
- informed by a knowledge of risks which attach to particular groups of young people because of their gender, race or current status – for example being homeless or remanded away from home;
- accompanied by a positive programme for addressing risks identified;
- supported by research evidence which backs up the course of action to be proposed – for example citing Home Office evidence that more than 7 out of 10 young people subject to a conditional discharge do not reoffend while that discharge is in force – the effectiveness of such a course of action in terms of the likelihood of further offending can then be emphasised;
- accompanied where necessary by a clear statement of risks attached to courses of action which are not being proposed, but may be under consideration by the court – such as custody;
- backed up by gatekeeping systems specifically set up for risk assessment. The brief of gatekeepers ought to be to test assessments to see if they contribute to outcomes which diminish or increase risk to or by the young person; and
- followed through by measures to ensure that specific risk assessments are not available for later use out of context. Risk assessments in PSRs, for example, reflect particular offences and life circumstances. On a later occasion these factors will have altered. Use of the risk assessment elements of 'old'

reports in further hearings, or in discharge plans from institutions, are therefore likely to be particularly unreliable. Steps need to be taken to limit this potential damage.

Young people and restorative justice

Across Europe there is a growing interest in what may be termed restorative juvenile justice. While there is some merit in this approach there are also some major problems which need to be discussed. As this section will demonstrate, these problems are quite serious and necessitate a cautious rather than headlong rush into restorative approaches to the treatment of offenders.

The first problem with restorative justice is one of definition. Just what is restorative justice? If the concept is to have meaning, and if this meaning is to be of some practical value in guiding or shaping our response to offenders, then it must be coherent and have some internal consistency. In short, for restorative justice to make sense there must be some logic to it that helps to understand what is being done and why. The logic of restorative justice, however, is not entirely clear. A leading UK proponent defines restorative justice as 'a form of criminal justice based on reparation', where reparation, in turn, is defined as:

> Actions to repair the damage caused by the crime, either materially (at least in part) or symbolically. Usually performed by the offender, in the form of payment or service to the victim, if there is one and the victim wishes it, or to the community, but it can include the offender's co-operation in training, counselling or therapy. Reparative actions can also be undertaken by the community. (Wright 1996: iv)

So, according to this definition restorative justice can be almost anything, excluding sanctions which aim to punish directly – direct payment to victims, mediation, community service, fines and compensation, various forms of supervision – and all of these things, it seems, can be called restorative justice when they involve the offender[3] making some form of payment (financial, material, symbolic) to the victim.

Thus in practice the operationalisation of Wright's version of restorative justice centres around the offender–victim nexus, and actions taken by the offender and others (directly and indirectly) that address the act of victimisation in such a manner as to ameliorate the crime and its effects in respect of the victim. It is the victim, and not the offender, which is the principle focus of much of this sort of thinking.

Not all versions of restorative justice, however, focus on restoring the victim. There are models which focus on the offender and his or her rehabilitation or 'reintegration' back into the law-abiding community. The most notable international proponent of these sorts of ideas is John Braithwaite (1989, 1993; see also Braithwaite and Mugford 1994) whose favoured mechanisms for successful reintegration can and do involve victims, but where the main focus of activity is on the offender and their place in the community or society. Braithwaite's theory of reintegrative shaming is based on the observation that societies with the lowest crime rates are those that 'shame potently and judiciously' (Braithwaite 1989), and that by shaming offenders in particular ways that are 'reintegrative', it is possible to reduce further offending.

Summarising this approach: reintegrative shaming is most successful when carried out by people who respect and care for the offender, who are not normal 'representatives of the state' (for example police or judges) but who identify themselves with law-abiding behaviour; when clear messages are given that what the offender did was wrong (but that they, in themselves, can be ok), both for the particular victim and as an activity in general; when a consensus can be engendered between all parties (offender, victims and others) around some collective morality, and when this can be symbolically acted out in some practical and meaningful manner[4] (see Braithwaite and Mugford 1994).

Braithwaite's articulation of restorative justice is more humanitarian than some traditional approaches to juvenile misconduct, and is clearly more liberal and tolerant than many approaches. But even this model makes it clear that although others will do some work, it is the offender who must change. Restoring the offender in Braithwaite's terms means getting the offender to see sense in, and to agree with, the dominant law-abiding consensus, and then to behave in line with these beliefs. In this way the problems of a community or a society (that is, crime) are encapsulated in the behaviour of the young and we are led to believe that it is they who must change.

The notion that offenders are socially aberrant and should be manipulated back into right ways of thinking leads us into our second major difficulty with restorative justice – that is, to questions of a moral or ethical nature. Are we justified in taking *any* action against a juvenile once they have offended? Or must our action (response) be based on some principles? Crime is at best unpleasant; being a victim of a crime, even of a fairly minor crime, can be very distressing; victims, generally, get a pretty raw deal from the criminal justice system and wider society; but does all of this justify doing anything to offenders? Beating children with a stick may give the victim or some other adults a sense of justice, and responding with fierce punishment to minor infractions may lead to a reduction in re-offending,[5] but are such responses justifiable?

Punishment must be proportionate; administered with a sense of justice, in a context of justice. A disproportionate response to offending behaviour is likely to leave the offender feeling unjustly treated and less, not more, inclined to conform in the future. It is equally important for victims, criminal justice professionals and the wider community to perceive a sense of justice in the operation of the criminal justice system. While fully recognising the difficulties over definitions of terms such as proportionate and sense of justice (while not believing that the achievement of a broadly acceptable outcome in individual cases should be blown out of proportion), it is important that this test is applied to our activities.

Is it justifiable for youth justice workers to take the victim's perspective (following Wright above) and to base one's interventions with the offender on what will be the best for the victim? Victims of crime deserve a response from society (see Winkel 1991), but this response should not come from local authority social workers who are charged with acting in the best interests of the child. It seems to us to be morally unacceptable to promote victims' interests at the expense of the child's. Children have rights too.

What of Braithwaite in this respect? The approach he advocates appears to be much more benign and tolerant, but is it morally acceptable? Chapter 1 showed how contemporary society tends to treat young people as an excluded group, deserving of few if any services as of right. If this was a society which valued young people, if this society had an equitable distribution of wealth, and if this society gave everyone an equal chance then Braithwaite's approach may be morally acceptable. But our society does not operate like that. Too many children are the victims of inadequate or inappropriate state provision and intolerance in society, too many are victimised by adults, and too many are exposed to the ravages of adult life unprotected by a family or community or the state which owes them a duty of care to make an approach which simply says 'you have done wrong, you must not do things which damage others, you must conform' morally acceptable.

A society which actively denies young people access to so many of the culturally defined attributes of pleasure and success must expect some young people to try to take those things they are denied, or to find alternative means of gaining access to the otherwise unobtainable. A society which then forces the marginalised and excluded to apologise to those who *have*, or to assimilate the beliefs of those who *have*, heaps injustice upon immorality in ways which are ethically and morally unacceptable.

It is all too tempting in the context of contemporary society to sweep away moral considerations as irrelevant or too complex and differentiated to reconcile. This is an unacceptable attitude or response. Exposing immoralities and acting in ways which are ethically and morally consistent are important, not just in their own right but in effective approaches to the treatment of offenders (see Chapter 6).

Whatever the morality of restorative justice, in criminal justice terms it is absolutely essential that what is done is effective; and this leads us to our third problem with the restorative justice approach as it is currently outlined, that is demonstrating that it works.

Restorative justice of a victim's persuasion works in the sense that it has an appeal to liberally-minded intellectuals[6] who are opposed to bland punishment-oriented responses to offenders, but who share a concern about ameliorating the negative consequences of crime for victims. This approach has similar appeal to more right-wing 'thinkers', and especially politicians who believe that paying lip-service to victims (or victims' rights generally) will have some personal/political pay-off, especially if this approach reinforces the individual responsibility and culpability of juvenile offenders. But to believe that this approach deals genuinely with the problem of crime, and effectively with individual offenders, is a considerable leap of faith.

The difficulty of being precise about what restorative justice actually is has already been noted; it seems that a whole range of things could, and do, fall into this category, ranging from paying financial compensation to victims, through symbolic verbal or material exchanges to reintegrative shaming. But where is the evidence which shows us that these approaches work? Where is the evidence (theoretical or empirical) that says a restorative approach shows promise? Where is the evidence from individual projects that says particular restorative justice approaches work in · practice? There is a lot written about restorative justice, most of it broadly in favour of increasing the extent to which restorative approaches are used, but there is very little *evidence* that it works.

If advocates of restorative justice expect their ideas to achieve a wider currency then they must begin to produce evidence which shows that particular restorative projects actually work. More so, they must demonstrate not only the efficacy of particular projects but the acceptability (morally and ethically) of what they are doing. The victim-oriented approach of Wright, and the reintegrative approach of Braithwaite, remain wanting in these respects.

There is an area of interventions, however, that broadly falls into the restorative justice nomenclature, which does show promise. The characteristics and limitations of the victim-oriented and reintegrative approaches have been highlighted above. The former places an emphasis on the victim and changing the victim's status, not the offender's. The second places an emphasis on changing the status of the offender, but only at the cost of the offender and in neglect of wider social factors. But if restorative justice is taken to mean restoring the offender into the community in ways which recognise the responsibilities of that society as well as those of the individual, then there are greater prospects for successful interventions. Indeed, this is exactly the sort of approach outlined in Chapter 6 where the research evidence on the effectiveness or otherwise of different intervention approaches was reviewed. While there is much work that needs to be done in practice to give expression to an offender-oriented restorative perspective, it is possible to summarise what such an approach might look like given what is known about effective offender intervention. Offender oriented restorative justice:

- is not work that is carried out for the benefit of the victim;
- is not work which victimises the offender through unethical and amoral treatments;
- is work which recognises the needs of the offender and sets about tackling these needs;
- is work which recognises the responsibility of others to the offender and tackles others in the delivery of their responsibilities (schooling, housing, benefits and so on);
- is work which promotes positive behaviour in youth through setting good examples; and
- is work which supports the offender and their family or community.

Young people and criminal responsibility

This chapter ends with consideration of an issue which runs as a linking theme between much of the content of this book and the criminal justice context in which it is written. The argument advanced has been for an approach to youth justice which is rooted in a recognition of the youthfulness of the young person in trouble, and which argues for a response to juvenile crime based upon the particular developmental needs and status of such an individual. Such an approach sets youth crime in relation to other social events, processes and structures. It places a premium upon developing a stake for young people in a society which seeks to include them more than it wishes to control them. It argues that addressing youth crime is a *shared* responsibility, in which adult obligations are accepted and acted upon by those with the power to do so.

The very different framework within which British criminal justice policy is conduced was set out in Chapter 1. The present government has continued in office with the approach it had developed in opposition. The twin pillars of blame and punishment remain far more to the fore than any more *sotto voce* efforts to tackle the causes of crime in the lives of young people. The basis of this shift is a changing concept of responsibility which goes beyond criminal justice policy. The communitarianism of Etzioni (1993) which is influential in the thinking of those at the heart of the administration has been summarised by Morgan (1995: 14) in this way:

the responsibility for any problem or situation belongs first to those nearest to the problem and then only if a solution cannot be found by the individual does responsibility devolve to the family. If the family cannot cope, then the local community should become involved. Only after these possibilities have been tried and the problem found too intractable should the state intervene.

As Morgan concludes, 'this type of thinking justifies levying fines on all who do not comply and imposing "workfare" instead of welfare on the unemployed'. It also underpins many of the policies which are proposed for young people in trouble: the abolition of the 'absurd' and 'archaic' *doli incapax* rule, 'final warnings', abolition of the conditional discharge, the confirmation of secure training centre orders, tagging and curfews for juveniles, tougher regimes of community interventions, and so on.

In all these proposals criminal justice policy is based upon an ascending scale of responsibility. It begins with the individual, the dangerous youth from whom outdated protections are to be removed in order, as the Home Secretary announced, to 'make it clear to young people that they will not get away with offending'. It moves on to 'bad' families, and confirms the efficacy of punishment as the preferred way of making them face up to their responsibilities. If failure continues at both these levels it ends with the state ensuring that adequate machinery is in place to deal with those who continue to give offence.

In the space available here, only one of the propositions which emerge from the paradigm can be considered. *Doli incapax*, however, provides a suitable test-bed for these issues, being the most time-honoured concept under reform and one which has attracted most Ministerial scorn. The basic doctrine, enshrined as long ago as Saxon times, has rested in an understanding within the law that young children should not be held criminally responsible until reaching the age of maturity (Moore 1995). The view that younger people were likely to be less-developed in their understanding of right and wrong than their older contemporaries was embodied in common law and, in recent times, has taken the form of a rebuttable presumption that a child aged between 10 and 14 is incapable of committing a crime because s/he lacks the necessary appreciation to distinguish between actions that 'were seriously wrong and [those caused by]...mere childish mischief or naughtiness' (*T* v. *DPP*, 1989, *Criminal Law Review*, 498, as reported in Moore 1995).

On a diminishing scale, as a child moved from 10 to 14, the prosecution were obliged to establish beyond a reasonable doubt that s/he knew what had gone on to be wrong.

This basic premise was called into question in the case of *C* (*A Minor*) v. *Director of Public Prosecutions* (1994) at the Queen's Bench Divisional Court, by Lords Justice Mann and Laws who determined that the presumption no longer existed in English law (*The Times* 30 March 1994). Lord Justice Mann, delivering the principal judgement, declared that the

> approach was unreal and contrary to common sense... It was not surprising that the presumption took root in an era when the criminal law was altogether more draconian but the philosophy of criminal punishment had obviously changed out of all recognition since those days ... the presumption had no utility whatever in the present era. (quoted in Davies 1994)

The case was taken to appeal at the House of Lords. Here Lord Justice Lowry and his fellow adjudicators determined that the principle of *doli incapax*, while 'inconsistently applied and which was certainly capable of producing inconsistent results' (in Moore 1995), was too established and central to be altered other than by Act of Parliament. The issue, said his Lordship, was 'a classic case for Parliamentary investigation, deliberation and legislation'.

It was against this background that the present government formed its proposals for reform. In the view of Ministers, young people aged as young as 10 are indistinguishable in terms of developed moral understanding from their adult contemporaries. No different test of *mens rea* needs be applied in each case. This text rejects such an argument, both in its particular application and in the wider view it embodies of the relationship between young people and the society in which they live. Specifically, a children-first approach exposes the evident flaw in treating young people as though their understanding, knowledge and ability to reason (to use the formula adopted in the 1990 White Paper, *Crime, Justice and Protecting the Public*) were fully-formed. A developmental understanding which makes an allowance for immaturity, and which recognises the impact upon development which adults produce, would lead to a strengthening of the protections which children are afforded in legal processes rather than their abolition. More generally, the relationship between the responsibility which adult society owes children, and judgements made concerning their own behaviour, needs to be redrawn. Children-first in youth justice depends upon redrawing that balance differently in education, employment, social security and housing. A view of 'fairness' and 'responsibility' which relies upon sharpening up criminal processes to the neglect of the social context runs the serious risk of producing no justice at all.

If responsibility is to be the watchword of youth justice policy, powerful figures in government and elsewhere who talk loudly of the obligations which far less-powerful people must bear, should expect to have their actions tested against the dangers of authoritarianism and repression. In the case of children in particular, these tests deserve to be narrowly drawn and deal with the long-term impact of policies as well as their short-term attractions. Today's curfews, crack-downs and lock-ups need to be weighed against tomorrow's embittered and excluded adults, in whom waywardness will have been inculcated by the treatments handed out in the name of responsibility.

At the end of 1997 the Labour administration published two key documents in its criminal justice strategy: the Crime and Disorder Bill and, in particular, the White Paper *No More Excuses* (Home Office 1997) retained and emphasised two increasingly familiar anti-child themes; (i) the focus upon young people as a source of society's ills, and (ii) the disporting of young people as deliberately and self-consciously anti-authority and anti-establishment. In this way Jack Straw, the Home Secretary, peppered his Preface to the White Paper with a series of suppositional attacks upon young people in trouble, the youth justice system and those who work within it. Young people had been 'excused too often'; the system 'excuses itself for its inefficiency'; those within it have become enmeshed in an 'excuse culture'. In short, the Government sought to promote the view that the youth justice system was in an impoverished state of collapse.

The Government's response was to rearticulate the philosophy underpinning its understanding of and approach to young offenders, and to bring about structural change within the youth justice system. Both sets of changes were, however, predicated on the Government's belief that it was time to tolerate 'no more excuses' from children or from those responsible for working with children. Thus some of the main features of the White Paper were:

- Ten-year-olds were to be prevented from excusing themselves by sweeping away the established defence of doli incapax.
- No excuse for parents, either. A new Parenting Order would allow the Courts to impose compulsory counselling and other additional requirements upon them.
- No escape from the harsh light of publicity. The softer minds of a century earlier might have thought it best to avoid the stigma which newspaper attention might bring to children in trouble. The less squeamish administration of 1 May 1997 announced the implementation of the 'name and shame' proposals of its Conservative predecessor in October 1997 assisting, once again, to 'end the excuse culture'.

To these were added a list of proposals drawn largely unamended from Labour's pre-election policies and consultation documents: Curfews, Final Warnings, Detention and Training Orders and new powers to remand younger individuals to secure accommodation.

Of course, it is possible to quarry from the White Paper and the Bill nodding references to more constructive ideas and even to the effects of social disadvantage upon the chances which young people have of leading law-abiding lives. The text, however, is shot through with an agenda of reactionary authoritarianism.

The central assertion of the White Paper – and it is asserted rather than argued – is that young people do not grow out of crime. Rather, any propensity to anti-social behaviour must be 'nipped in the bud' through new Youth Offending Teams whose primary and statutory duty is to be the prevention of offending. The Government's policies are deliberately aimed at forcing more and more young people to penetrate deeper into the youth justice system and its increasingly interventionist measures. These plans, if implemented, will reverse one of the central principles of the juvenile justice movement. By repeating the unfocused, catch-all 'preventative' practices of the 1970s the mistakes of that decade are set to be repeated, but this time with a far more explicitly repressive intent – especially for those whose behaviour is not nipped, but amplified, labelled and distorted by drawing them ever earlier and ever closer into a system which cannot but do more harm than good.

For a final time, therefore, we attempt to reassert a different set of priorities and practices, on the basis, once again, that these represent a real agenda for reducing crime and promoting community safety. Youth justice practitioners, more than any other, know that they have the ability to shape the local response to national legislation. Compliance or resistance is a choice not a given. Practitioners and managers must look for a criminal justice policy and a government which offers no excuses for those who seek to reduce the political and legal rights of those less able to defend themselves; no more excuses for those who seek to make young people answer for the sins of their parents and those adults who made the society in which they have to live; no more excuses for those who take money away from the poorest members of our society, leaving their children go cold and hungry; no more excuses for an adminstration which fails its young people by turning its back on the pursuit of social justice and relying instead upon the short-term repression of criminal justice.

The Children First approach which this book has tried to articulate is based upon the opposite premise: that children come first when social policy, rather than criminal policy, drives the actions of governments towards them.

Conclusion

A concluding chapter has not been included in this text in the hope that its main themes will have remained consistent and have emerged clearly as each chapter has developed. In this final chapter, therefore, it has been our aim to show how a revived approach to systems management, animated with the principles of Children First and extended to related systems beyond the narrow confines of criminal justice itself, can be applied to new challenges as well as old.

National Standards represent a threat to the survival of that knowledgeable, skilful and critical practice which is the hallmark of worthwhile youth justice practice. Yet, when interrogated from the children-first perspective, and with determination to make maximum use of every ounce of discretion to be bleached from them, it is still possible to act in the best interests of young people caught up within them. In a systemic sense it is the duty of management to ensure that good quality practice – rather than the redundancies of rote-bound, by-the-rule-book mechanicals – remains valued and supported by youth justice organisations. In the worst places good practice becomes threatened, carried out covertly against the grain of agencies dominated by the dictats of National Standard procedures. It is management's responsibility to ensure that these powerful currents are resisted.

The view of risk assessment set out here has been guided by the warning of professionals in other fields (see Crichton 1995) that 'dangerousness is a dangerous concept'. Risk assessment should not be about predicting the future, but about providing an informed and defensible commentary upon the factors which are likely to influence that future. In the case of young people in particular, that places a priority upon the ways in which they are treated by other more powerful individuals and organisations, and the ways in which their own conduct may be shaped by such encounters and the life-chances which result. The focus of risk assessment, in other words, should not be upon the young person as a source of risk to others, but as an individual whose chances of improvement are potentially placed at risk by the actions of others.

Restorative justice, differs from the other areas of contemporary concern, in being more diffuse and, as yet, less prescriptive in practice. It contains within it, however, all the central threads outlined so far. A children-first approach should alert any practitioner to the hidden power imbalances within the restorative justice project, imbalances which are all the more acute in the case of young people generally, and of specific acuity when applied to young people who face additional issues of race, gender, disability, poverty and so on.

This book ends where it began. An agenda for youth justice practice over the foreseeable future needs to be rooted in a celebration of past success and a reinvigoration of principles which have made social work with young people in trouble different, distinctive and worthwhile. Our touchstone for that distinction, and that worth, is the extent to which youth justice organisations, managers and practitioners are prepared to strive to put the interests of young people first. Our prescription has been for a systems management approach which re-engages the social dimension of young people's lives and makes explicit the links between the denial of social justice and the impossibility of criminal justice. In a threatening climate these messages are unlikely to be easily communicated or comfortably received. That is precisely why, of course, the power and resources of youth justice services have to be shaped and applied to the task of assisting those who carry the burden of that hostility. Putting children first means counteracting the burden of negativity which is projected upon young people in our society and, for those in trouble, reassembling the props of a rewarding lifestyle amongst the ruins of exhausted and desperate families and the assault upon their social rights. Even in destructive times, only a concentration upon the painstaking construction of useful and valuable futures holds out hope for the sake of young people themselves, and for the prospective well-being of us all.

Notes

2 Juvenile Justice: a Recent History

1. The nature and development of Intermediate Treatment is discussed in more detail later in this chapter.
2. Shortly after it was elected the Labour government established a Youth Justice Task Force to advise the Home Secretary on possible changes to the youth justice system. In a Commons written answer on 18 June, the Home Secretary announced that, 'The role of the Task Force on Youth Justice is to advise Home Office Ministers on Government proposals for the development of youth justice polices and, in particular, to provide advice on taking forward an action plan as agreed by the interdepartmental Ministerial group on Youth Justice.' There were no independent academics or youth justice practitioners represented amongst the 18 members of this Task Force.
3. The introduction of the youth court is dealt with in Chapter 3.
4. Although Borstal Training was a sentence only available in the Crown Court until the early 1980s. The 1982 Criminal Justice Act abolished Borstal Training, replacing it with Youth Custody and making the sentence of 'Detention in a Young Offender Institution' available to both the juvenile and Crown Courts.
5. This development was buttressed in the case of IT as many of the newly appointed IT workers came from a youth work background. This was significant as traditionally youth work was not inhibited by notions of labelling or stigmatisation and tended to operate with a more open and inclusive philosophy.
6. It is, perhaps, true to say that the Criminal Justice Act (CJA) 1991 represents the culmination of justice-based thinking in criminal justice philosophy and legislation in the legal history of England and Wales; and that this represents an ideological victory for the back-to-justice movement. The CJA 1991 enshrined a justice-based philosophy for the processing and sentencing of all offenders (children and adults), based on the just deserts model (von Hirsch 1985; Home Office 1988, 1990).
7. Under the terms of the Initiative the money was to be paid to voluntary bodies who had to apply for funding in conjunction with a local authority SSD. The use of voluntary bodies in this way was

partly politically expedient (avoiding conflict with the Home Office, and a mechanism for funding locally-based developments at a time when central government sought to restrict local expenditure), but it was also expressly designed to bring about rapid change: using voluntary bodies with no necessary prior involvement in IT and giving them the funds to develop a new type of provision. Many new projects were in fact developed by large voluntary organisations (NACRO 1991), but in some areas new voluntary organisations were created by local authorities keen to drive changes in tune with local circumstances (Bottoms *et al.* 1993; Haines 1996).

8.   s.1(2) of the Children and Young Persons Act 1969 allowed 'care proceedings' to be brought in respect of various non-criminal matters such as non-school attendance and being beyond parental control; such proceedings might (but did not necessarily) result in a care order. The law has been remodelled by the Children Act 1989.

9.   Although in 1984 Jones was *questioning* the emergence of this 'new orthodoxy' to the extent that it seemed to ignore the needs of children.

10. 'This sociological concept refers to the tendencies to be found in advanced welfare societies whereby the capacity for conflict and disruption is reduced by means of the centralisation of policy, increased government intervention, and the cooperation of various professionals and interest groups into a collective whole with homogeneous aims and objectives' (Unger 1976). Quoted in Pratt (1989: 245).

11. As, for example, was experienced during the implementation of the youth court and the requirements placed on Social Services Departments and Probation Services to work together both at the highest levels of local management and in terms of direct service delivery – see, HOC 30/1992 *Young People and the Youth Court*, as discussed in Chapter 3.

12. It is important to recognise that practice varied across the country in this respect and that in most teams basic grade juvenile justice officers did get involved with the welfare issues of their clients. It is essential to realise, however, that whereas welfare issues were the main focus of report writing and direct work with children in the 1970s, as the 1980s progressed any consideration of welfare matters in SERs and any intervention aimed at tackling welfare needs ran very much against the dominant trend. Thus welfare issues were almost universally excised from Social Enquiry Reports; juvenile justice workers tended exclusively to justify their intervention with young people solely on the basis of the seriousness of their offending, and although the nature of this intervention did sometimes involve attempts to meet the needs of young people such work was no longer the norm and more often the exception.

3   Developing a Youth Justice Philosophy

1. Although, once established, philosophy does tend to shape the way knowledge is acquired and understood, and shape which skills are acquired and applied.
2. Consistent, in this sense, refers to the *consistent application* of sentencing *principles*.
3. Post-CJA 1991 legislative changes mean that courts may now take fully into account an individual's previous offending history when determining sentence. The framework of the CJA 1991 as amended is still desert-based, i.e. these changes do not diminish in any way the basic principle that sentences should be individualised – only those factors which courts may take into account when making individualised assessments have changed.
4. Also issued jointly by the Department of Health as LAC (92) 5 and by the Welsh Office as Welsh Office Circular 21/92.
5. Many, similarly damaging, social policies have been directed towards children and young people – see Chapter 1.
6. And little is written or said about young people as victims of crime (see Morgan and Zedner 1992; Pearson 1994).
7. The only brake on this process seems to be that of cost and the general unwillingness of government to increase public expenditure (and taxes). In the criminal justice sphere, however, this is not always an effective braking mechanism as the willingness of the last Conservative Home Secretary to spend vast sums on prison building, for both adults and juveniles, shows.

4   Managing Youth Justice Systems

1. As Spencer (1994) laconically remarked, while the revelation that 8% of those dealt with in this way had already received two or more cautions was not 'altogether satisfactory...it is true that recidivism applies to those placed in custody, as well as those who are cautioned'.

6   Effective Work with Young Offenders

1. Although it is worth noting that there is no evidence that juvenile crime in particular is increasing. Indeed recent Home Office research (Graham and Bowling 1995) shows that larger numbers of young people are continuing to offend into their early 20s; a finding which indicates that increases in crime may be located with this older age-group.
2. Maximising efficiency and economy, and enhancing control within community sentences are rhetorical justifications for National Standards, but research has shown (Haines and O'Mahony 1995) that the rhetoric is not borne out by experience and that the procedural con-

trol mechanisms associated with National Standards are quite ineffective in achieving these objectives.

3. During the extended general election campaign of 1997, Labour's Shadow Home Office spokesperson, Alun Michael, repeatedly used exactly this phrase in defence of his Party's proposals for reform of the youth court and its flirtation with the 'zero tolerance' policy of American policing. In his first speech to the House of Commons as Home Secretary on 19 May 1997, Jack Straw made the point central to his attack on the policies of the former administration, claiming that a situation had been produced in which, 'Far from nipping bad behaviour in the bud, the present youth justice system perversely reinforced much bad behaviour'.

4. This is not to claim that criminal careers researchers make such claims. Farrington (1997), for example, is cautious about any claims that criminal careers research is effective in the early identification of future criminal behaviour in individuals. For Farrington criminal careers research is helpful to the extent that it can clarify a range of problem behaviours in families or communities which may then be tackled by effective social programmes (Farrington 1997a).

5. Indeed, criminal careers researchers present the category of antisocial behaviours as if all members of society were in agreement about such matters, in a manner which obfuscates value judgements in the guise of scientific research.

6. The flaw in the US crime statistics which shows a declining crime rate is a little technical. The statistics which show such a decline are based on a telephone victim survey which 'captures' a distorted picture of the true crime level. For certain categories of crime the telephone victim survey records fewer offences than police recorded crime. This level of under-reporting and police recording is on average about one-third of real crime levels. The conclusion that crime in the US is going down, therefore, is fallaciously based on significant levels of under-reporting actual crime rates.

7. This material is included here not because of a belief there are plans to introduce US-style boot camps for juveniles in England & Wales, but because the boot camp experiment shows where excessively punitive policies can take youth justice practice and because the boot camp experiment provides hard data on the negative effects of punitive custodial regimes.

8. The significance of employment, for example, will be different for young people than for adults. It may be the case, however, that young people are more amenable to such a community-oriented approach and that their social bonds may be more malleable.

7 Some Contemporary Concerns

1. Jointly issued by the Department of Health and Welsh Office, but originating in the Home Office.

2. And, in some cases, strengthened and intensified as epitomised by the introduction of electronic tagging.
3. Wright also argues that 'reparative actions can be undertaken by the community', but it is not entirely clear what he means in this respect. It could mean, for example, that the community takes action to restore the offender to a law abiding position in society. But this interpretation does not really fit with the overall timbre of the definition above, and in this context is much more likely to mean that the community can take action to 'restore' the victim.
4. Braithwaite and Mugford articulate a total of 14 separate conditions for successful reintegration ceremonies – these have been summarised and collapsed above. So confident are they that their approach is effective that one of the last conditions is to repeat the process until it works!
5. Although, in fact, there is scant criminological evidence to suggest that individual deterrence works.
6. While this appeal, no doubt exists, questions have been raised as to just how beneficial such an approach is to actual victims of crime (Davis *et al.* 1988, Dignan 1992, and Marshall and Merry 1990).

Bibliography

Ahmad, B. (1990) *Black Perspectives in Social Work* (Birmingham: Venture Press).

Allen, R. (1990) 'Punishment in the community', in *Social Work and Social Welfare Yearbook*, vol. 2, pp. 29–41 (Buckingham: Open University Press).

Allen, R. (1991) 'Out of jail: the reduction in the use of penal custody for male juveniles 1981–88', *The Howard Journal*, vol. 30, no. 1, pp. 30–52.

AMA (1995) *A Future for Youth Justice Services*, a discussion paper by the ACC, AMA, ADSS, NACRO and ACOP (London: AMA).

Anderson, S., Kinsey, R., Loader, I. and Smith, C. (1994) *Cautionary Tales, Young People, Crime and Policing in Edinburgh* (Aldershot: Avebury).

Ashworth, A., Cavadino, P., Gibson, B., Harding, J., Rutherford, A., Seago, P. and Whyte, L. (1992) *The Youth Court* (Winchester: Waterside Press).

Askey, S. and Ross, C. (1988) *Boys Don't Cry: Boys and Sexism in Education* (Milton Keynes: Open University Press).

Bailey, R. and Ward, D. (1993) *Probation Supervision: Attitudes to Formalised Help* (Centre for Social Action: University of Nottingham).

Balding, J. (1993) *Young People in 1992*, Schools Health Education Unit (Exeter: Exeter University School of Education).

Baldwin, S. (1995) 'Youthful drinking in Scotland and France: reflections on some cross-cultural comparisons', *Social Sciences in Health*, vol. 1(2), pp. 73–9.

Baldwin, S. and Barker, P. (1995) 'Uncivil liberties: the politics of care for younger people', *Journal of Mental Health*, vol. 4(1), pp. 41–50.

Ball, C. (1983) 'Secret justice: the use made of school reports in the juvenile court', *British Journal of Social Work*, vol. 13, pp. 197–206.

Banks, M., Bates, I., Brakewell, G., Bynner, J., Emler, N., Jamieson, L. and Roberts, K. (1992) *Careers and Identities* (Buckingham: Open University Press).

Beck, U. (1992) *Risk Society, Towards a New Modernity* (London: Sage).

Bell, A. (1996) 'The Northamptonshire Diversion Unit', unpublished paper presented to Gwent Youth Justice Strategy Forum, Cwmbran.

Bell, C. and Haines, K. (1991) 'Managing the transition: implications of the introduction of a youth court in England and Wales', in Booth, T. (ed.), *Juvenile Justice in the New Europe* (Sheffield: Joint Unit for Social Services Research).

Berger, P., Berger, B. and Kellner, H. (1974) *The Homeless Mind: Moderniza-tion and Consciousness* (New York: Vintage Books).

Blagg, H., Pearson, G., Sampson, A., Smith, D. and Stubbs, P. (1988) 'Inter-agency co-operation: rhetoric and reality', in Hope, T. and Shaw, M. (eds), *Communities and Crime Reduction* (London: HMSO).

Blumner, R.E. (1994) 'No: curfews treat law-abiding teens like criminals', *ABA Journal*, April.

Bocock, R. (1993) *Consumptions* (New York: Routledge).

Bottoms, A. (1995) *Intensive Community Supervision for Young Offenders: Out-comes, Process and Cost* (Cambridge: Institute of Criminology Publica-tions).

Bottoms, A. (1995a) 'The philosophy and politics of punishment and sentencing', in Clarkson, C. and Morgan, R. (eds), *The Politics of Senten-cing Reform* (Oxford: Clarendon Press).

Bottoms, A.E. (1974) 'On the decriminalisation of English juvenile courts', in Hood, R. (ed.), *Crime, Criminology and Public Policy* (London: Heine-mann).

Bottoms, A., Brown, P., McWilliams, B., McWilliams, W., Nellis, M. and Pratt, J. (1990) *Intermediate Treatment and Juvenile Justice* (London: HMSO).

Bottoms, A., Haines, K. and Nellis, M. (1993) *Community Penalties for Young Offenders: Part A: The Processual Study*, Final Report to the DHSS from Phase Two of the Intermediate Treatment Evaluation Project.

Bottoms, A., Haines, K. and O'Mahony, D. (forthcoming) 'Youth justice and crime prevention in England and Wales', in Walgrave, L. and Mehlbye, J. (eds), *Confronting European Youth* (Copenhagen: AKF).

Bottoms, A. and McClintock, F. (1973) *Criminals Coming of Age* (London: Heinemann).

Bourdieu, P. (1977) *Outline of a Theory of Practice* (Cambridge: Cambridge University Press).

Bourdieu, P. (1984) *Distinction* (London: Routledge).

Bourne, J., Bridges, L. and Searle, C. (1994) *Outcast England: How Schools Exclude Black Children* (London: Institute of Race Relations).

Bowden, J. and Stevens, M. (1986) 'Justice for juveniles: a corporate strat-egy in Northampton', *Justice of the Peace*, vol. 150, pp. 326–9 and 345–7.

Box, S. (1981) *Deviance, Reality and Society* (London: Holt, Rinehart & Winston).

Bradley, S. (1994) 'The youth training scheme: a critical review of the evaluation literature', *International Journal of Manpower*, vol. 16(4), pp. 30–56.

Braithwaite, J. (1989) *Crime, Shame and Reintegration* (Cambridge: Cam-bridge University Press).

Braithwaite, J. (1993) 'Shame and modernity', *British Journal of Criminology*, vol. 33, pp. 1–18.

Braithwaite, J. and Mugford, S. (1994) 'Conditions of successful reintegra-tion ceremonies: dealing with juvenile offenders', *British Journal of Crim-inology*, vol. 34, pp. 139–171.

Brake, M. (1980) *The Sociology of Youth Culture and Youth Subcultures* (Lon-don: Routledge & Keegan Paul).

Breakwell, G. (1992) 'Changing patterns of sexual behaviour in 16–29 year olds in the UK. A cohort-sequential longitudinal study', in Meeus, W., de Goede M., Kox, W. and Hurrelmann, K. (eds), *Adolescent Careers and Cultures* (Berlin: de Gruyter).

Browne, D. (1993) 'Race issues in research on psychiatry and criminology', in Cook, D. and Hudson, B. (eds), *Racism and Criminology* (London: Sage).

Brown, S. (1996) 'Crime and safety in whose "Community"?: age, everyday life and problems for youth policy', *Youth and Policy*, vol. 55, pp. 27–48.

Buchan, A., Wheal, A. and Barlow, J. (1995) *How to Stay Out of Trouble: The Views of Young Offenders in Wiltshire* (Barkingside: Barnardos).

Bullock, R., Little, M. and Milham, S. (1994) *The Experiences and Careers of Young People Leaving Youth Treatment Centres*, Dartington Social Research Unit.

Bullock, R., Little, M., Mulham, S. and Mount, K. (1995) *Child Protection: Messages from Research* (London: HMSO).

Burney, E. (1985) *Sentencing Young People: What Went Wrong with the Criminal Justice Act 1982?* (Aldershot: Gower).

Burney, E. and Pearson, G. (1995) 'Mentally disordered offenders: finding a focus for diversion', *Howard Journal*, vol. 34(4), pp. 291–313.

Campbell, B. (1997) 'Zero homework', *Guardian*, 15 January.

Carlen, P. (1996) *Jigsaw – A Political Criminology of Youth Homelessness* (Buckingham: Open University Press).

Cavadino, P. (1995) 'The Criminal Justice and Public Order Act 1994 and young offenders', *Youth and Policy*, vol. 48, pp. 71–83.

Celnick, A. and McWilliams, B. (1991) 'Helping, treating and doing good', *Probation Journal*, vol. 38, pp. 164–70.

Chapman, T. and Cook, J. (1988) 'Marginality, youth and government policy in the 1980s,' *Critical Social Policy*, vol. 8(1), pp. 41–64.

Children's Society (1994) *Psychiatric Admissions: A Report on Young People Entering Residential Psychiatric Care* (London: The Children's Society).

Children's Society (1995) *Six Years Severe Hardship*, Coalition on Young People and Social Security, Children's Society, London, reported in *Childright*, April 1995, p. 115, 'Teenagers beg to bridge benefit act'.

Childright (1995a) 'Remand can deliver: remand fostering reduces jail risk', no. 117.

Childright (1995b) 'Severe hardship: conditions tighten', no. 117.

Christie, N. (1993) *Crime Control as Industry: Towards GULAGS Western-style?* (London: Routledge).

Crichton, J. (1995) *Psychiatric Patient Violence: Risk and Response* (London: Duckworth).

Coates, R. (1981) Community-based services for juvenile delinquents: concept and implications for practice, *Journal of Social Issues*, vol. 37, no. 3, pp. 87–101.

Coates, R., Miller, A. and Ohlin, L. (1978) *Diversity in a Youth Correctional System: Handling Delinquents in Massachusetts* (Cambridge: Ballinger).

Cochrane, D. (1989) 'Poverty, probation and empowerment', *Probation Journal*, vol. 38(1), pp. 20–4.

Coles, B. (1995) *Youth and Social Policy* (London: UCL Press).

Collins, M. and Kelly, G. (1995) 'The relationship between crime and justice', *Child Care in Practice*, vol. 2(2), pp. 30–8.

Convery, P. and Taylor, D. (1994) 'Youth unemployment: 16 and 17- year-olds', in *Working Brief 49* (London: Unemployment Unit and Youthaid).

Coppock, V. (1996) 'Mad, bad or misunderstood? a critical analysis of state responses to young people whose behaviour is defined as "disturbed" or "disturbing"', *Youth and Policy*, vol. 53, pp. 53–65.

Courtnay, G. and McAleese, I. (1993) 'England and Wales youth cohort study. Cohort 5: aged 16–17 years old in 1991', *Report on Sweep 1. Youth Cohort Series no. 21* (Sheffield: Employment Department, Research and Development Series).

Crane, S. and Coles, B. (1995) 'Alternative careers: youth transitions and young people's involvement in crime', *Youth and Policy*, vol. 48, pp. 6–26.

Crichton, J. (ed.) *Psychiatric Patient Violence: Risk and Response* (London: Duckworth).

Crown Prosecution Service (1986) *Code of Practice for Prosecutors* (London: CPS).

Dalrymple, J. and Burke, B. (1995) *Anti-Oppressive Practice* (Buckingham: Open University Press).

Davies, E. (1994) *They All Speak English Anyway* (Gwasanaethau Golwg, Cardiff: CCETSW Cymru).

Davies, F.G. (1994) 'The presumption of doli incapax', *Justice of the Peace*, vol. 158 (19), pp. 158–60.

Davies, H. and Bourhill, M. (1997) '"Crisis": the demonisation of children and young people', in Scraton, P. (ed.), *'Childhood' in 'Crisis'?* (London: UCL Press).

Davis, G., Boucherat, J. and Watson, D. (1988) 'Reparation in the service of diversion: the subordination of a good idea', *The Howard Journal* vol. 27, pp. 127–32.

Delors, J. (1993) 'Giving a new dimension to the fight against exclusion'. Closing speech at Copenhagen Conference, 3–4 June.

Department of Health (1994) *Responding to Youth Crime: Findings from Inspections of Youth Justice Sections in Five Local Authority Social Services Departments* (London: HMSO).

Dignan, J. (1992) 'Repairing the damage: can reparation be made to work in the service of diversion?' *British Journal of Criminology*, vol. 32, no. 4 pp. 453–72.

Dodds, M. (1986) 'The restrictions on imposing youth custody and detention centre sentences – some recent cases', *Justice of the Peace*, 7 June, pp. 359–62.

Dominelli, L., Jeffers, L., Jones, G., Sibanda, S., and Williams, B. (1996) *Anti-racist Probation Practice* (Aldershot: Arena).

Downes, D. and Morgan, R. (1994) 'The politics of law and order', in Maguire, M., Morgan, R. and Reiner, R. (eds), *The Oxford Handbook of Criminology* (Oxford: Clarendon Press).

Drakeford, M. (1993) 'But who will do the work?' *Critical Social Policy*, vol. 38, pp. 64–76.

Drakeford, M. (1994) 'The appropriate adult', *Probation Journal*, vol. 41(3), pp. 135–9.

Drakeford, M. (1996) 'Parents of young people in trouble', *Howard Journal*, vol. 35, no. 3 pp. 242–55.

Drakeford, M. and Vanstone, M. (1996a) 'Rescuing the social', *Probation Journal*, vol. 43(1), pp. 16–19.

Drakeford, M. and Vanstone, M. (1996b) *Beyond Offending Behaviour* (Aldershot: Arena).

Edwards, H. (1994) *Wales, Land of Low Pay* (London: Low Pay Unit).

Edwards, H. (1996) *Wales, Land of Low Pay: supplementary report* (London: Low Pay Unit).

Edwards, S. (1992) 'Parental responsibility: an instrument of social policy', *Family Law*, vol. 22, pp. 113–18.

Eekelaar, J. (1991) 'Parental responsibility: state of nature or nature of the state?', *Journal of Social Welfare and Family Law*, vol. 37, pp. 37–50.

Etzioni, A. (1993) *The Spirit of Community* (New York: Eima & Selter).

Evans, K. (1995) 'Competence and citizenship: towards a complementary model for times of critical social change', *British Journal of Education and Work*, vol. 2.

Evans, R. (1993) 'The conduct of police interviews with juveniles', *Royal Commission on Criminal Justice Research Study no 8* (London: HMSO).

Evans, R. and Wilkinson, C. (1990) 'Variations in police cautioning policy and practice in England and Wales', *Howard Journal of Criminal Justice*, vol. 29, pp. 155–76.

Fagan, J. A., Slaughter, E. and Hartstone, E. (1987) 'Blind justice? The impact of race on the juvenile justice process', *Crime and Delinquency*, vol. 33, pp. 224–58.

Farrington, D. (1994) 'Human development and criminal careers', in Maguire, M., Morgan, R. and Reiner, R. (eds), *The Oxford Handbook of Criminology* (Oxford: Clarendon Press).

Farrington, D. (1997) 'Early prediction of violent and non- violent youthful offending', *European Journal on Criminal Policy and Research*, vol. 5, no. 2, pp. 51–66.

Farrington, D. (1997a) *Understanding and Preventing Youth Crime* (York: Joseph Rowntree Foundation).

Fenwick, C.R. (1982) 'Juvenile court intake decision-making: the importance of family affiliation', *Journal of Criminal Justice*, vol. 10(6), pp. 443–53.

Ford, J. (1992) 'Young adults use of credit', *Youth and Policy*, vol. 37, pp. 22–32.

Fossey, E., Loretto, W. and Plant, M. (1996) 'Alcohol and youth', in Harrison, L. (ed.), *Alcohol Problems and the Community* (London: Routledge).

Foster, J. (1990) *Villains* (London: Routledge).

France, A. (1996) 'Youth and citizenship in the 1990s', *Youth and Policy*, vol. 53, pp. 28–43.

Freedland, J. (1997) 'Age of consent goes up in smoke', *Guardian*, 15 July.

Furlong, A. (1993) 'The youth transition, unemployment and labour market disadvantage', *Youth and Policy*, vol. 41, pp. 24–35.

Furlong, A. and Cartmel, F. (1997) *Young People and Social Change* (Buckingham: Open University Press).

Garland, D. (1989) 'Critical reflections on the Green Paper', in Rees, H. and Williams, E.H. (eds), *Punishment, Custody and the Community: Reflections and Comments on the Green Paper* (London School of Economics).

Gelsthorpe, L. and Morris, A. (1994) 'Juvenile justice 1945–1992', in Maguire, M., Morgan, R. and Reiner, R. (eds), *The Oxford Handbook of Criminology* (Oxford: Clarendon Press).

Gendreau, P. (1983) 'Success in corrections, programs and principles', in Corrado, R., LeBlanc, M. and Trepanier (eds), *Current Issues in Juvenile Justice* (Canada: Butterworth and Coy).

Giddens, A. (1991) *Modernity and Self Identity. Self and Society in the Late Modern Age* (Oxford: Polity Press).

Giller, H. and Morris, M. (1981) *Care and Discretion* (London: Burnett Books).

Glueck, S. and Glueck, R. (1964) *Ventures in Criminology* (Cambridge: Harvard University Press).

Glueck, S. and Glueck, R. (1974) *Of Delinquency and Crime: A Panorama of Years of Search and Research* (Springfield: Charles C. Thomas).

Graham, J. and Bowling, B. (1995) *Young People and Crime*, Home Office Research Study 145 (London: HMSO).

Gray, A. and Jenkins, W. (1986) 'Accountable management in British central government: some reflections on the financial management initiative', *Financial Accountability and Management*, vol. 2, pp. 171–86.

Guardian, 12 November 1996, 'Young offenders rampant, say police'.

HCC 588 (1986/7) *The Financial Management Initiative*, Report by the Comptroller and Auditor General/National Audit Office.

HM Inspectorate of Probation (HMIP) (1993) *The Criminal Justice Act 1991 Inspection* (London: Home Office).

HM Inspectorate of Probation (HMIP) (1994) *Young Offenders and the Probation Service* (London: Home Office).

Hagell, A. and Newburn, T. (1994) *Persistent Young Offenders* (London: Policy Studies Institute).

Haines, K. (1996) *Understanding Modern Juvenile Justice* (Aldershot: Avebury).

Haines, K. (1997) 'Young offenders and family support services: an European perspective', *International Journal of Child and Family Welfare*, issue 3.

Haines, K., Bottoms, A. and O'Mahony, D. (1996) *Providing and Managing Youth Court Support Services*, Report of the Cambridge Institute of Criminology submitted to the Home Office.

Haines, K. (1995) 'Tribulations des tribunaux de la jeunesse en Angleterre et au Pays de Galles', *Les Politiques Sociale*, vols iii and iv, pp. 61–72.

Haines, K. and O'Mahony, D. (1995) *Providing and Managing Youth Court Services*, a report submitted to the Home Office.

Haines, K. and O'Mahony, D. (1995a) 'The youth court: a national survey of service delivery and management arrangements', *Research Bulletin*, Home Office Research and Statistics Department, no. 37, pp. 2–31.

Hansard (1997a) 19 May, cols 387–90.

Hansard (1997b) 30 July, cols 341–4.

Hartless, J.M., Ditton, J., Nair, G. and Phillips, S. (1995) 'More sinned against than sinning. A study of young teenagers' experience of crime', *British Journal of Criminology*, vol. 35, pp. 114–33.

Hebdige, D. (1979) *Subcultures: The Meaning of Style* (London: Macmillan).

Hirschi, T. (1969) *Causes of Delinquency* (Berkeley: University of California Press).

Hollin, C. (1995) 'The meaning and implications of programme integrity', In McGuire, J. (ed.), *What Works: Reducing Reoffending* (Chichester: John Wiley).

Holman, B. (1995) 'Urban youth – not an underclass', *Youth and Policy*, vol. 47, pp. 69–77.

Holland, J., Ramazanoglu, C. and Sharpe, S. (1993) *Wimp or Gladiator: Contradictions in Acquiring Masculine Sexuality*, WRAP/MRAP Paper 9 (London: Tufnell).

Home Office (1968) *Children in Trouble*, Cmnd. 3601 (London: HMSO).

Home Office (1980) *Young Offenders*, Cmnd 8045 (London: HMSO).

Home Office (1984) Cautioning by the Police: A Consultative Document (London: HMSO).

Home Office (1985) *The Cautioning of Offenders*, Circular 14/1985 (London: Home Office).

Home Office (1988) *Punishment, Custody and the Community*, Cm. 424 (London: HMSO).

Home Office (1990) *Crime, Justice and Protecting the Public*, Cm. 965 (London: HMSO).

Home Office (1990a) *Supervision and Punishment in the Community* (London: HMSO).

Home Office (1990b) *The Cautioning of Offenders* Circular 59/90 (London: HMSO).

Home Office (1992) *National Standards for the Supervision of Offenders in the Community* (London: HMSO).

Home Office (1993a) *Criminal Justice Act 1993: Commencement of Certain Provisions on 16 August and 20 September 1993*, Circular 38/1993 (London: Home Office).

Home Office (1993b) 'Cautioning', draft circular, November.

Home Office (1995) *National Standards for the Supervision of Offenders in the Community* (London: Home Office).

Home Office (1995) 'Statistics of drug seizures and offenders dealt with in the UK, 1994', *Statistics Bulletin*, 24/95 (London: Home Office).

Hood, R. (1992) *Race and Sentencing* (Oxford: Clarendon Press).

House of Commons Debates (1990) *Hansard*, vol. 151, col. 767.

Howard League (1997) *The Howard League Troubleshooter Project: Lessons for Policy and Practice on 15 Year Olds in Prison* (London: Howard League for Penal Reform).

Hucklesby, A. (1994) 'The use and abuse of conditional bail', *Howard Journal*, vol. 33(3), pp. 258–70.

Hudson, B. (1992) 'Family trends and public policy', *Health Visitor*, vol. 65, pp. 20–21.

Hudson, B. (1993) *Penal Policy and Social Justice* (Basingstoke: Macmillan).

Huizinga, D. and Elliott, D.S. (1987) 'Juvenile offenders: prevalence, offender incidence, and arrest rates by race', *Crime and Delinquency*, vol. 33, pp. 206–23.

Humphrey, C. (1993) 'Reflecting on attempts to develop a financial management information system (FMIS) for the Probation Service in England and Wales: some observations on the relationship between the claims of accounting and its practice', *Accounting, Organisations and Society*,

Humphrey, C., Carter, P. and Pease K. (1992) 'A reconviction predictor for probationers', *British Journal of Social Work*, vol. 22, pp. 33–46.

Humphries, S. (1991) *The Secret World of Sex* (London: Sidgwick & Jackson).

Hutton, W. (1995) *The State We're In: Why Britain is in Crisis and How to Overcome it* (London: Jonathan Cape).

Ignatieff, M. (1989) *A Just Measure of Pain* (London: Penguin).

Imich, A. (1994) 'Exclusions from school: current trends and issues', *Educational Research*, vol. 36.

Irwin, S. (1996) *Rights of Passage: Social Change and the Transition from Youth to Adulthood* (London: University College London Press).

Jackson, P. (1985) 'Policy implementation and monetarism', in Jackson, P. (ed.), *Implementing Government Policy Initiatives the Thatcher Administration 1979–1983* (London: RIPA).

Jacobson, L.D. and Pill, R.M. (1997) 'Critical consumers: teenagers in primary care', *Health and Social Care in the Community*, vol. 5(1), pp. 55–62.

Jacobson, L.D. and Wilkinson, C. (1994) 'A review of teenage health: time for a new direction', *British Journal of General Practice*, vol. 44, pp. 420–4.

Jarvis, G., Parker, H. and Sumner, M. (1987) 'An ambivalent service', *Probation Journal*, vol. 34 pp. 103–4.

Jeffs, T. and Smith, M.K. (1996) '"Getting the Dirtbags Off the Street": Curfews and Other Solutions to Juvenile Crime', *Youth and Policy*, vol. 53, pp. 1–14.

Jones, D. (1989) 'The successful revolution', *Community Care*, 30 March.

Jones, D. (1990) 'The rise and fall of the 7 (7) care order', *AJJUST*, February 1990, pp. 5–7.

Jones, D. (1993) 'The successful revolution in juvenile justice continues – but for how long?', *Justice of the Peace*, vol. 157, pp. 297–8.

Jones, G. (1995) *Leaving Home* (Milton Keynes: Open University Press).

Jones, G. and Wallace, C. (1992) *Youth, Family and Citizenship* (Milton Keynes: Open University Press).

Jones, R. (1984) 'Questioning the new orthodoxy', *Community Care*, 11 October.

Karabinas, A., Sheptycki, J.W.E. and Monaghan, B. (1996) 'An evaluation of the Craigmillar Youth Challenge', *Howard Journal*, vol. 35(2), pp. 113–30.

Kay, H. (1994) *Conflicting Priorities: Homeless 16 and 17- year-olds: A Changing Agenda for Housing Authorities?* (London: CHAR/Chartered Institute of Housing).

Kemshall, K. (1995) 'Risk in probation practice: the hazards and dangers of supervision', *Probation Journal*, vol. 42, no. 2, pp. 67–72.

Kemshall, H. (1996) 'Risk assessment: fuzzy thinking or "Decisions in Action"?' *Probation Journal*, vol. 43, pp. 2–7.

Kerslake, A. (1987) 'Unintended consequences?', *Community Care*, 10 March, pp. 18–21.

Kiernan, K. (1992) 'The impact of family disruption in childhood transitions made in young adult life', *Population Studies*, vol. 46, pp. 213–34.

Knott, C. (1995) 'The STOP programme: reasoning and rehabilitation in a British setting', in McGuire, J. (ed.), *What Works: Reducing Reoffending* (Chichester: John Wiley).

Krisberg, B. and Austin, J. F. (1993) *Reinventing Juvenile Justice* (London: Sage).

Labour Party (1964) *Crime: a Challenge to Us All*, Report of a Labour Party Study Group chaired by F. Longford (London: Labour Party).

Labour Party (1996) *Tackling Youth Crime: Reforming Youth Justice* (London: The Labour Party).

Lash, S. and Urry, J. (1987) *The End of Organised Capitalism* (Cambridge: Polity Press).

Lavelette, M., Hobbs, S., Lindsay, S. and McKechnie, J. (1995) 'Child employment in Britain: policy, myth and reality', *Youth and Policy*, vol. 47, pp. 1–15.

Law Commission (1994) *Binding Over*, Report no. 222 (London: HMSO).

Lee, M. (1993) *Consumer Culture Reborn: The Cultural Politics of Consumption* (London: Routledge).

LeClair, D. (1984) 'Community reintegration of prison releases', in Carter, R., Glaser, D. and Wilkins, L. (eds), *Probation, Parole and Community Corrections* (New York: John Wiley).

LeClair, D. (1985) 'Community-based reintegration', in Carter, R., Glaser, D. and Wilkins, L. (eds), *Correctional Institutions* (New York: Harper & Row).

Leonard, P. (1975) 'Towards a paradigm for radical practice', in Bailey, R. and Brake, M. (eds), *Radical Social Work* (London: Edward Arnold) pp. 46–61.

Lilly, J., Cullen, F. and Ball, R. (1989) *Criminological Theory: Context and Consequences* (Newbury Park: Sage).

Lipsey, M. (1992) 'Juvenile delinquency treatment: a meta- analytic inquiry into the variability of effects', in Cook, T. *et al.* (eds), *Meta-Analysis for Explanation* (New York: Russell Sage Foundation).

Lipsey, M. (1995) 'What do we learn from 400 research studies on the effectiveness of treatments with juvenile delinquents?', in McGuire, J. (ed.), *What Works: Reducing Reoffending* (Chichester: John Wiley).

Littlechild, B. (1996) *The Police and Criminal Evidence Act 1984: The Role of the Appropriate Adult* (London, BASW).

Lister, R. (1991) *The Exclusive Society: Citizenship and the Poor* (London: Child Poverty Action Group).

Lowe, R. (1993) *The Welfare State in Britain since 1945* (London: Macmillan).

Lucas, J., Raynor, P. and Vanstone, M. (1992) *Straight Thinking on Probation One Year On* (Bridgend: Mid-Glamorgan Probation Service).

Lyon, C. (1996) 'Adolescents who offend', *Journal of Adolescence*, vol. 19, pp. 1–4.

MacDonald, R. (1995) 'Youth, crime and justice', editorial, *Youth and Policy*, vol. 48, pp. 1–5.

MacDonald, R., Banks, S. and Hollands, R. (1993) 'Youth and policy in the 1990s', editorial, *Youth and Policy*, vol. 40, pp. 1–9.

Maguire, M., Morgan, R. and Reiner, R. (ed), (1994) *The Oxford Handbook of Criminology* (Oxford: Clarendon Press).

Mackenzie, D., Brame, R., McDowall, D. and Souryal, C. (1995) 'Boot Camp Prisons and Recidivism in Eight States', *Criminology* vol. 33, No. 3, pp 327–57.

McCarney, W. (1996) *Juvenile Delinquents and Young People in Danger in an Open Environment* (Winchester: Waterside Press).

McEwan, J. (1983), 'In search of juvenile justice, the Criminal Justice Act 1982', *Journal of Social Welfare Law*, vol. xx, pp. 112–17.

McLaughlin, H. (1989) 'School reports: a cause for concern', *Practice*, vol. 4(2), pp. 110–16.

McMahon, M. (1992) *The Persistent Prison?: Rethinking Decarceration and Penal Reform* (Toronto: University of Toronto Press).

McWilliams, W. (1992) 'The rise and development of management thought in the English probation system', in Statham, R. and Whitehead, P. (eds), *Managing the Probation Service: Issues for the 1990s* (Harlow: Longman).

Malek, M. (1991) *Psychiatric Admissions: A Report on Young People Entering Residential Psychiatric Care* (London: Children's Society).

Manpower Services Commission (1985) *Development of the Youth Training Scheme: a Report* (Sheffield: MSC).

Marshall, T.H. (1950) *Citizenship and Social Class* (Cambridge: Cambridge University Press).

Marshall, T. and Merry, S. (1990) *Crime and Accountability: Victim/Offender Mediation in Practice* (London: HMSO).

Maung, N. (1995) *Young People, Victimisation and the Police. British Crime Survey Findings on Experiences and Attitudes of 12 to 15 Year Olds*, Home Office Research Study 140 (London: HMSO).

Mayhew, P., Maung, N. and Mirrlees-Black, C. (1993) *The 1992 British Crime Survey*, Home Office Research Study no. 132 (London: HMSO).

Measham, F., Newcombe, R. and Parker, H. (1994) 'The normalisation of recreational drug use amongst young people in north-west England', *British Journal of Sociology*, vol. 45, pp. 287–312.

Merchant, J. and MacDonald, R. (1994) 'Youth and the rave culture, ecstacy and health', *Youth and Policy*, vol. 45, pp. 16–38.

Merry, G.B. (1984) 'Curfews for teen-agers gain support as curb on drunk driving', *The Christian Science Monitor*, 18 July.

Miles, S. (1995) 'Towards an understanding of the relationship between youth identities and consumer culture', *Youth and Policy*, vol. 51, pp. 35–45.

Miller, A. and Ohlin, L. (1985) *Delinquents and Community: Creating Opportunities and Controls* (Beverly Hills: Sage).

Mizen, P. (1993) 'Youth training: consensus or conflict in the 1990s', *Youth and Policy*, vol. 41, pp. 36–43.

Moore, T.G. (1995) 'In Defence of Doli Incapax', *Justice of the Peace*, vol. 159(21), pp. 159–60.

Morgan, J. and Zedner, L. (1992) *Child Victims: Crime, Impact and Criminal Justice* (Oxford: Clarendon Press).

Morgan, P. (ed.) (1995) *Privatisation and the Welfare State* (Aldershot: Dartmouth).

Morris, A. and Giller, H. (1983) *Providing Criminal Justice for Children* (London: Edward Arnold).

Morris, A. and Giller, H. (1987) *Understanding Juvenile Justice* (London: Croom Helm).

Morris, A., Giller, H., Szued, M. and Geech, H. (1980) *Justice for Children* (London: Macmillan).

Morris, E. (1985) *Looking After Yourself – Some Issues from 15 to 19-Year-Olds on Health and Illness – Special Report Series 73*, pp. 95–6 (Wellington: New Zealand Department of Health).

Morrow, V. and Richards, M. (1996) *Transitions to Adulthood: A Family Matter?* (York: Joseph Rowntree Foundation).

Murray, C. (1990) *The Emerging British Underclass* (London: Institute of Economic Affairs, Health and Welfare Unit).

Murray, C. (1994) *Underclass: The Crisis Deepens* (London: Institute of Economic Affairs, Health and Welfare Unit).

Murray, I. (1994) 'Vacancies "bait" to jobless', *Working Brief*, July 1994.

National Association for the Care and Resettlement of Offenders (NACRO) (1987) *Diverting Juveniles from Custody* (London: NACRO).

National Association for the Care and Resettlement of Offenders (NACRO) (1989) *Replacing Custody: Findings from Two Census Surveys of Schemes for Juvenile Offenders Funded Under the DHSS Intermediate Treatment Initiative, Covering the Period January to December 1987* (London: NACRO).

National Association for the Care and Resettlement of Offenders (NACRO) (1991) *Seizing the Initiative: NACRO's Final Report on the DHSS Intermediate Treatment Initiative to Divert Juvenile Offenders from Careand Custody: 1983–1989* (London: NACRO).

National Association for the Care and Resettlement of Offenders (NACRO) (1994) *Prison Overcrowding – Recent Developments* (London: NACRO).

National Association for the Care and Resettlement of Offenders (NACRO) (1994) *Good Practice after the Criminal Justice and Public Order Act 1994* (London: NACRO).

National Association for the Care and Resettlement of Offenders (NACRO) (1995) *A Crisis in Custody: Findings from a Survey of Juveniles in Prison Awaiting Trial* (London: NACRO).

National Childrens Home (1996) *Factfile* (London: NCH Action for Children).

National Institute of Justice (1994) *Boot Camps for Adult and Juvenile Offenders: Overview and Update* (Washington, DC: US Department of Justice).

NHS Health Advisory Service (1995) *Bridges Over Troubled Waters: A Report on Services for Disturbed Child and Adolescent Mental Health Services* (London: HMSO).

Nee, C. (1993) *Car Theft. The Offender's Perspective* (London: Home Office).

North, J., Adair, H., Langley, B., Mills, J. and Morten, G. (1992) *The Dog that Finally Barked: The Tyneside Disturbances of 1991 a Probation Perspective* (Northumbria Probation Service).

Northumbria, Probation Service (1994) *Survey of Probation Practice on Poverty Issues* (Northumbria Probation Service).

O'Mahony, D. and Haines, K. (1993) 'Magistrates' views on the proposals for secure training centres,' *Justice of the Peace*, vol. 157, no. 46, pp. 722–8.

Oppenheim, C. and Lister, R. (1996) 'Ten years after the 1986 Social Security Act', in May, M., Brunsdon, E. and Craig, G. (eds), *Social Policy Review 8* (London: Social Policy Association), pp. 84–105.

Orme, J. and Pritchard, C. (1996) 'Health', in Drakeford, M. and Vanstone, M. (eds), *Beyond Offending Behaviour* (Aldershot: Arena), pp. 87–96.

Paley, J. and Thorpe, D. (1974) *Children: Handle with Care* (Leicester: National Youth Bureau).

Parker, H. and Measham, F. (1994) 'Pick'n'mix: changing patterns of illicit drug use amongst 1990s adolescents', *Drug Education, Prevention and Policy*, vol. 1(1), pp. 5–13.

Parker, H., Sumner, M. and Jarvis, G. (1989) *Unmasking the Magistrates: The 'Custody or Not' Decision in Sentencing Young Offenders* (Milton Keynes: Open University Press).

Pearson, G. (1983) *Hooligan: A History of Respectable Fears* (London: Macmillan).

Pearson, G. (1994) 'Youth, crime and society', in Maguire, M. *et al.* (eds), *The Oxford Handbook of Criminology* (Oxford: Clarendon Press).

Peelo, M., Stewart, J., Stewart, G. and Prior, A. (1992) *A Sense of Justice: Offenders as Victims of Crime* (London: Association of Chief Officers of Probation).

Peters, A. (1986) 'Main currents in criminal law theory', in van Dijk, J. *et al.* (eds), *Criminal Law in Action* (Arnheim: Gouda Quint BV).

Pincus, A. and Minahan, A. (1973) *Social Work Practice: Model and Method* (Itasca: F.E. Peacock).

Pitts, J. (1988) *The Politics of Juvenile Crime* (London: Sage).

Pitts, J. (1990) *Working with Young Offenders* (Basingstoke: Macmillan).

Pitts, J. (1995) 'Scare in the Community', *Community Care*, 4–10 May.

Pitts, J., Pearce, J. and Burr, C. (1996) 'Juvenile Justice', *Research Matters*, vol. 1, pp. 14–16.

Plant, M. and Plant, M. (1992) *Risk Takers: Alcohol, Drugs, Sex and Youth* (London: Tavistock).

Pollitt, C. (1993) *Managerialism and the Public Services* (Oxford: Blackwell Business).

Pond, C. and Searle, A. (1991) *The Hidden Army: Children at Work in the 1990s* (London: Low Pay Unit).

Pratt, J. (1989) 'The punishment of juveniles and the commodification of time', in Jones, S. (ed.), *British Criminology Conference Proceedings* (Bristol: Bristol and Bath Centre for Criminal Justice).

Pritchard, C., Cotton, A., Godson, D., Cox, M. and Weeks, S. (1992) 'Mental illness, drug and alcohol misuse and HIV risk behaviour in 214 young adult (18–35 year) probation clients: implications for policy practice and training', *Social Work and Social Sciences Review*, vol. 3(3), pp. 227–42.

Raynor, P. (1991) 'Sentencing with and without reports', *Howard Journal*, vol. 30, no. 4, pp. 293–300.

Raynor, P. (1995) 'The Pembrokeshire bail support scheme: an evaluation' (Carmarthen: Dyfed Probation Service).

Raynor, P. (1996) 'The criminal justice system', in Drakeford, M. and Vanstone, M. (eds), *Beyond Offending Behaviour* (Aldershot: Arena), pp. 11–21.

Raynor, P., Smith, D. and Vanstone, M. (1996) *Effective Probation Practice* (London: Macmillan).

Rickford, F. (1993a) 'Children "dumped" in mental hospitals', *The Independent on Sunday*, 4 April.

Rickford, F. (1993b) 'And everyone seemed weird and terrifying', *The Independent on Sunday*, 4 April.

Rickford, F. (1995) 'The treatment of troubled minds', *Guardian*, 8 March.

Roberts, K., (1986) 'Young people in society 16–19 initiative. A sociological view of the issues', ESRC review document.

Roberts, K. (1987) 'ESRC – young people in society', *Youth and Policy*, vol. 22, pp. 15–24.

Roberts, K. (1993) 'Career trajectories and the mirage of increased social mobility', in Bates, I. and Riseborough, G. (eds), *Youth and Inequality* (Buckingham: Open University Press).

Roberts, K. and Parsell, G. (1989) 'The stratification of youth training', *ESRC 16–19 Initiative Occasional Paper No 11*, London.

Roberts, K. and Parsell, G. (1991) 'Young people's sources and levels of income and patterns of consumption in Britain in the late 1980s', *Youth and Policy*, vol. 35, pp. 20–5.

Roberts, C., Moore, L., Blackey, V. and Payle, R. (1995) 'Drug use amongst 15–16 year olds in Wales, 1990–94, *Drug Education, Prevention and Policy*, vol. 2(3), pp. 305–16.

Rogers, S. (1997) 'Interview with Tony Blair', *Big Issue*, 6 January.

Rogowski, S. (1995) 'Youth crime and community based initiatives: a critical look at their development and some thoughts on a radical practice', *Practice*, vol. 7(4), pp. 43–52.

Ross, R. (1988) 'Reasoning and rehabilitation', *International Journal of Offender Therapy and Comparative Criminology*, vol. 32, pp. 29–35.

Ross, R. and Bilson, A. (1939) *Social Work Management and Practice* (London: Jessica Kigsley).

Ruefle, W. and Reynolds, K.M. (1995) 'Curfews and delinquency in major American cities', *Crime and Delinquency*, vol. 41(3).

Rutherford, A. (1983) 'The Criminal Justice Act '82 and the use of Custody', *Probation Journal*, vol. 30, no. 3, pp. 93–5.

Rutherford, A. (1985) *Growing Out of Crime* (London: Penguin).

Rutherford, A. (1992) *Growing Out of Crime – The New Era* (Winchester: Waterside Press).

Rutherford, A. (1996) *Transforming Criminal Policy* (Winchester: Waterside Press).

Rutter, M. and Smith D.J. (1996) *Psychosocial Disorders in Young People: Time Trends and their Causes.*

Sampson, R. and Laub, J. (1993) *Crime in the Making: Pathways and Turning Points Through Life* (Cambridge: Harvard University Press).

Schur, E.M. (1973) *Radical Non-Intervention: Re-Thinking the Delinquency Problem* (Englewood Cliffs: Prentice-Hall).

Sharp, L. (1994) 'Underage drinking in the United Kingdom since 1970: public policy, the law and adolescent drinking behaviour', *Alcohol and Alcholism,* vol. 29 (5), pp. 555–63.

Simon, J. (1988) 'The ideological effects of acturial practices', *Law and Society Review,* vol. 22, no. 4, pp. 771–800.

Sinclair, I. (1971) *Hostels for Probationers,* Home Office Research Study No. 6 (London: HMSO).

Singer, S.I. (1996) *Recriminalizing Delinquency: Violent Juvenile Crimes and Juvenile Justice Reform* (Cambridge: Cambridge University Press).

Smith, D. (1984) 'Law and order: arguments for what?' *Critical Social Policy,* vol. 11, Winter, pp. 33–45.

Smith, D. (1996) 'Reforming the probation service', in May, M., Brunsdon, E. and Craig, G., (eds), *Social Policy Review 8* (London: Social Policy Association), pp. 227–46.

Smith, T. and Noble, M. (1995) *Education Divides, Poverty and Schooling in the 1990s* (London: CPAG).

Social Action Today (1996) 'Briefing: housing benefit changes threaten young people', vol. 1, pp. 11–13.

Social Services Inspectorate (SSI) (1994) *Responding to Youth Crime: Findings from Inspections of Youth Justice Services in Five Local Authority Social Services Departments* (London: HMSO).

Spencer, J.N. (1994) 'Cautionary Tales: The Use of the Police Caution, *Justice of the Peace and Local Government Law,* 9 July, pp. 445–550.

Springhall, J. (1986) *Coming of Age: Adolescence in Britain* (London: Gill & Macmillan).

Stanley, C. (1988) 'Making statutory guidelines work', *Justice of the Peace,* vol. 8, October, pp. 648–50.

Stenson, K. and Factor, F. (1994) 'Youth work, risk and crime prevention', *Youth and Policy,* 1–15.

Stern, V. (1997) 'Crime pays big dividends', *Guardian,* 15 January.

Stewart, F. (1992) 'The adolescent as consumer', in Coleman, J.C. and Warren-Anderson, C. (eds), *Youth Policy in the 1990s: The Way Forward* (London: Routledge) pp. 203–26.

Stewart, J. and Smith, D. with Stewart, G. and Fulwood, C. (1994) *Understanding Offending Behaviour* (London: Longman).

Stockley, D., Canter, D. and Bishop, D. (1993) *Young People on the Move* (University of Surrey: Department of Psychology).

Stone, C. (1989) 'Public interest case assessment: final report of the probation initiative "Diversion from custody and prosecution" ' (New York: Vera Intitute of Justice).

Stone, N. (1995) 'An early face-lift for pre-sentence reports', *Justice of the Peace and Local Government Review* vol. 159(4), pp. 140–3.

Straw, J. and Anderson, J. (1996) *Parenting* (London: The Labour Party).

Tain, P. (1994) 'Remanding young people', *Practitioners' Child Law Bulletin*, vol. 89, pp. 104–6.

Financial Times (1996) 'Morals adrift in the marketplace', 9 March.

Guardian (1996) 'Young "have never had it so good" ', 26 August.

Guardian (1997) 'Straw threatens to merge probation and prisons', 17 July.

Sunday Times (1995) 'Sick trustees of posterity', 4 June.

Times (1995) 'Youth Crime', 7 June.

Thompson, N. (1995) *Anti-Discriminatory Practice* (London: BASW/Macmillan).

Thornton, D. Curran, L., Grayson, D. and Holloway, V. (1984) *Tougher Regimes in Detention Centres: Report of an Evaluation by the Young Offender Psychology Unit* (London: HMSO).

Thorpe, D., Smith, D., Green, C. and Paley, J. (1980) *Out of Care – The Community Support of Juvenile Offenders* (London: George Allenand Unwin).

Tildesley, W.M. and Bullock, W.F. (1983) 'Curfew orders: the arguments for', *Probation Journal*, vol. 30, pp. 139–42.

Tittle, C. (1996) *Control Balance: Towards a General Theory of Deviance* (Oxford: Westview Press).

Trades Union Congress (1996a) *Underworked and Underpaid* (London: TUC).

Trades Union Congress (1996b) *Testament of Youth* (London: TUC).

Trotter, C. (1993) *The Supervision of Offenders – What Works?* (Clayton, Victoria: Monash University, Report to the Australian Criminology Research Council).

Tutt, N. (1982) 'Justice or welfare', *Social Work Today*, vol. 14, no. 7, pp. 6–10.

Tutt, N. and Giller, H. (1987) 'Manifesto for management – the elimination of custody', *Justice of the Peace*, vol. 151, pp. 200–2.

Vanstone, M. (1995) 'Managerialism and the ethics of management', in Hugman, R. and Smith, D. (eds), *Ethical Issues in Social Work* (London: Routledge).

von Hirsch, A. (1985) *Past or Future Crimes* (Manchester: Manchester University Press).

Walker, B. M. (1997) ' "You learn it from your mates, don't you?": young people's conversations about sex as a basis for informal peer education', *Youth and Policy*, vol. 57, pp. 44–54.

Ward, D. (1987) *The Validity of the Reconviction Prediction Score*, Home Office Research Study 94.

Wardaugh, J. (1995) 'Exclusion of young homeless people', *Childright*, December, pp. 16–17.

Warner, G. (1995) 'Vulgarity has been translated into a lifestyle', *Sunday Times*, 1 January.

Weaver, C. and Bensted, J. (1992) 'Thinking for a change', *Probation Journal*, vol. 39, pp. 196–200.

Webb, T. (1996) 'Reconviction prediction for probationers', *Probation Journal*, vol. 43, no. 2, pp. 8–12.

Wilkinson, C. and Evans, R. (1990) 'Police cautioning of juveniles: the impact of Home Office Circular 14/1985', *Criminal Law Review*, pp. 165–76.

Wilkinson, J. (1994) 'Using a reconviction predictor', *British Journal of Social Work*, vol. 24, pp. 461–75.

Wilson, P. (1995) 'A mentally healthy young nation', *Youth and Policy*, vol. 51, pp. 60–3.

Winkel, F. (1991) 'Police, victims and crime prevention', *British Journal of Criminology*, vol. 31, no. 3, pp. 250–65.

Woodroffe, C., Glickman, M., Barker, M. and Power, C. (1993) *Children, Teenagers and Health. Key Data* (Buckingham: Open University Press).

Worrall, A. (1990) *Offending Women: Female Lawbreakers and the Criminal Justice System* (London: Routledge).

Wright, M. (1996) *Justice for Victims and Offenders: A Restorative Response to Crime* (Winchester: Waterside Press).

Index